Economics of Sport and Recreation

Economics of Sport and Recreation

Chris Gratton and Peter Taylor

London and New York

First published 2000
by Spon Press
11 New Fetter Lane, London EC4P 4EE

Simultaneously published in the USA and Canada
by Spon Press,
29 West 35th Street, New York, NY 10001

Spon Press is an imprint of the Taylor & Francis Group

© 2000 Chris Gratton and Peter Taylor

Typeset in Baskerville by Graphicraft Limited, Hong Kong
Printed and bound in Great Britain by Biddles Ltd,
Guildford and King's Lynn

British Library Cataloguing in Publication Data
A catalogue record for this book is available from the British Library

Library of Congress Cataloging in Publication Data
Gratton, Chris, 1948–
    Economics of sport and recreation/Chris Gratton and Peter
Taylor – 2nd edn.
        p.   cm.
    Rev. edn. of: *Sports and Recreation*. 1985.
    Includes bibliographical references (p. 223) and index.
    ISBN 0-419-18960-2 (pbk)
    1. Leisure – Economic aspects.   2. Recreation – Economic
aspects.   3. Sports – Economic aspects.   I. Taylor, Peter, 1949–.
II. Gratton, Chris, 1948–. Sports and recreation.   III. Title.
GV181.3.G73   2000   99-41898
338.4'7796–dc21   CIP

ISBN 0-419-18960-2

Contents

To Joe, William, and Anderson

Preface

The purpose of this book is to apply economic analysis to the sports industry. It is now generally recognised that sport is an industry accounting for a significant share of Gross Domestic Product, consumer expenditure and employment. However, there has been little systematic study of this industry by economists. This book attempts to fill the gap.

The book started out as a second edition of our *Sport and Recreation: An Economic Analysis* which was published in 1985. So much has changed in the area of the economic analysis of sport since then, however, that this book contains little of the earlier book. The change in title to *The Economics of Sport and Recreation* is a recognition of the fact that this is essentially a new book, although it will replace the 1985 edition. In the past 15 years a wide range of studies have been carried out that substantially enhance our understanding of the way the sports industry works. Whereas in 1985 we had to search around for examples that could be included under the broad heading 'sport and recreation', now we have to make decisions about which examples to include and which to leave out. The bibliography at the end of the book is testimony to the wealth of information now available on the sports industry, and contrasts sharply with the bibliography of the 1985 edition in which general references, rather than sport-specific references, dominated.

The 1985 book was original in its attempt to treat sport both as an industry and as a recognised area of applied microeconomics. Unlike other areas of applied microeconomics such as health, education, housing, or transport, sport had not then had the benefit of 20 to 30 years of economic research in which to inform a book about the industry. The result was that the 1985 book asked the relevant questions, provided the analytical framework, but lacked answers to analytical questions in a large percentage of the topics covered. In this new book, that percentage is much lower.

Ideally, readers of this book will already possess an introductory knowledge of economics. However, we are confident that, even without such a knowledge, the discussions in the various chapters will be understandable to those who are interested in the study of sport as an industry.

We gratefully acknowledge the support of our wives, Christine and Janice, in providing the time and space we needed to complete this book, and Lizzie Watts and Louise Dungworth who did a large share of the word processing, editing, and formatting.

Part I
Introduction

1   Sport and economics

Introduction

This book is about the economic analysis of the sports market, i.e. the demand for and supply of sporting opportunities. Sport is now recognised as an important sector of economic activity, part of the increasingly important leisure industry which accounts for over a quarter of all consumer spending and over 10 per cent of total employment in the UK, and brings in over £20 billion per annum in foreign exchange. Sport is not the largest sector of the leisure industry, but it is among the fastest growing.

Many articles and books have been written about money in sport, and when the phrase 'economics of sport' is used, most people think of it as the analysis of the 'sports business', or the élite sector of the sports market that attracts massive amounts of money through sponsorship, payments for broadcasting rights, and paying spectators. Although money generated through professional sport, international sports competitions, and the televising of major sports events is both substantial and increasing, this is a relatively small part of the total sports market.

It is relatively easy to identify the amounts of money involved at the élite, increasingly professional, end of the sports market. It is less straightforward to identify the expenditure on sport in a country as a whole and the balance between the élite of the sports market and the broad base of recreational sport. We will show that it is now possible to estimate the money value of the broad flow of resources in and out of sport, and such estimates indicate that the economic value of the recreational base of sport far exceeds that of the top of the sports hierarchy.

Figure 1.1 shows the hierarchical nature of the sports market, with a relatively small group of top athletes at the top of the pyramid competing in national and international competitions. At this level, money flows into sport from sponsorship, from paying spectators, from the National Lottery, and from television companies eager to broadcast this top level of competition.

Although the élite end of the sports market appears to be essentially commercial, it is also subsidised by government. Economics can help to provide a rationale for and to assess the cost-effectiveness of such subsidy. Every country wishes to see its own sportsmen and sportswomen as international champions. There is a national demand in every country for international sporting success. Governments fund the top end of the sports market in order to 'produce' sporting excellence

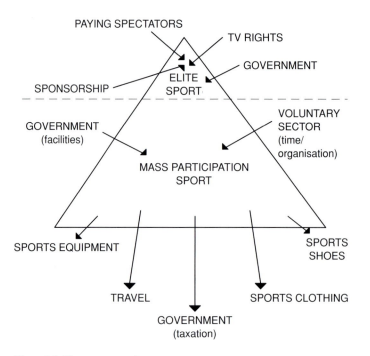

PAYING SPECTATORS

TV RIGHTS

GOVERNMENT

ELITE
SPORT

SPONSORSHIP

GOVERNMENT
(facilities)

VOLUNTARY
SECTOR
(time/
organisation)

MASS PARTICIPATION
SPORT

SPORTS EQUIPMENT

SPORTS
SHOES

TRAVEL

SPORTS CLOTHING

GOVERNMENT
(taxation)

Figure 1.1 The sports market.

and international sporting success, both through their own direct expenditure and through their control of sports lottery funds through government agencies.

At the bottom end of the pyramid we have recreational sport: people taking part in sport for fun, for enjoyment or maybe in order to get fitter and healthier. This part is also subsidised by government (including lottery funds), but predominantly by local government through subsidies to sports facilities in the community and in schools. Again, economic analysis explores both the rationale and the efficiency of such government intervention. Government subsidies at this level are much higher than those directed at the élite end of the sports market. Figure 1.1 also identifies another important source of resources into sport: the voluntary sector. The resources the voluntary sector contributes to sport are massive, but the most important resource is the time that volunteers contribute to sport without payment, and it is not easy to put a monetary valuation on this (although we do attempt it in this book!).

Although government and the voluntary sector support the recreational end of the sport market, there are substantial monetary flows from sports participants to the commercial sector through their expenditures on sports equipment, sports clothes and sports shoes. These same participants also contribute to government revenue in the form of taxation on sport-related expenditures and incomes. In fact, in Britain the amount that sportspeople give back to the government in taxation through sport participation is greater than the amount of government subsidies to sport. Sport gives more to government than government gives to sport.

One final important area that is just starting to be recognised and measured as a sport-related expenditure is sport-related travel. Leisure travel is an important part of travel expenditure, accounting for over 30 per cent of all travel expenditure. Sport-related travel has increased its share of all leisure travel consistently over the past 20 years so that it now accounts for about 10 per cent of leisure travel.

Figure 1.1 indicates the complex nature of the sports market. The supply side of the sports market is a mixture of three types of provider: the public sector, the voluntary sector, and the commercial sector. Government supports sport both to promote mass participation and to generate excellence, but government also imposes taxation on sport. The commercial sector sponsors sport both at the élite level and at grassroots. Some of these sponsors (e.g. Nike, Adidas, Reebok) do so in order to promote their sports products and receive a return on this sponsorship through expenditure by sports participants on their products. Most of sports sponsorship is, however, from the non-sports commercial sector (e.g. Coca-Cola, McDonalds), where the motives for the sponsorship are less directly involved with selling a product to sports participants. Squeezed between government and the commercial sector is the voluntary sector, putting resources into sport mainly through the contribution of free labour time, but needing also to raise enough revenue to cover costs since it cannot raise revenue through taxation as government can.

If the supply side of the sport market is complicated, then so is the demand side. The demand for sport is a composite demand involving the demand for free time; the demand to take part in sport; the demand for equipment, shoes, and clothing; the demand for facilities; and the demand for travel. Taking part in sport involves, therefore, the generation of demand for a range of goods and services which themselves will be provided by the mixture of public, commercial, and voluntary organisations discussed above.

To this complexity of the demand to take part in sport can be added the complication that the sports market is a mixture of both participant demand and spectator demand of different types. As we move up the hierarchy towards élite sport, there is an increasing demand to watch sporting competitions. Some of these spectators may also take part, but many do not. The spectators may go to a specific sports event, or watch at a distance on television. Alternatively, they may not 'watch' at all, preferring to listen on the radio or read about it in newspapers. All of these activities are part of the demand side of the sports market.

In fact, market demand is even more complicated than this rather complex picture, since Figure 1.1 represents only the flows into and out of a national sports market. Increasingly it is more appropriate to talk about the global sports market. A small, but increasing, part of every country's sports market is international or global. There already exist sporting competitions that are of truly global dimensions: over two-thirds of the world's population (over 3.5 billion people) watched some part of the global television coverage of the 1996 Atlanta Olympic

Games. The cumulative television audience for the 1998 football World Cup was over 40 billion. Equally there are commercial companies that produce, distribute, and market their product on a global basis. Nike designs its sports shoes in Oregon, USA, contracts out the production of these shoes to factories in Thailand, Indonesia, China, and Korea, and markets the shoes on a global basis using a symbol (the swoosh) and, in the past, three words that have been understood throughout the world ('Just Do It'). Nike, in 1997, rose to 167th in the world's top 500 companies with a market capitalisation of $17.5 billion.

This book attempts to increase understanding of this complex, increasingly global, market. However, at this early stage it is worth pausing to consider what we mean by sport.

The definition of sport

All researchers concerned with the study of sport face the difficult problem of how to define sport. Sport is a part of a broad range of activities that we call leisure. Leisure researchers, however, have struggled for some time to answer the simple question: what is leisure? Many leisure researchers would argue that it is impossible to have an objective definition of a leisure activity since it depends crucially on the perceptions of the individual participant. The argument is that the same activity can be leisure to one person and non-leisure to another. In fact, it would be quite possible to write a whole book on the question of the definitions of leisure, recreation and sport; but we do not intend to do that here.

The *European Sport for All Charter* (Council of Europe, 1980) gives a classification of activities that might solve the problem, by dividing sport into four broad categories:

1   competitive games and sport which are characterised by the acceptance of rules and responses to opposing challenge;
2   outdoor pursuits in which participants seek to negotiate some particular 'terrain' (signifying in this context an area of open country, forest, mountain, stretch of water or sky); the challenges derive from the manner of negotiation adopted and are modified by the particular terrain selected and the conditions of wind and weather prevailing;
3   aesthetic movement which includes activities in the performance of which the individual is not so much looking beyond himself and is responding to the sensuous pleasure of patterned bodily movement, for example dance, figure-skating, forms of rhythmic gymnastics and recreational swimming;
4   conditioning activity, i.e. forms of exercise or movement undertaken less for any immediate sense of kinaesthetic pleasure than from long-term effects the exercise may have in improving or maintaining physical working capacity and rendering subsequently a feeling of general well-being.

The Council of Europe's *European Sports Charter*, adopted in 1992, uses a more concise definition:

'Sport' means all forms of physical activity which, through casual or organised participation, aim at expressing or improving physical fitness and mental well-being, forming social relationships or obtaining results in competition at all levels.

The main question to be answered is how to distinguish between active sport and more general leisure and recreation activities. Certain activities fall easily into one category or the other. Football, athletics, and gymnastics are clearly Olympic sports and will be recognised by every country as active sport. Going to the cinema, going out for a meal, and watching television are other activities done in leisure time that are clearly non-sport. It is at the margin the problem arises. Are darts and snooker sports or leisure activities?

It could be argued that they are sports, since television coverage of such activities occurs in sports programmes, and newspaper coverage is in the sports section. The activities are also competitive, with well-publicised world championships. In countries where these activities are popular, they are normally included as sports in sports participation surveys. However, they involve little or no physical exertion, so they do not fulfil the criterion of 'physical activity'.

Another set of activities, which are physical but not competitive, are also often included in national sports participation surveys. Activities such as gardening are physical but generally regarded as non-sport, although this activity is included in some participation surveys, normally when the survey is of 'sports and physical activities' rather than just sports. More problematical in this category of activities is walking. Although many types of walking, such as strenuous walking in mountains and the countryside, are clearly active recreation giving the same sort of health benefits as sport, there is a serious problem in interpreting the category 'walking' when it appears in sports participation surveys. Normally, it will represent a wide range of types of activity, some of which we would not want to include as sport. Walking is an activity that is particularly problematical for international comparisons of sports participation, since it tends to have a very high participation rate in northern European countries and a relatively low rate in central and southern European countries.

Rodgers (1977) considered the same problems and argued that four basic elements should ideally be present in a sport, and the first two should always be present. Sport should involve physical activity, be practised for a recreational purpose, involve an element of competition, and have a framework of institutional organisation. To these we add the criterion of general acceptance that an activity is sporting, e.g. by the media and sports agencies. Rodgers developed a core list of sporting activities that could be used for all countries and suggested that a supplementary list could be drawn up to fit the specific needs of each country. The general categorisation of sports and non-sports is shown in Figure 1.2.

The inner circle represents activities that are accepted as sport in all countries and fulfil all of Rodgers' criteria. The second circle represents those which cannot be classified as core sport but have the two key characteristics of being physical and recreational, as well as commonly being regarded as sporting activity.

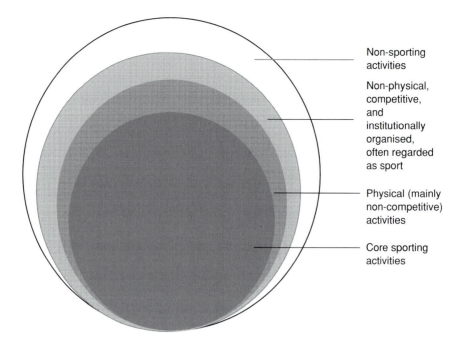

Non-sporting
activities

Non-physical,
competitive,
and
institutionally
organised,
often regarded
as sport

Physical (mainly
non-competitive)
activities

Core sporting
activities

Figure 1.2 Conceptual classification of sporting and non-sporting activities.

The inclusions in this group may vary from country to country; in the UK it would include walking. The third ring from the centre represents activities that are non-physical but are competitive, organised and commonly regarded as sports; in the UK it would include darts and snooker. The white outer area represents activities that are clearly regarded as non-sport in all countries.

The economic characteristics of sport: sport as a commodity

Sport can provide both psychic and physical benefits to participants. Psychic benefits can arise from the sense of well-being derived from being physically fit and healthy, the mental stimulation and satisfaction obtained from active recreation, and the greater status achieved in peer groups. Physical benefits may relate directly to the health relationship with active recreation. Physical exercise, it is argued, is a direct, positive input into the health production function. There is some evidence to indicate that those who regularly engage in physical exercise are likely to live longer, have higher productivity over their working lives, and have greater life satisfaction and an improved quality of life. We will consider these arguments and the related evidence in later chapters. For the moment, it is useful to consider these potential benefits of sports participation within an economic discussion of what type of commodity sport is. The discussion follows similar approaches used by health economists (e.g. Cullis and West, 1979).

It is possible to classify sport under three headings. First, sport is a *non-durable consumption good*: that is, the benefit that matters to the consumer is generated at the time of consumption. Most sports spectating fits within this category of consumer demand: the aesthetic appreciation and enjoyment of watching gymnastics or ice-skating; the tension and excitement of watching a Premier League football match. Each consumer will weigh up the potential satisfaction or 'utility' from consuming the product and make a judgement on whether this is worth more or less than the asking price. If more, then the consumer will be willing to pay for the admission ticket. Equally, most participation in sport is of this non-durable consumption type: people take part because they enjoy it and derive more satisfaction than it costs them to take part.

Participation in sport, however, can generate benefits that are not immediate. If taking part in sport results in the participant being physically in better shape, this is a *durable consumption good* since the benefits of sports consumption accrue over time: the activity (sport) gives utility (satisfaction) in the future as well as in the present. Furthermore, like a durable good, the stock (of fitness) depreciates without regular participation.

In the case of both a non-durable and a durable consumption good the analysis of consumer demand is similar, in that we are seeing pleasure as the motivation for consumption. In one case (non-durable) it is immediate; in the other (durable) there is a time dimension to the pleasure. However, there is another motivation to the consumption of sport that has nothing to do with pleasure. Sport can possess the characteristic of a *capital good*, one that yields a return as part of a *market production process*. If sport makes a person fitter and healthier then this improved health status may lead to a 'pay-off' in terms of increased productivity in the labour market and higher labour market income. This is an extension of Becker's (1964) human capital theory. In the same way that machines can be of different qualities, so can people. A person can 'invest' in himself or herself in order to increase this productivity. The obvious way to do this is through education, and it is in this area that human capital theory has been developed. However, health status is also a pecuniary investment in these terms and since exercise contributes to health status, it becomes an investment good.

There is another aspect to sport as a pecuniary investment, yielding a rate of return in the market, that does not relate to the health connection referred to above. This is the investment of time and effort in training that increases skill and performance to the point that a pecuniary return results from the sporting activity itself. The obvious examples of this are the élite sportsmen and sportswomen who earn their living through participation in sport. This is the classic case of human capital theory. The individual invests time and effort in training in order to become a capital good in the production process of producing a saleable market good. For example, the professional footballer is an integral part of the production process of producing a football match. Although the returns depend to a large extent on innate ability of the player, the harder he or she trains and acquires new skills, the greater is the reward. The increased reward is the return on the investment in training.

There is another sense in which sport can be regarded as a capital good. Becker (1965) adopted the term 'household production' to refer to the way in which consumers can combine their own time with market-purchased inputs of goods and services to 'produce' a leisure activity. In Becker's view, both non-work time and the goods and services purchased on the market should be regarded as necessary inputs for the production of the activity. For instance, to 'produce' a game of badminton requires the time input of the players, the purchase (or hire) of rackets and shuttlecock, and the hire charge for a court.

The relevance of Becker's household production concept for the classification of sport as a commodity is that some evidence exists that people who regularly take part in sport are also more active in a wide range of other leisure activities (socialising, going out for a drink, going out for a meal, etc.). If this is the case, the sport can be regarded as a *capital good* that yields a return in the *non-market production process*. On this reasoning, sport is a 'non-pecuniary investment' in that it increases the 'productivity' of household production.

Different sports are likely to confer a different mix of benefits on participants. This mix of benefits is also likely to change with age and experience in the activity. Young participants are likely to be unaware of durable consumption good benefits or non-pecuniary and pecuniary investment benefits. They will be more interested in immediate pleasure and will not be keen to participate in an activity that does not give it. As they grow older, however, it is likely that awareness of the other three types of benefit will increase, with a possible change in participation to take advantage of them.

Many of the benefits referred to in the classification above relate directly to the relationship between participation in sport and health. Fentem and Bassey (1978, 1981) and the Department of Health (1997) have indicated numerous potential physical and psychological benefits that follow from increased exercise. The benefits are wide-ranging, and exercise is particularly beneficial to the elderly and the chronically sick. On the other side of the coin we have health disbenefits from sport. Sports injuries, and deaths from dangerous sports such as mountaineering and hang-gliding, are negative health aspects associated with sport. We need more quantitative research into the relative size of these positive and negative aspects of the sport–health connection. Recent evidence (Nicholl *et al.*, 1994) seems to indicate that whether the net effect is positive or negative depends on the choice of sport and the age of the participant. For participants over 45, the net effect seems to be clearly positive but participants of this age are less likely to take part in dangerous sports or sports that produce high levels of sports injuries (such as football and rugby).

What this discussion reveals is the difficulty that the consumer faces in making a rational decision when it comes to sport. Economics assumes that consumers are perfectly knowledgeable and make rational choices. The rather complicated nature of the commodity that is sport makes rational decision-making difficult, since the consumer is unlikely to have sufficient knowledge about present and future benefits that will follow from taking part in sport.

Thus, the private demand curve of an individual is not a simple affair. The question is not simply: is the satisfaction I will get from taking part greater than the price I have to pay? Other factors complicate the issue. Some part of the satisfaction does not accrue immediately. The decision to participate depends to some extent on how we value today satisfaction that will be obtained in the future, i.e. the consumers' time discount rate. Also, a person may participate now even though there is no present or future satisfaction from the activity itself. He or she participates purely as an investment that will yield a return. The decision depends again on their personal discount rate, i.e. the value of future financial returns compared with the benefits now of spending the time and money on something else. In general, for any one individual, participation will give aspects of all the benefits discussed above, but the relative weight of each category of benefits is likely to vary substantially from one individual to another.

A framework for the economic analysis of the sports market

Most of this chapter has indicated the difficulties of applying economics to sport. The rest of this book aims to show how these difficulties can be overcome (at least to some extent) so that economics can help us to understand how the sports market works.

As a first stage to this understanding, in Chapter 2 we discuss the measurement of the flows of money and resources in and out of sport as depicted in Figure 1.1. Chapter 2 is the only part of the book to concentrate on a macroeconomic approach to the analysis of sport. The chapter uses a national income accounting framework to estimate the economic importance of sport in the United Kingdom. Chapter 2 also discusses the inadequacies of this methodology, in particular its lack of ability to identify the economic importance of sports events and sports tourism since the impact is normally identifiable only at local rather than national level. The approach also fails to measure the broader economic benefits of sports participation, usually referred to as the social significance of sport.

After the important context of this macroeconomic study of sport, the rest of the book looks at the microeconomics of sport. Part II is concerned with the analysis of demand for sport. Chapter 3 looks first at the question of the demand for leisure time since, as we have seen, time is an essential input into the household production of leisure activities. Next we look at the various theoretical approaches to the demand for sport (Chapter 4) before looking at evidence available on sports participation and the economic factors that determine the demand for it (Chapter 5).

Although the framework for the analysis of the demand for sport is the standard economic theory of consumer demand, we broaden the discussion to include both psychological and sociological factors in the analysis of consumer behaviour in sport, to reflect the increasing importance of the areas of psychological economics and socio-economics for the understanding of consumer decision-making.

Part III of the book looks at the supply side of the market. As indicated earlier, the 'production' side of the sports market is a complicated mixture of the public, commercial, and voluntary sectors. We have one chapter for each sector: Chapter 6 looks at the government sector; Chapter 7 the voluntary sector; and Chapter 8 the commercial sector.

In the mid-1980s it was easy to distinguish between these three sectors, as each had different objectives and different means of satisfying them. In the late 1990s, that distinction is not so clear-cut. In the intervening period, the market sector has become dominant and all three sectors concentrate on using resources efficiently and effectively. However, there are clear differences in the spatial arena in which the different sectors operate. The voluntary sector is dominant at the club level, often operating in conjunction with the public sector, to provide sporting opportunities within a relatively small radius of the clubhouse or sports facility.

Government co-ordinates both the voluntary sector and public sector facilities at the broader community level. Thus government, i.e. local government, has strategic responsibility over its administrative area for the provision of sporting opportunities. It often does this independently by direct supply. However, increasingly it does it in partnership with voluntary sector clubs and charitable trusts across all sports in that area. It also has an interface with the commercial sector in the area, at the very least through the application of planning regulations.

If government and the voluntary sector operate primarily at the local level, there is an important, and strategic, national presence for these two sectors. The first national impact is through the governing bodies of sports, which have responsibility for the organisation and administration of national and international competitions. The second impact is through national government sports agencies, which have responsibility for the 'production' of international sporting success.

Where does the commercial sector fit into this structure? The commercial sector is the most diverse and fragmented of the three sectors involved in the provision of sporting opportunities.

The commercial sector has an increasingly strong presence at the local level in direct competition with both local government and the voluntary sector in the provision of sporting opportunities, particularly through the provision of sport, health and fitness facilities. The commercial sector, however, will only compete in certain sectors of the sports market: fitness centres, country clubs, golf clubs, and the like. In these areas, the commercial sector will aim to give a similar product but provide a higher quality product at a higher price. This allows the commercial sector to have a national presence in the sense of a national network of sports facilities with an established brand and quality.

The national presence of the commercial sector in sport, however, is dominated by the professional sports sector, which grew enormously in importance in the 1990s through the escalation in the price of broadcasting rights for major national and international sports competitions. The alliance between professional sport and the changing structure of broadcasting (involving terrestrial, cable, satellite, and digital) is the largest single influence on the economics of sport in the 1990s.

These changes are increasingly global rather than local or national, and are intrinsically linked to the third major player in the global commercial sports business: the sports shoe, equipment, and clothes suppliers. The word 'suppliers' rather than 'manufacturers' is used since many of these operators contract out the manufacturing side of their products to factories in South-East Asia. Their operations are local in the sense that the design and marketing of their products is handled locally. Manufacturing and distribution are global operations. An important part of this global operation is their relationship with the global broadcasting of major sports events where globally recognised athletes promote the products of these companies.

Although the voluntary, government, and commercial sectors of sport overlap in the markets in which they operate and the economic theories that relate to them, the spatial dimension of these sectors differentiates them. The voluntary club is the most local provider of sporting opportunities; the local government sector co-ordinates and supplements voluntary sector provision; the commercial sector is a relatively small player in competition with the voluntary and the local government sector at the local level but is the leading edge in the globalisation of the sports market.

Part III attempts to analyse these forces, but again to understand what is happening on the supply side of the sports market we will need to go beyond the conventional neo-classical economic analysis of the theory of the firm, economic analysis of government intervention, and theories of the non-profit sector. Although we will use relevant parts of this conventional analysis, we will also attempt to integrate them with more modern approaches to the organisation of economic activity. One major area of this modern approach is the globalisation of markets driven by the development of new technology in communication, media, and broadcasting. The other is the growing importance of the management of contractual relationships which blur the distinctions between public, commercial, and voluntary sector organisations.

Part IV gives a more in-depth analysis of the major contemporary developments on the supply side of the sports market identified in Part III, in particular in the commercial sector of sport. Chapter 9 examines the economics of sports sponsorship; Chapter 10 investigates the economics of major sports events; Chapter 11 looks at the economics of professional team sports and Chapter 12 at the economics of sports broadcasting.

2 The economic importance of sport

Introduction

One of the reasons that the economics of sport has become much more important in the late 1980s and early 1990s is the proliferation of studies in Europe
attempting to estimate the economic importance of sport.

There have been three studies of the economic importance of sport for the
UK economy (Henley Centre for Forecasting, 1986, 1992a; Leisure Industries
Research Centre (LIRC), 1997), estimating the economic importance of sport on
a consistent basis for the years 1985, 1990, and 1995. In addition there have
been three studies for Wales for the years 1988, 1993, and 1995 (Henley Centre
for Forecasting, 1990; Centre for Advanced Studies in the Social Sciences, 1995;
LIRC, 1997b), two for Scotland for 1990 and 1995 (Pieda, 1991; LIRC, 1997c),
and two for Northern Ireland for 1989 and 1995 (Henley Centre for Forecasting, 1992b; LIRC, 1997d). Many other European countries (e.g. the Netherlands,
Belgium, Finland, Denmark, France, and Germany) carried out similar studies
in the 1980s; some of these countries repeated the exercise in the 1990s. Jones
(1989) reviewed all the first round of European economic impact studies and
Andreff (1994) reviewed developments in the early 1990s. LIRC (1997a) reviewed
all the studies that had been carried out in the UK.

All but one of the British studies have used the same approach – the National
Income Accounting framework – to the estimation of the economic importance
of sport, the exception being the study of the Northern regional economy (Pieda,
1994), which used a multiplier approach. Although British studies have concentrated on the National Income Accounting framework, most other European
studies have used alternative approaches. This chapter will concentrate on the
National Income Accounting framework, and the results from the UK studies,
although we do discuss alternative approaches and comparisons between Dutch
and UK estimates at the end of the chapter. The main reason for our emphasis
on the National Income Accounting framework is that a major review of methodologies for estimating the economic importance of sport (LIRC, 1997a) concluded that this method was the most appropriate in the UK context.

However, before we look at the details of the estimation of the economic
importance of sport, we need to look at a model of the flow of goods and services
within the economy.

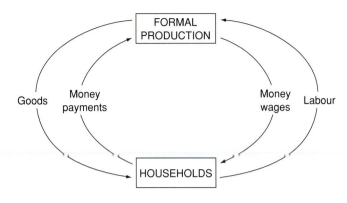

Figure 2.1 The formal economy.
Source: Gershuny (1979)

A model of the economy

Figure 2.1 shows the circular flow of income model of the economy at its simplest. Households spend their money on the goods and services produced by firms. We have a flow of money (consumer expenditure) from households to firms and a flow of goods and services (output) from firms to households. Households also sell their labour services to firms in return for the payment of income. Thus on the right-hand side of Figure 2.1 we see again a flow of money (income), this time from firms to households, and a 'real' flow of labour services from households to firms.

Since all factor services are owned by households, the total amount paid out for these services by firms makes up National Income. In the simple model of Figure 2.1 the total amount of income is spent on goods and services so that total expenditure equals total income, and both correspond to the total value of goods and services produced (total output).

If we wish to measure the economic importance of sport in such a model we have three choices: total expenditure on sports goods and services by households, which would be exactly matched by the value of sports goods and services produced by firms, which also would match the incomes of households supplying factor services to firms producing sports goods and services. The measurement of these totals would be a subset of the National Income accounts, which measure all flows of expenditure (Total Final Expenditure), income (National Income), and output (National Product).

Obviously the model in Figure 2.1 is unrealistic since there is no government, no saving and investment, and no foreign countries. The model can easily be adapted to take account of flows to and from an overseas sector and a government sector, and a financial markets sector (saving and investment). Any flow from households out of total expenditure that does not go to purchase goods and services from firms (e.g. saving) is a 'leakage' from the circular flow of income.

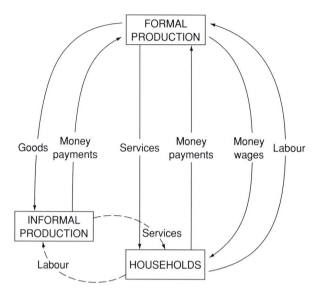

Figure 2.2 The informal economy.
Source: Gershuny (1979)

Any flow entering the circular flow from one of these other sectors (e.g. investment) is an injection into the system. Thus taxation, saving, and imports are leakages, while government expenditure, investment expenditure and exports are injections. If leakages and injections are equal then the size of National Income is constant. If injections are greater then leakages in total, then total expenditure increases as does output and income. Conversely, if leakages are greater than injections then total expenditure falls. The introduction of new sectors to Figure 2.1, and the move to a more realistic model of the economy, allows national income to grow and decline, which of course is what happens in reality.

The circular flow of income model incorporating these other sectors is the conceptual model of the economy that lies behind the National Income Accounting approach to the estimation of the economic importance of sport. The estimation is now more complicated since we must measure sport-related expenditure flows to and from the overseas sector and government, but essentially the principle is the same.

One other sector that plays a crucial role in sport must be added to the model: the voluntary sector.

Figure 2.2 uses concepts of the formal and informal economy derived from Gershuny (1979) to incorporate the voluntary sector. The formal economy is the one depicted in Figure 2.1 which is represented by market transactions. The informal economy refers to those activities where households contribute their own time together with market-purchased goods for the production of services they themselves consume. Unlike in the formal economy, the flow of labour services to the informal economy is not matched by an income flow in the opposite direction. In the informal economy, the household sector is part of the production sector: it is essentially the same as Becker's (1965) household production concept except that here several households combine together in the voluntary sector and 'produce' a product from which they can all derive benefit. The voluntary sector sports club is an example of such an informal economic activity. Members contribute their time and effort without payment for the 'production' of sporting opportunities. There is some formal sector economic activity, since members will pay subscriptions to the club, but the formal sector payments and receipts will be an underestimate of the true level of economic activity (i.e. the true level of income, expenditure, and output).

The National Income Accounting framework

National Income Accounting is the name given to the process of measurement of the flows of income, expenditure, and output in the economy as represented by the model of the previous section. All government statistical services carry out this measurement exercise: it is their core business. Our interest is in that part of the national accounts that relates to sport. We can try to isolate sport-related output, sports-related income, or sports-related expenditure. In the UK the tradition has been to identify sport-related final expenditure. In effect, the process attempts to measure the expenditure flows into and out of the sports market represented in Figure 2.1.

The National Income Accounting framework indicates how expenditure in one particular sector of the economy flows as income to other sectors and hence generates value-added and employment. Applied to sport, seven different sectors are identified:

- central government
- local government
- commercial sport
- commercial non-sport
- consumer sector
- voluntary sector
- overseas sector.

The commercial non-sport sector is the only one of these that is not self-explanatory. It consists of commercial firms supplying sports organisations with non-sports goods and services which are required by the sports organisations, e.g. catering for sports outlets, transport for sports trips.

The advantage of the sector-based method is that a large proportion of the estimates of sport-related final expenditure is based on expenditure figures that form part of the UK National Income Accounts and therefore the sports sector is clearly identified as a distinct sector within the national economy. The method categorises each element of total sport-related final expenditure to one of the seven sectors above and then shows the flows from expenditure to income, indicating how expenditure in any one sector can contribute to income in several other sectors.

The sectoral accounts are the main output of the National Income Accounting framework, but these are essentially a description of the monetary flows between the sectors (a flow-of-funds framework). They are not an economic importance calculation for the whole sports economy because they 'double count' a lot of the economic activity, e.g. expenditure on a stock of sports goods by a retailer will double count the expenditure by manufacturers on materials to make the goods.

To move from these sectoral accounts to the economic importance of the whole sports economy, it is necessary to estimate the value-added created in each destination sector by the sport-related final expenditure. Value-added is exactly what the term suggests: it is the value that is added to a product at each stage of production/retailing. For example, a retailer buys sports goods at wholesale prices, then provides a retail outlet, staff to advise customers, promotion for the product, etc., and sells the product at a higher price than the wholesale price paid. The difference in price is equivalent to the value added, and is reflected in the retailer's wages and profits.

Value added estimation for sport in the UK uses information from relevant business monitors or (in the commercial non-sport sector) input–output tables are used to identify the share of the total turnover that is wages and salaries and profit. These shares are then used to turn income into value-added (i.e. wages, salaries, and profits; or alternatively turnover minus other inputs). This estimation process is therefore an *ad hoc* 'add-on' to the essentially flow-of-funds approach of the National Income Accounting framework.

Similarly, the National Income Accounting framework does not directly generate estimates of employment. Employment is estimated again by an *ad hoc* method. Average wages in each sector are calculated from the New Earnings Survey, and the total wages in each sector are divided by their average wages to give employment estimates. For sectors where this method cannot be used, other *ad hoc* solutions are found (e.g. Census of Employment is used for local government employment in sport; results from a survey of voluntary sports organisations are used to estimate employment in the voluntary sector).

Despite the rather piecemeal approach that has to be incorporated to move from sectoral accounts to the economic importance of sport, we feel that the method is particularly appropriate in identifying the economic contribution made by one industrial sector of the economy, particularly a sector like sport that is not clearly identified as an industry in official statistics.

The Leisure Industries Research Centre (1997a) has constructed a spreadsheet model that estimates the economic impact of sport. The model requires the input of published data for the required year, then performs all the relevant calculations to derive first sports-related expenditure, then all the relevant sectoral accounts, and finally value-added and employment. The model has been used to reproduce the economic impact calculations for 1985 and 1990 for the UK, and also to calculate the economic impact of sport for the latest year for which complete data are available, 1995.

Table 2.1 Consumers' expenditure (£ million) on sport-related goods and services (current prices)

	1985	1990	1995
Participant sports: subscriptions and admission charges	593.92	1,214.08	2,010.81
Clothing sales	435.00	1,157.00	1,407.00
Footwear sales	290.00	795.00	938.00
Travel	274.78	334.20	473.92
Gambling:			
football pools	355.62	522.84	633.29
horse racing	1,199.26	2,076.06	2,299.27
Other consumer expenditure on sport	1,927.24	2,343.26	2,649.27
Total	5,075.82	8,442.44	10,411.56

Source: LIRC (1997a)

The economic importance of sport in the UK, 1985–1995

The latest UK estimates indicate that:

- consumers' expenditure on sport in 1995 was £10.4 billion, or 2.33 per cent of total consumers' expenditure
- value-added to the UK economy in 1995 by sport-related economic activity was £9.8 billion, or 1.6 per cent of Gross Domestic Product
- employment in sport was 415,000 in 1995, compared to 324,470 in 1985; employment in sport accounted for 1.61 per cent of total employment in 1995 compared to 1.52 per cent of total employment in 1985.

Table 2.1 indicates the time series for the major elements of consumers' expenditure on sport-related goods and services from 1985 to 1995. The values are all in terms of current prices and hence reflect the rise in prices (i.e. inflation) as well as the increased volume of purchasing between 1985 and 1995.

Table 2.2 gives consumers' expenditure on sport in constant 1987 prices and the real rate of growth of expenditure on sport over the 10 year period. Overall real consumers' expenditure on sport grew by 30 per cent between 1985 and 1995, with the strongest growth being in subscriptions and charges for participation sports, and expenditure on sports clothing and sports footwear. These three items all doubled in volume terms (i.e. at constant prices) over the period, which is consistent with the strong growth in sports participation between 1985 and 1995 as revealed by General Household Survey sports participation data (see Chapter 5).

Overall growth in consumers' expenditure on sport was greater than growth in consumers' expenditure in total, which itself grew strongly over the 1985 to 1989 period, so that sport accounted for a higher share of consumers' expenditure in 1995 than it did in 1985 (2.33% in 1995 compared to 2.01% in 1985).

Table 2.2 Consumers' expenditure (£ million) on sport-related goods and services (constant 1987 prices)

	1985	1995	% increase 1985–1995
Participant sports:			
subscription and fees	627.82	1,348.63	115
Clothing sales	459.83	943.66	105
Footwear sales	306.55	629.11	105
Travel	290.47	317.85	9
Gambling:			
football pools	375.91	424.74	13
horse racing	1,267.72	1,542.09	22
Other consumer			
expenditure on sport	2,027.25	1,776.84	−13
Total	5,365.56	6,982.93	30

Source: LIRC (1997a)

Table 2.3 Percentage share in value-added by sector

	1985	1990	1994
Commercial sport	20.10	22.34	20.92
Voluntary	6.15	10.93	14.98
Commercial non-sport	64.40	57.83	54.31
Central government	0.27	0.36	0.47
Local government	9.08	8.54	9.32

Source: LIRC (1997a)

Table 2.3 gives the changing contribution of each sector to value-added. In 1985 value-added was dominated by the commercial non-sport sector. This was still the case in 1995 although its share dropped, the drop being matched by a large rise in the voluntary sector contribution to value-added. This rise in the share of the voluntary sector is almost certainly due to some of the economic activity that formerly took place in the informal economy having switched to the formal economy. That is, some of the jobs done by volunteers in 1985 were being done by paid labour in 1995. Overall value-added in sport accounts for 1.61 per cent of GDP in 1995 compared to 1.34 per cent of GDP in 1985.

Table 2.4 gives employment in sport at 415,000 in 1995, compared to 324,470 in 1985. Employment in sport accounted for 1.61 per cent of total employment in 1995, compared to 1.52 per cent of total employment in 1985.

International comparisons: sports expenditure in the UK and the Netherlands

As indicated earlier, at the same time as studies of the economic importance of sport were being carried out in Britain, similar studies were being carried out in

Table 2.4 Employment in sport in the UK, 1995

Sector	Employment (000s)
Commercial sport	
Spectator clubs	21.84
Participation clubs	12.46
Retailers	66.58
Manufacturing (exports)	7.76
TV and radio	5.40
Subtotal	114.05
Voluntary sport	49.06
Commercial non-sport	197.03
Central government	
Transport	1.11
Administration	0.76
Subtotal	1.87
Local government	
Sports facilities	32.08
Education	16.41
Transport/police	4.44
Subtotal	52.93
Total	414.95

Source: LIRC (1997a)

other European countries. The methodologies employed varied across countries, as did the definition of sport-related expenditure, and this has made comparisons between countries difficult. However, it is possible to make comparisons between the UK estimates of sport-related expenditure and the Dutch estimates. As in the UK, studies were carried out in the Netherlands in both the 1980s (van Puffelen *et al.*, 1988) and the 1990s (Oldenbroom, *et al.*, 1996).

Figure 2.3 compares sports expenditures in the UK and the Netherlands for 1994. Total sports expenditures are at similar levels in the two countries. However, the distribution of expenditures within these totals is different. The Dutch spend substantially more on admission fees and subscriptions than the British, and although this has been the area of sports spending that has grown the most between 1985 and 1994 in Britain, which has narrowed the gap, the Dutch still spend about twice as much per capita as the British on subscriptions. One major reason for this is the much higher level of sports club membership in the Netherlands – over twice as high as Britain – with around 25 per cent of the population being members of sports clubs. Another reason is that high state spending on sport in the Netherlands has led to a much higher quality of sports facility provision, on average, in the Netherlands compared to Britain, particularly for outdoor sport. Thus the Dutch pay more but for a higher quality.

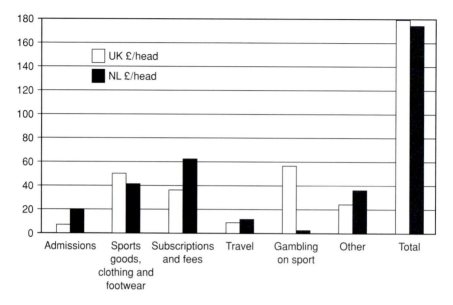

Figure 2.3 Comparison of UK and Dutch consumers' expenditure on sport (1994).

The higher levels of expenditure on sport subscriptions have more to do with factors such as this than with higher levels of participation in sport in general, as indicated by comparable levels of expenditure on sports goods, clothing, and footwear. Two items of expenditure do reflect, however, differences in levels of participation in particular activities – cycling and skiing – where the Dutch participation rate is considerably higher than the British. One final major difference between sport-related consumer expenditure in Britain and the Netherlands is the relative importance of expenditure on gambling on sport in the two countries. In Britain it is the largest single item of sports-related expenditure; in the Netherlands it is the smallest.

Inadequacies of national estimates of the economic importance of sport

All the estimates provided in this chapter on the economic importance of sport in the UK are consistent in that they have all been calculated in the same way with the same assumptions. However, they almost certainly consistently underestimate the true economic importance of sport due to the underestimation of three areas of economic activity: the voluntary sector, sports events, and sports tourism.

The voluntary sector

The lack of availability of any information on the voluntary sector in sport is a long-standing problem. The level of detailed economic information required for an economic impact study is simply not available. Virtually all the studies carried out in the UK have attempted to solve this problem with primary data collection using questionnaires. The outcome of such primary data collection, however, is very uneven.

In The Henley Centre for Forecasting's (1986) study, no new survey work was carried out and data on the voluntary sector was compiled from the accounts of thirty-five clubs across seven sports that the Sports Council had on record as a result of applications for grants. The report acknowledged that clubs making grant applications to the Sports Council were unlikely to be representative of all sports, but no mechanism for correcting for any bias was employed.

In the second study (Henley Centre for Forecasting, 1992a), new primary data collection was carried out, but only six sports were surveyed (athletics, cricket, football, golf, rugby, and sailing) and only 232 questionnaires were returned from clubs in these sports.

Obviously, wide margins of error will be associated with estimates of voluntary sector economic activity based on such small surveys across a small number of sports. This is not so much the fault of the researchers carrying out the work as the very nature of the voluntary sector which makes it difficult to record in normal statistical assessments.

However, there is a more fundamental reason why conventional estimates of the economic importance of sport underestimate the true size of economic resources in sport. This relates to the discussion earlier on the formal and informal economy. Conventional estimates of the economic importance of sport only represent the contribution of the voluntary sector to the formal economy: that is, these estimates only look at the income and expenditure accounts of voluntary sector clubs. They take no account of the unpaid labour service of volunteers, which is the essential resource element of the voluntary sector. A true estimation of the resources involved in sport would include these unpaid labour services. Studies in several countries have shown that if we included such services in the estimate of the economic importance of sport, this would add up to 50 per cent to the estimate. We return in Chapter 7 to this problem of measuring the value of voluntary labour in UK sport.

Sports events

The Family Expenditure Survey estimates of expenditure on entrance charges for spectating at sports events are the only source of this component recorded in the economic impact studies of sport. This records only a small fraction of the sport-related expenditure associated with spectating at sports events. The entrance charge is only a fraction of the total expenditure associated with the day and/or night out generated by the sport event. Expenditure on accommodation, food and drink dominates the economic impact generated by visitors to sports events. This will be greatest for overseas tourists, but the relatively small importance of spectating at sports events in the overall tourist market means that aggregate statistics make it impossible to estimate the economic importance of this specific market.

There is also an important spatial element to the sports events spectator market. Normal domestic competitions are dominated by a small number of areas in the economic importance of events, particularly since overall football spectating accounts for over a half of all sports spectating. Thus, London, Manchester, Birmingham, Liverpool, Glasgow, Newcastle, and Leeds together account for a major share of total football attendances. Nationally this spatial element is lost in the aggregation process. Thus, UK economic impact of sport studies do not pick out specific areas that benefit more from sport than others. However, visitors from outlying areas to attend football matches will contribute substantially to the local economy of the cities mentioned above. Thus, major sports events have the potential to attract significant additional expenditure to a local economy even though they may only attract domestic visits from other areas close by. This inter-regional redistribution of income due to sports events has never been seriously studied, and therefore we have no idea of its economic importance.

When we move to international events such as the Euro 96 football championships, this spatial redistribution of income is extended to the international field, but still includes a large element of inter-regional redistribution of income. This means that national studies record very little economic effect for such events, but locally based studies would show a substantial economic impact on the local economy in which the events were based. The importance of this effect can be seen from this quote from the *Investors Chronicle* (June 14th 1996):

> Euro 96 is big business – the third-largest sporting event after the football World Cup and the Olympic Games. When England hosted the World Cup finals in 1966, the tournament's revenues were just over £2m (worth about £20m in today's money). This time ticket sales alone will total £55m. On top are £45m of TV rights and a hierarchy of sponsorship deals, worth around £50m.
>
> This £150m is just for starters. According to Licensed Properties International (LPI), the buy-out from Time Warner which is licensed to sell Euro 96's merchandising rights to the UK's retailers, sales of licensed goods should fetch at least £120m. The 11 official sponsors are expected to splurge a further £100m between them on marketing. The British Tourist Association reckons 250,000 tourists will arrive for the championships, spending £120m mainly on accommodation and entertainment. And Ladbroke believes UK punters will bet around £80m on the event.

The nature of these 'special events' is that they are under-recorded or not recorded at all in the standard expenditure and tourism surveys, which reflect 'normal' rather than 'special' behaviour. Chapter 10 analyses the economics of staging major sports events, but the important implication for this chapter is that the economic impact of sport studies seriously underestimates the true economic importance of sports events.

Sports tourism

Sports tourism is treated in different ways in different studies. The Henley Centre studies made no attempt to identify the economic importance of sports tourism. They identified two items of expenditure, travel and skiing holidays, of which some elements can be classified as sports tourism. The first study carried out in Scotland (Pieda, 1991) did have a specific item on sports tourism in the 'Outside Scotland' sector. However, the estimate was highly suspect since it was based on the proposition that 'inward' tourism for sport is largely accounted for by golfing holidays (Pieda, 1991), thus ignoring sports tourism relating to salmon fishing, skiing, walking, hunting and shooting, and mountaineering, all of which are major activities for tourists to Scotland. The second Welsh study (Centre for Advanced Studies in the Social Sciences, 1995) identified 'other sporting holidays' which accounted for £53 million of consumer expenditure, compared with the £31 million estimated for this category in Scotland by Pieda (1991). This suggests that sports tourism in Scotland is substantially less than that in Wales, a result that conflicts with a priori expectations.

This rather piecemeal approach to sports tourism in the economic impact of sport literature contrasts sharply with recent evidence from the tourism field that suggests that sports-related tourism may be a significant, and increasing, part of the tourism market. UKTS (1998) indicated that 55 per cent of all holiday trips taken by UK residents in the UK involved some type of sport and recreation activity. For 20 per cent of all trips, such activities were the main purpose of the holiday.

The *European Travel Monitor* indicates that in Europe as a whole, of all holiday trips, 5 per cent are for the purpose of winter sports, 1 per cent of tourist trips are for the purpose of summer sport, 6 per cent are for mountain recreation, and a further 10 per cent are for countryside recreation. Thus up to 22 per cent of tourist trips in Europe have something to do with active physical recreation.

There is clearly a need for a systematic research project aimed at estimating the value of sports tourism. In particular, the way tourism data is collected almost certainly underestimates two important elements of sports tourism, as follows.

- Sports tours by recreational sports clubs. These are most common in team sports such as football, rugby, hockey, and cricket. Such tours conventionally take place at the end of the season, which means early spring for winter sports and early autumn for summer sports. The random sample approach to data collection for tourism statistics means that these peaks in sports tourism are almost certainly underestimated. Given the underestimation of the economic importance of the voluntary sector in general and voluntary sector sports clubs in particular, referred to above, this suggests a serious underestimation of this element of sports tourism.
- At the élite level of sport, national squad members are spending up to 100 days and nights a year away from home for competition and training. This involves nights away from home in both Britain (training camps and domestic

competition) and abroad (competitions and warm weather training). Although the number of people involved is small in relation to the total population, the large number of nights away from home makes this a not insignificant contribution to the economic importance of sports tourism (see Reeves and Jackson, 1996).

The essential problem associated with the estimation of the economic importance of sports tourism is the same one identified in the discussion of the voluntary sector above: there has been no systematic attempt to identify the size and importance of this form of tourism. Conventional approaches to data collection in the broad area of tourism behaviour will almost certainly seriously underestimate the economic importance of sports tourism because of its tendency to show sharp peaks outside of the normal tourism season. Only targeted studies involving new primary data collection will identify the size of this form of tourism.

Although sports events are an important generator of sports tourism, this is only one part of the sports tourism industry. The other major contribution that sports tourism makes to the local and regional economy is from the spending of visitors to areas for participation in sport and recreation. In Britain this is dominated by tourism for the purposes of outdoor recreation.

- The Highland and Islands Enterprise (1996) estimated the economic impact of hillwalking, mountaineering and associated activities in the Highlands and Islands of Scotland. It estimated that these activities generated £160 million in gross expenditure and over 6,000 full-time equivalent jobs in the Highlands and Islands. This compares with £35 million expenditure supporting some 2,200 jobs for sporting shooting in Scotland, £34 million supporting some 3,400 jobs for salmon fishing, and £14.5 million supporting 365 jobs for skiing in the Cairngorms and Glencoe.

The total size of the UK sports tourism market was estimated at around £1.5 billion in 1995, and the examples cited show the potential for economic regeneration through sport in both urban and rural areas. At the moment national estimates of the economic importance of sport underestimate these economic effects.

The broader economic benefits of sports participation

Even if we could obtain reasonably accurate estimates of all the items of sport-related expenditure so far referred to in this chapter, the estimate of the economic importance of sport derived from the National Income Accounting, input–output or multiplier models would still be a considerable underestimate of the true economic importance of sport in society. The reason is that there is a broader set of economic benefits of sport that so far no economist has attempted to measure. Such benefits include the economic value of:

- improvements in health and fitness
- reductions in anti-social behaviour
- contribution of sport to the quality of life
- inward investment.

Such benefits are often put forward as the arguments for government subsidy of sport, and we will deal with them in detail in Chapter 6. However, it is important to recognise here that conventional estimates of the economic importance of sport take no account of such benefits.

Alternative approach for the estimation of the economic impact of sport

Input–output analysis

Input–output models differ from the flow-of-funds (income and expenditure) approach of national income accounting in that the focus of the input–output approach is production: inputs to the production process and outputs from it. In theory, these inputs and outputs are expressed in physical terms and the technology of production is presented in a matrix which shows (row by row) the input of each sector required for the production of output in all sectors.

Fletcher (1989) identified the benefits of using an input–output approach in the estimation of the economic impact of tourism, including a comprehensive view of the whole economy, attention on the sectoral interdependencies which exist in the economy, and improvements in the level and quality of data available for the economy in general and for the national accounts in particular.

The major disadvantages of the input–output approach are particularly relevant to its potential in measuring the economic importance of sport.

- The input–output tables available normally relate to an earlier year than the one for which the economic impact is being calculated. Previous economic impact studies in tourism have used the 1979 and 1984 tables. Any studies carried out in the next few years would have to use the 1990 tables.
- The industrial categories used are very broad, and a sub-sector such as sport is lost in broad aggregate groupings. For instance, the production of boats for sporting use comes under the general category of 'shipbuilding', and bicycles come under 'other vehicles'.

Sport-related production is a small part of these industries, and the Central Statistical Office has advised that it considers the input–output tables inappropriate for the estimation of the economic importance of sport for this reason.

As a check on the sensitivity of the economic importance of sport estimates to the methodology used, the input–output approach was used to estimate value added for sports for 1990, the latest year for which input–output tables are available. The input–output approach gave a figure of £7,732 million, which is close to the

£7,560 million generated by the LIRC model using a National Income Accounting framework. The two approaches therefore appear to give similar results.

The multiplier

The multiplier approach is the method most commonly used to estimate the economic importance of tourism and the arts in a specific region. However, there are problems in using it at national level. The arguments about using the multiplier for a microeconomic economic impact study are discussed in the Henley Centre for Forecasting's (1986, 1992a) studies, and mainly relate to adverse effects of additional spending on financial markets effectively reducing the multiplier to zero. There is also a fundamental issue of whether it is appropriate to use a multiplier approach to estimate the economic importance of a specific industry such as sport. The multiplier essentially refers to effects of an *additional* injection of spending into the economy. It shows the direct, indirect, and induced effects of a specific *change* in expenditure. Thus in tourism impact studies, the tourism expenditure is considered as an addition to the normal flow of expenditure in the local economy. At the national level, it is not appropriate to treat all expenditure associated with sport as additional in this way.

The multiplier, however, is particularly appropriate for the estimation of the economic impact of special events, such as sports events, because they clearly generate additional expenditure, income, and employment to the economy. It is more appropriate also to use the multiplier to estimate the local and regional impacts rather than national impacts. We discuss this in more detail in Chapter 10, where we analyse the economic impact of major sports events on the local economy of host cities.

Census of Employment-based estimates

Vaughan (1986) provides a framework for estimating tourism employment directly from the Census of Employment. The Census of Employment approach is completely different from the other three approaches above since it moves straight to an employment estimate rather than to expenditure, value-added and then employment. We mention the approach for completeness, since it has been used in tourism studies and is being used to estimate employment in the arts.

Only two industrial categories (sport and recreational services and sports goods manufacturers) relate directly to sport. Employment in these categories from 1981 to 1994 is recorded in Table 2.5.

The apparent large drop in employment in sports goods from 9,000 in 1991 to 6,300 in 1993 is not necessarily an actual drop in employment. A new Standard Industrial Classification was introduced in 1992, and whereas the sport and recreational services category is broadly the same in the new classification as in the old, the new sports goods category excludes several areas of production included in the old sports goods categories. This problem applies to all the other categories of employment that have some sport-related employment. Not only

Table 2.5 Employment in sport and recreational services and in sports good manufacture (000s)

	Sport and recreational services	*Sports goods manufacture*
1981	272.4	9.8
1984	277.7	10.1
1987	301	9.6
1989	308.9	10.2
1990	324.4	
1991	338	9
1993	356.4	6.3
1994	355.2	

will these categories be non-comparable post-1992 with pre-1992, but also the assumptions needed to estimate the sport-related element of employment from a broader employment category are much more tenuous than used in the expenditure categories. We suggest then that this is not a viable method for the estimation of sport-related employment.

Conclusion

The estimates of the economic importance of sport show that sport has grown substantially in economic importance between 1985 and 1995. Sport-related consumers' expenditure accounted for 2.33 per cent of total consumers' expenditure in 1995 compared to 2.01 per cent in 1985; value-added in sports accounted for 1.61 per cent of GDP in 1995 compared to 1.34 per cent of GDP in 1985; sport-related employment accounted for 1.61 per cent of total employment in 1995 compared to 1.52 per cent of total employment in 1985. These estimates are very much the minimal estimates of the size of the sports sector, as indicated earlier.

This growth in the sports industry is likely to have accelerated in the period 1996 to 2000. Sports events are growing in economic importance, as Euro 96 proved, and are not fully reflected in these estimates. Lottery grants in sport, though included in the 1995 estimates, will be much larger in future years and their economic benefits will start to multiply.

The biggest single change, however, to the economic importance of sport will be the large rise in the sale of television rights for sports events, which we investigate in Chapter 12. Many of the deals have already been completed (e.g. £670 million by BSkyB for Premier League football matches for the period 1997–2001), so we already know that there will be substantial increases in the revenues of professional sports clubs. However, it is estimated that the arrival of digital television could add another £2.5 billion pounds per year to the revenue of professional sports clubs through the sale of television rights. Changes of this magnitude over the next few years will make it worthwhile to re-estimate the economic importance of sport on an annual basis, since year-on-year changes could be substantial.

Part II
Demand

3 The demand for leisure time

Introduction

Economic analysis of the demand for a commodity normally takes as its starting point the relationship between the quantity demanded, the price of the commodity and the income of the consumers. For leisure commodities, however, the resources available to the consumer are wider than simply his or her income. To enjoy leisure commodities consumers need time, and for some consumers the lack of availability of time is a bigger constraint on leisure consumption than the lack of availability of money. When people are asked in surveys either why they do not participate in sport or why they do not participate more often, the single biggest response is typically lack of time. For this reason we dedicate a whole chapter to the demand for and availability of leisure time.

The income/leisure trade-off

Neo-classical economic analysis assumes that rational utility-maximising consumers are faced with a continuous choice over how to allocate their time between work and leisure. Work is treated as disutility and consumers need compensation in terms of income to persuade them to give up their leisure time. In this income/leisure trade-off analysis, any time spent in leisure or other non-paid work activities means losing potential earnings, so that the opportunity cost, or *price of leisure* is the forgone earnings. If people behave rationally, they will only enter the labour market and continue to work as long as the benefits from income outweigh the benefits from leisure time.

If a decision is made to enter the labour market, the next decision concerns how many hours to work. The more hours the consumer works, the more valuable each hour of leisure time that is left becomes, as leisure time becomes increasingly scarce. Eventually there will come a point when the additional income earned from an additional hour of work (i.e. the hourly wage rate) is not sufficient to compensate for the loss of another hour of leisure time. The optimum trade-off between time spent at work and time spent at leisure will be at the point when the valuation of an hour of leisure time is equal to the wage rate. Working longer hours than this optimum would mean that the consumer was irrationally choosing to trade-off an hour of leisure time for income that was less than their valuation of that hour of leisure time.

This choice mechanism has been used in economics to analyse individual decisions concerning whether or not to work, whether to take part-time or full-time employment, whether to work more hours in a week (overtime) or whether to take a second job (moonlighting).

A crucial part of the analysis is how people react to a change in the wage rate, the price of leisure time. Since over time we expect wage rates to rise, we will consider here the effect of a rise in the wage rate. How does this affect the income/leisure choice? There are two contrasting influences: the substitution and the income effects of the rise in the price of leisure. First, because the price of leisure time is rising, there is an inducement to take less leisure time and devote more time to work. This is the normal demand relationship: for any commodity, as the relative price rises, we demand less of it. This is the substitution effect.

Second, because rates of pay for all existing work hours are higher, total income will rise even if the amount of time spent at work does not change. Some of this extra income may be used to 'buy' more leisure time, by working fewer hours. If leisure time is a 'normal good', which in economics means that demand for it rises as incomes rise, than we would expect demand for leisure time to rise as wage rates rise. This is the income effect.

Thus we have two effects pulling in opposite directions, and the net effect on the demand for leisure time is difficult to predict. Whether leisure time increases or decreases as wage rates rise is an empirical question. In the next section we examine the evidence.

Leisure time demand indicators

The main indicators of leisure time are commonly indicators of paid work, since leisure time in its broadest sense is time free from such work. However, a more acceptable notion of leisure time is time free from work and obligated time such as sleeping and household chores. There are, though, 'grey areas' in the use of time which are partly obligated or work and partly leisure, such as eating, shopping, travelling, and DIY.

The most reliable data source on working hours in the UK is the Labour Force Survey (LFS). The survey requires each respondent to record the number of hours that they worked in the previous week. Figure 3.1 shows the change in the number of hours worked per week between 1975 and 1995 as recorded in the LFS. Working hours fell for full-time employees between 1975 and 1984. This downward trend was so significant during this period that the average working day fell by around 1 hour. By 1985, full-time male workers were working an average of 40.3 hours per week. However, 1985 signalled the end of the post-war trend of decline in working hours in Britain. By 1989 the average working week for full-time male workers had increased to 44.1 hours. The rate at which working hours for men was increasing slowed in the early 1990s, so that it had

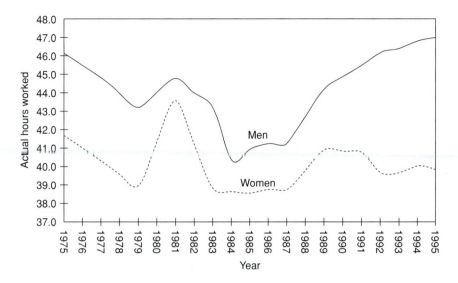

Figure 3.1 Actual number of hours worked by full-time employees 1975–1995.

increased to 46.8 hours per week for male full-time employees by 1995, which is higher than the figure for 1975. Full-time female employees' hours also reached a low point in 1985 at 38.5 hours per week. They had reached 39.7 hours by 1995. These male and female time patterns to working hours demonstrate a dominant income effect until the mid-1980s, causing a rise in demand for leisure time. Thereafter, however, there has been a dominant substitution effect.

One of the features of the UK labour market is the predominance of overtime working in manual jobs. Typically over half of men in manual jobs work an average of ten hours a week paid overtime, and a fifth of men in non-manual jobs work an average of six hours a week paid overtime. The percentage of female workers working overtime has risen steadily to a current position whereby 30 per cent of female manual workers work an average of over six hours a week paid overtime and 17 per cent of female non-manual workers work an average of nearly four hours paid overtime. The economic logic of overtime for employers is its flexibility and the fact that there are far lower fixed costs of employment associated with overtime than with taking on extra employees. The logic for employees is that the higher overtime rate of pay will encourage only a substitution effect, i.e. demanding less leisure time, because leisure time is more expensive at the margin during overtime hours.

Another indicator of trends in leisure time availability is the percentage of working age people that are in the workforce (i.e. the labour force activity rate). The long-term trend in labour force activity rates demonstrates a steady decrease in the percentage of working age men (16–65 years) working in paid employment, and a steady increase in the percentage of women of working age (16–60

Table 3.1 Labour force economic activity rates* in the UK by gender and age (%)

	16–24	25–44	45–59	60–64	65 and over	All aged 16 and over
Males						
1984	81.8	96.1	90.0	57.5	8.7	75.9
1991	81.2	95.7	88.1	54.2	8.6	74.9
1994	75.1	94.1	86.1	51.0	7.6	72.6
Females						
1984	69.1	65.6	63.3	21.8	3.1	49.2
1991	71.3	73.0	66.9	23.9	3.1	53.1
1994	64.6	73.5	69.3	25.3	3.2	53.0

Source: Labour Force Survey, Central Statistical Office, in *Social Trends*, **26**, 1996.

* The percentage of the population that is in the labour force.

Table 3.2 Holiday entitlement, 1995

Days' entitlement per year	Full-time employees (%)	Part-time employees (%)
0	4.1	36.0
1–5	0.4	4.3
6–10	2.2	9.0
11–15	7.2	12.2
16–20	22.8	15.4
21–25	38.1	13.5
26–30	16.5	4.6
31+	8.7	5.0

Source: Department of Employment.

years) in the paid workforce (see Table 3.1). In 1994 just under 73 per cent of men of working age were in paid employment, one of the main factors being that just over half of men aged 60–65 years were still working, probably due to early retirement in the case of those that weren't. By 1994, 53 per cent of women of working age were in paid employment, and there is every expectation that this will continue to rise. Interestingly, the rise in the percentage of women in paid work applies to the oldest group – in 1994 over a quarter of 60–65 year old women were in paid employment. The only age group for women demonstrating a declining labour force activity rate in the 1990s has been the youngest, 16–24 years, probably due to higher numbers of women entering higher education.

The principal ways in which any expansion in leisure time has been achieved have been through increases in paid holiday entitlement and earlier retirement by men. Table 3.2 gives the paid holiday entitlement for full-time and part-time employees in 1995 (not counting public holidays). The average entitlement for full-time employees is 23 days for men and 25 days for women, while for part-time

Table 3.3 Time allocation by full-time employed men and women (hours per week)

	1986	1987	1988	1989	1990	1991	1992
Men							
Paid work	39.0	41.8	40.9	41.6	41.4	40.1	NA
Travel	6.9	6.7	6.8	7.3	6.7	6.2	6.2
Personal*	22.7	22.3	23.1	25.9	24.1	26.0	25.0
Free time†	50.4	48.2	48.2	44.2	46.6	45.4	47.7
Women							
Paid work	33.8	36.1	37.8	37.5	37.0	37.6	36.9
Travel	6.6	6.3	7.0	6.1	5.6	5.3	4.7
Personal*	41.2	37.1	43.2	42.2	39.6	44.3	42.1
Free time†	37.4	39.5	31.0	33.2	36.8	31.8	35.3

Source: *Leisure Futures*, Henley Centre for Forecasting.

* House cleaning, everyday cooking, other chores, personal hygiene and appearance, essential shopping, essential childcare.
† Free time = 168 − paid work − travel − personal − sleep (7 hours a day if not given).

workers the averages are 6 days for men and 14 for women. Perhaps the most remarkable part of Table 3.2 is the 4 per cent of full-time employees who have no paid holiday entitlement beyond statutory public holidays. Historical evidence from the Department of Employment shows that the paid holiday entitlement for full-time manual workers steadily increased over time, from a norm of three weeks or less in 1971 to a norm of four weeks or more in the late 1980s.

Evidence on the changing use of time by individuals emerges from an annual survey of 2,000 people for the Henley Centre for forecasting (reported in *Leisure Futures*). The results for the period 1986 to 1992 are summarised in Table 3.3. Not surprisingly, the era of 'the new man' has made little impression on the inequality of free time between the sexes: men have 12 to 13 hours a week more free time than women. Accounting for what it terms 'secondary activities' (e.g. non-essential child care and shopping), the Henley Centre estimates that the leisure component of free time was approximately 38 hours a week for men and 27 hours a week for women. Table 3.3 shows that since 1986 the total amount of time free from work, obligations such as cooking, housework, essential shopping and child care, and personal hygiene has declined by three hours a week for men in full-time employment and by two hours a week for women in full-time employment.

The lack of an increase in free time for the full-time employed is partly due to the increasing work hours shown in Figure 3.1. It may also reflect the difficulty of further savings in time spent doing essential activities, once the standard time-saving technology (microwave oven, dishwasher, washing machine, etc.) has been purchased.

So far, the analysis of demand for leisure time has dealt mainly with quantitative choices, such as how many hours to work in a week. The purpose of this section is also to examine qualitative considerations. Shiftwork, in principle, provides workers with an opportunity for a qualitative choice over hours of work. However, in practice, it is not so much a choice as a requirement to work anti-social hours. The amount of shiftworking being worked has a long-term upward trend. By 1990, 22 per cent of male manuals received shift pay, as did 14 per cent of female manuals, 10 per cent of female non-manuals and 6 per cent of male non-manuals.

Such qualitative considerations as shiftwork and choices of different types of leisure time point to a major qualitative choice constraint, i.e. the fixed time of day, week and year that many activities are limited to. This is called time-dating. The clichéd nine-to-five job is the most obvious example of this time-dating, but other activities, eating and sleeping in particular, are just as inflexible. Many sport and recreation activities are similarly undertaken by the majority of people at certain specific times of the day, week and year: football, rugby, darts, even country walks, all display peak demand at certain times. Shiftworking is probably damaging to participation in recreation activities, particularly those of a more social nature, such as team sports, since such sports take place at a very specific time of the week, e.g. Saturday afternoons. However, for other sports, particularly indoor sports, time-dating leads to demand peaks in the evening and at weekends, and shiftworkers at least get the opportunity to use sports facilities at off-peak times when they will almost certainly be cheaper as well as less congested.

Overall, then, the quantity of leisure time does not seem to have expanded significantly in the UK over the recent past. Although there are two indicators of increasing leisure time – holiday entitlement and early retirement by men – there are strong indicators of reductions in leisure time, particularly for men in full-time employment. The increasing proportion of women in paid work and their higher working hours means that, on average, leisure time for women has fallen. There has been a clear reversal since 1985 in the post-war trend in the UK of decreases in working hours for those in work.

We will return to the British situation with regard to work and leisure later in the chapter, but first it is interesting to compare this situation in the UK with that in other countries.

Leisure and work in the USA: the 'overworked American' hypothesis

Juliet Schor (1991), in her book *The Overworked American: The Unexpected Decline of Leisure*, found that in the USA in the period 1969 to 1987, against all expectations, America had chosen to take all the benefits of productivity gains in more money rather than more leisure time. In fact, rather than working time being reduced over this period, it actually increased substantially. Schor (1996) indicates the similarity of this pattern of increasing working time with that seen in Britain since 1985:

Since 1969 American workers have experienced a substantial rise in hours of work. The rise is very small for the population as a whole but if we look at people with jobs, it is quite substantial. The average employed person in America, excluding people who are under-employed or unemployed, increased his or her market hours over the period 1969 to 1987 by an average of about 160 hours a year, or by what I have referred to as the 'extra month of work'. For women, the increase in market hours was much larger, just over 300 hours a year. This has been brought about by a number of factors. Over the period there has been a substantial rise in the numbers of women in full-time jobs. Increasingly, these are career jobs which require both more hours of work per week and a more continuous labour force participation around the year than has conventionally been associated with female employment.

However the increase in working time has not been confined to women. Men also experienced an increase in their hours of work over this period by an average of about 100 hours. Around two-thirds of the rise is accounted for by a larger fraction of the year that people are working and about a third of it is due to longer weekly hours. Increasingly, Americans can be described as overworked in what I would say is the technical rather than the popular sense of overwork. That is, increasing numbers of people say they are working more hours than they would like to and are willing to trade off income in order to work fewer hours. A variety of polls in the last five years indicate that between 15% and just over 50% of workers feel this way, depending on the form of worktime and income reduction proposed and the wording of the question.

Schor's evidence is in direct contradiction to the neo-classical income/leisure trade-off model outlined above. She argues that rigidities in the labour market prevent people from choosing to work the hours they would prefer. The main factor explaining the unexpected decline in leisure time in the USA over this period is that the USA has become enmeshed in what she calls 'the cycle of work and spend':

> The cycle of work and spend is an explanation for the following paradox: the United States has almost tripled its productivity level since the end of the Second World War. It has not used any of that increase in productivity to reduce working hours. Instead it has channelled it all into increases in income and in fact, not just income, but consumption. Consequently we have just about tripled the average goods and services that a person or a household consumes, but we have not given ourselves any more leisure.

> Why is this paradoxical? Economists typically think of leisure as a normal good, something that people will buy more of as they get richer. Certainly historically this has happened since the mid-nineteenth century. The fact that the USA has not done this since the Second World War despite substantial increases in productivity is therefore a paradox from the standard

perspective. It also stands in great contrast to Western Europe where a much more significant fraction of productivity growth was channelled into reducing working hours.

(Schor, 1996)

Schor argues that there is an economic incentive for employers to make existing workers work longer hours rather than take on new employees because there are a series of fixed costs (medical insurance, pension benefits, etc.) associated with taking on any employee. The more hours each employee works, the lower are the fixed costs per hour. She also argues that a culture of long working hours has developed in American organisations. This culture gets stronger the higher you go up the jobs hierarchy. In effect, the only choice faced by those in high-ranking, well-paid jobs is to work long hours or not to work at all. This situation, she argues, is leading a significant minority of people to take the latter option and exit the formal labour market. This phenomenon is referred to as 'downshifting'.

Leisure and work in Japan: the 'corporate warrior' culture

Japan has traditionally had substantially higher working hours than either Britain or the USA. Table 3.4 shows the trend in working hours in the UK, USA, and Japan from 1870 to 1970. In 1870, all three countries had remarkably similar working hours per year. Even by 1929, there was little difference between the three countries in terms of hours worked. The difference is that Japan has not seen the rapid decline in working hours in the post-war period (at least until 1970) that Britain and the USA have experienced.

If we examine Table 3.5, Britain seems to be closer to the position in other European countries in terms of the availability of leisure time than to the USA or Japan. The European worker is most different when it comes to paid holiday entitlement. Whereas 5 or 6 weeks is common in Europe, the Japanese worker takes only 9 days, and the American 16 days. In fact, the Japanese have many more statutory holidays (20 days per year) than Europeans or Americans, so that in fact Americans have the lowest number of paid holidays in total, supporting

Table 3.4 Hours worked 1870–1970 (annual totals)

	UK	USA	Japan
1870	2,984	2,964	2,945
1929	2,286	2,342	2,364
1950	1,958	1,867	2,289
1970	1,688	1,754	2,195

Source: OECD and Becker (1991).

Table 3.5 International comparison of number of days off in 1989

	Japan	*US*	*UK*	*Germany*	*France*
Weekends	85	104	104	104	104
National holidays	20	9	8	11	8
Paid holidays	9	16	24	29	26
Absent	3	6	11	11	16
Total	117	138	147	155	154

Source: Nishi (1993).

Schor's argument. Because Japanese workers often work at weekends, the Japanese have the highest annual working hours at around 2,100 hours per year in the 1990s, closely followed by the Americans at 1924 hours. The average for Europe is 1,650, substantially below the other two major economic powers. Also, Table 3.5 shows that Europeans take more time off due to illness than the Japanese or Americans. This could be another indicator of a more leisurely approach to work.

Harada (1996) indicates the prevalence of a 'corporate warrior' culture in Japan as the main cause of the long working hours:

> They do not complain about working hours. Fighting stress and strain on all aspects of their job, they silently bear increasing overtime hours and long commuting time. These workers spend an amazing length of time at their jobs. . . .
>
> In the finance and insurance industry, where considerable unpaid overtime occurs, 30% of the actual hours worked are unpaid overtime, as indicated by Ono (1991), bringing the annual hours worked for the industry to 2,500 hours. If this is divided by 250 working days, that means 10 hours of work each day of work. People living in a large metropolis may require three hours of commuting time for the round-trip, leaving a meagre 10 hours for sleep, eating, bathing, and other daily living necessities. If we estimate that these workers spend no time whatsoever doing household chores, that gives them free time at home totalling a mere one hour per working day. This type of Japanese person is known for bringing work from the office home with him (it is mostly men). It is not unusual for this kind of person to carry home overtime work and to go to work on holidays. Almost all household chores and the raising of children is left up to the wife. Even if the wife is also maintaining a paid job, the responsibility for housework and taking care of the children rests entirely on her.

However, such corporate warriors tend to be the older generation. There are indications that the younger generation has much more interest in leisure and will not continue to work the long working hours traditionally associated with the Japanese economy.

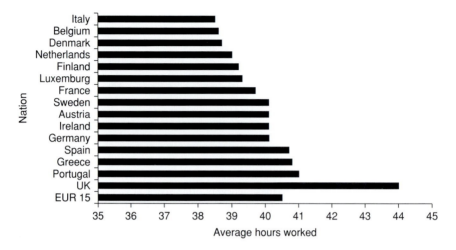

Figure 3.2 Average total usual weekly hours worked by full-time employees (1992).
Source: Eurostat

Leisure and work in Britain and the rest of Europe: the 'overworked British'?

Although Britain has more leisure time than both the USA and Japan, within Europe Britain has the longest working hours. Figure 3.2 shows that the average weekly hours worked by full-time employees is around 40 for the twelve countries of the European Union (prior to the enlargement to fifteen with addition of Austria, Sweden, and Finland). This average has not changed since 1983 for the EU as a whole, with small reductions in some countries matched by small increases in others. The UK has by the far the highest working hours in Europe with the Netherlands, Belgium, Italy and Denmark in the group with the lowest working hours.

Figure 3.3 emphasises this point by showing the proportion of employees who usually work over 48 hours per week. Again the UK has the highest proportion with the Netherlands the lowest.

There is evidence that, in Britain, working time is increasing and leisure time declining. However, it is not those at the bottom end of the income distribution that are working the longest hours, as might be expected. These are the ones most likely to be working less than they would like to. Rather it is the better-educated, the higher-paid, those in middle and senior management that are working the longest hours.

This point was highlighted by an Institute of Management survey (Charlesworth, 1996). The survey was a random sample of 3,000 managers who were members of the Institute of Management. One thousand and seventy-three questionnaires were returned. Of these 12 per cent were chief executives/managing director status and a further 36 per cent senior management, with 25 per cent junior

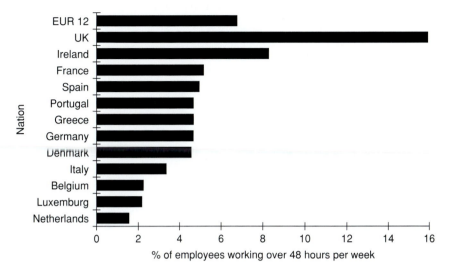

Figure 3.3 Proportion of employees who usually work more than 48 hours per week (1992+).
Source: Labour Force Survey 1998, Eurostat

management. Forty-seven per cent of the sample were aged between 45 and 54. Thus the sample included a high proportion of people at the top end of the jobs hierarchy.

The survey revealed that 60 per cent of British managers found it difficult to find enough time to relax, for hobbies/interests, and for one's partner. Nearly six in ten respondents to this survey of managers claimed that they always worked in excess of their official working week. Forty-nine per cent of the sample regularly took work home, with 18 per cent always doing so; 41 per cent of the sample regularly worked at weekends, with 14 per cent always doing so. More than eight in ten of respondents reported that their workload had increased over the past year, with 47 per cent stating that it had increased greatly.

Jonathan Gershuny (1996), Britain's most prominent economic researcher into time allocation, reports evidence from the British Household Panel Survey (BHPS) to indicate that those with the highest monthly income have clearly the longest working hours. He estimates that for men on average, excluding the unemployed, the best paid 20 per cent of the workforce work 10 hours longer per week than do the worst paid. As he points out: 'Those with the highest earnings now have the least time to spend them'. Gershuny suggests the reasons for this pattern:

> More of the top jobs in the economy require high levels of specific technical knowledge, which, combined with increasing levels of education, intensifies competition for advantageous positions that were once less meritocratically

Table 3.6 Weekly paid work (hours by income, BHPS 1994/5)

	Employed women	*Employed men*
Gross monthly income quintiles		
lowest	18	22
second	35	42
third	40	46
fourth	43	18
highest	47	50
Whole sample	33	45

Source: Gershuny (1996).

allocated. The freeing of women from the imperatives of the reproductive cycle allows them also to compete for these top jobs. And one of the main mechanisms in this competition for top jobs seems to be to work long hours. Add to this increased competitive pressure from government deregulation of industries, and underfunding of services leading to overwork of senior staff, and the punishingly long hours of the top jobs are quite unsurprising.

And of course, going along with the economic pressures, are powerful social influences. Just as, at the beginning of the twentieth century, the fact that the richest and most socially prominent were also the most leisured, gave social cachet to leisure itself, so that in turn all the classes strove to achieve leisure, by the end of the same century, in Britain and America at least, the richest and most powerful groups now have the least leisure – and busy-ness acquires its own cachet, long hours of work denote superior social status.

Gershuny (1996) reports further evidence to show that there is a clear preference of those working the longest hours to reduce their working hours.

A staggering 57 per cent of women in the top 20 per cent of income earners and of working hours wanted to reduce their working hours in 1994/95. Table 3.7 shows that as you move up the hierarchy of either income or working hours the preference for reducing working hours grows. It rises more steeply for women than for men.

Part of the reason for higher preferences of women for shorter working hours may be the length of time they spend on domestic unpaid work. Gershuny (1997) shows that although there has been a slight reduction in women's housework (cleaning, clothes washing, and cooking) time since 1961, there has been a sharp rise in time spent on shopping and domestic travel and, perhaps more surprisingly, a massive rise in the amount of time women spend on childcare.

Despite the very substantial reduction in family size . . . it appears that childcare time has pretty much doubled, among men and women in every category. Indeed, full-time employed women with children in 1995 appear to devote more time to children than even non-employed mothers did in 1961.

Table 3.7 Percentage of all men and women with a work-time preference who wish to reduce their working hours ($N = 3648$)

	Work-time quintiles			Gross monthly pay quintiles	
	Women	Men		Women	Men
BHPS 1994/5 work time quintiles			BHPS 1994/5 gross income quintiles		
lowest	6	13	lowest	9	11
second	23	17	second	24	25
third	43	29	third	41	31
fourth	49	38	fourth	50	41
highest	57	50	highest	57	43
Whole sample	28	35	Whole sample	28	35

Source: Gershuny (1996).

Gershuny explains the rise in shopping and domestic travel time as due to the replacement of local shops by huge self-service stores in out-of-town sites that involve less cost to the retailers but more time from shoppers. He also discusses the reasons for the rise in childcare time:

> Children use all sorts of personal services – educational, medical, recreational – and as the scale of these facilities grows, their location becomes on average more distant from the child's own home. To these increasingly remote facilities must be added another factor: the lapse in children's 'licence to roam'. In the UK in 1961, children were allowed a considerable degree of freedom to travel about unsupervised. But, as Meyer Hillman has documented, traffic danger and the perceived growth in child assault mean that children are now mostly constrained to travel to these remote facilities in the company of adults.

On the more positive side, however, Gershuny also attributes the rise in childcare time to an increasing commitment by parents to find 'quality time' with their children. Such time could more realistically be called leisure time rather than unpaid work time.

Overall, though, Gershuny's evidence does suggest that in addition to increasing working hours there is also increasing time committed to other domestic chores, so that there is less and less time available for leisure activities such as sport.

Thus we see a clear difference between the USA, Japan, and Europe in the availability of leisure time and, within Europe, Britain has shown trends in working time closer to the trend in the USA than in the rest of Europe. We now turn to the question of whether different countries and cultures have different preferences for leisure time on the basis of cultural differences in their ability to enjoy leisure time. In fact, some commentators have argued that the more leisurely situation in Europe is an expression of a different way of life in Europe.

Is Eurocapitalism more leisurely?

According to Henzler (1992), Eurocapitalism is a different form of capitalism to that in America and Japan. The American capitalist system is based on free markets and individual action; the Japanese system is much less individualistic than its US counterpart and is more of a corporate capitalist system. Henzler argues that Eurocapitalism is a form of social democratic capitalism:

> Eurocapitalism supports a social compact to which the great majority of our people subscribe. . . . Although an actual written compact obviously does not exist, we Europeans explicitly accept our roles as members of society who must act responsibly within the bounds of that society. In return, we assume that society is, in the broadest sense, responsible for everyone in it. In this civic polity, jointly engaged in economic affairs, all sorts of people are bound together and responsible to one another.

The crucial question for Henzler is which of these capitalist systems will give its people the best quality of life. He argues that the European system will, and in no small part because of lower working hours and a greater emphasis on high-quality leisure experiences:

> Europeans place a high value on quality of life. American and Japanese observers routinely comment on the pleasures of life in Europe, from afford-able concerts to longer vacations to shorter working days. But achieving a decent quality of life for the largest number of people is a conscious social choice. For example theatres in Germany are heavily subsidised: ticket prices cover only about 30% of the cost; government picks up the rest. No one is eager for this largesse to disappear. This applies even more strongly to Germany's completely free university system and its generous health-care system.
>
> If it is possible to supply these benefits and run the country's economic engine more productively at the same time, well and good. If products can be made even more competitive around the world, even better. But if the choice appears to lie between maintaining economic performance or quality of life, public opinion will tilt toward the latter. Higher return on equity is abstract. Reasonably priced theatre tickets and affordable health care are tangible. And social cohesiveness is priceless.

Scitovsky (1976) also argues that Europe is very different to the USA in terms of preferences towards work and leisure. Americans, according to Scitovsky, are much more work-centred than Europeans. This is due to a strong Puritan heritage backed up by an education system that is geared to the acquisition of production skills rather than consumption skills. Not only do Americans have less interest in leisure than Europeans, they also lack appropriate consumption skills to allow them to enjoy fully their leisure time:

America's work ethic puts the earning of money ahead of the enjoyment of life. Every comparison of European and American work habits, among businessmen, professional people, administrative employees, and factory workers alike, shows that no matter whether we are driven by bosses or by internal compulsion, we always work harder, more persistently, more single-mindedly, and at a more relentless pace than the Europeans do. Our very much higher productivity, as shown by all the international comparisons, is one result of this difference; another result may well be our greater need for rest after work. Everybody, when exhausted, puts comfort ahead of pleasure. . . .

Whereas the average European seeks status by showing off his exper-tise as consumer, displaying his knowledge of good but obscure and cheap restaurants, or demonstrating his ability to provide pleasant entertainment through unexpected and simple means, we Americans are more inclined to go in for austere ostentation, displaying our ability to spend a lot of money on goods distinguished from their cheaper counterparts mainly by their conspicuous expensiveness. In that way, we maintain our puritanical disdain for the frivolous matter of consumption, as if if it were not dignified to aim at getting the lowest price, let alone to display skill at doing it.

So it seems that Europe and Europeans are different. We pay more taxes so that government can provide a rich and varied leisure lifestyle for its citizens. Our education system gives us the skills to appreciate and enjoy culture and leisure. And we work less so that we have the time to enjoy our leisure. As a result, by American standards, we have a leisurely lifestyle that delivers a good quality of life. This seems to be what Henzler and Scitovsky are arguing.

However, Henzler's 'Europe' would seem to be continental Europe on the basis of the evidence provided above. Although the British clearly have more leisure time than Americans or Japanese, they seem to be out of step with continental Europe in their tendency to work long hours.

Conclusion

It was generally thought by economists that as we approached the end of the twentieth century we would be faced by a problem of having too much time. Vickerman (1980) writing appropriately in a journal called *Futures*, analysed the policy implications of the then accepted scenario of leisure time becoming more and more abundant.

In this chapter we have shown that, at least for some countries in the world, notably the USA and Britain, most people seem to be faced with decreasing leisure time and would prefer to trade-off some of their income for more leisure time. Such evidence casts doubt on the validity of the income/leisure trade-off model. We will see in future chapters that time scarcity seems to be a bigger constraint on consumers' demand for sport than any scarcity of income.

4 The demand for sport

Theory

Introduction

Although the economics of the work–leisure choice is the essential context in which we study the demand for sport, the central core of the demand analysis is the participation decision. We are interested in analysing the factors that result in participation or non-participation in active sport.

The neo-classical economics approach starts the analysis at the most micro level, the individual consumer's demand for a specific activity. All other aspects of demand can then be deduced once we have analysed this consumer choice situation. The approach models the balancing act of the consumer to match the pleasure he or she obtains from taking part in sport with the costs of doing so.

However, we have shown in Chapter 1 that although sport generates immediate consumption benefits that fit the conventional consumer choice model, there is an investment demand element to the demand for sport because of the health benefits generated through long-term participation in active recreation. This makes the modelling of the demand for sport more complicated than it is for most other commodities.

In addition, there are serious reservations as to whether the neo-classical approach, however adjusted to take account of these complications, can ever completely explain the consumer's decision to take part in sport. This criticism is based on the assumptions on which the model is based.

In order to deal with these issues our analysis begins with the neo-classical approach, moves on to consider the issue of investment demand, and finally discusses a broader approach incorporating both economics and psychology.

The neo-classical approach

As economists, our starting point for the analysis of consumer behaviour in sport is the theory of consumer demand. This has remained virtually unaltered for over a century. It is a theory developed from the nineteenth century economist Alfred Marshall. The consumer is regarded as having a given set of tastes and preferences and, facing a given set of prices of goods and services, allocates his or her income in such a way as to maximise utility, which results in a spending pattern where the relative marginal utilities of different goods are equated to relative prices. Economic theory concentrates on such 'rational' maximising behaviour.

Consumer choice theory gives us a demand function where the quantity demanded of Good A (Q_{DA}) by a consumer is a function of the price of the good (P_A), the prices of other goods $(P_1, P_2, \ldots P_n)$ and the consumer's income (Y):

$$Q_{DA} = f(P_A, P_1, P_2, \ldots P_n, Y)$$

This simple framework provides a starting point for our investigation of the demand for sport and recreation activities, but we must adapt this general framework to the specific market we are studying.

The dependent variable: the quantity demanded

The first question to answer is what is meant by the 'quantity demanded' in the context of the market for sport? There are two approaches to tackling this question.

The first adopts a hierarchical approach to modelling the demand for sport, with the demand for the sporting activity playing the role of the parent demand function and the demand for sports facilities, sports equipment, sports clothing, and sports shoes treated as derived demands from this logically prior parent demand to take part in the activity.

In this case, the quantity demanded for the parent demand function is a measure of sports participation. In the case of the separate derived demand functions the quantity demanded will be the consumer's expenditure on the sports good or services (e.g. on sports equipment). Thus instead of one demand function we have one parent demand function and several derived demand functions for each element of the derived demands.

As an example of this approach, we can look at the demand for badminton. The parent demand function is concerned with the consumer's decision to take part in badminton or not. If the consumer decides to participate then he or she will require a racket, shuttlecocks, clothing and footwear. In addition, he or she will have to rent a court at a sports centre or club, and travel to and from the facility. All these extra demands, including the demand for sports-related travel, are treated as derived demands from the decision to participate in badminton.

Vickerman (1975a) argues that this is the most appropriate approach to the modelling of the demand for recreation. However, although the approach may be suitable for most sports, there are others where the hierarchical approach is less appropriate. For some activities all the elements are demanded simultaneously and it is not possible to distinguish such a parent/derived demand relationship.

For instance, for many people the decision to participate in skiing involves the purchase of a package holiday. The very name 'package' means that what is being purchased is a composite commodity with several different elements included. In the case of a ski holiday the package may include air travel to and from the country with the ski resort, transport from the airport to the accommodation and back, food and accommodation for the duration of the holiday, ski pass, ski school, and equipment hire. Some packages may include only some of these elements; others may include them all. When the consumer makes the decision to participate in skiing, a single price is paid for this composite commodity, the ski holiday. However, this single price is even then not the total cost of taking part in skiing. The consumer will still pay for travel to and from the airport, maybe parking at the airport, additional spending while on holiday, and maybe new clothes purchased for the holiday. Thus the composite commodity of taking part in skiing is larger than the package holiday.

In such circumstances, it is more appropriate to treat the quantity demanded as the total expenditure on the skiing trip. Even for other sports that are not packaged in this way it is possible to use such a 'composite commodity' model and treat the total expenditure on taking part in the sport as the relevant dependent variable in the model, even though it is the consumer that may do the packaging.

The determinants of demand

The price of the activity

Since goods normally give pleasure, most consumers 'want' most goods. Economics distinguishes 'want' from 'demand' by defining demand as effective demand, that is, not the amount consumers want, but the amount they are willing to pay for by paying the market price. Hence price is a major determinant of demand. The consumer will only purchase the commodity if the value of the satisfaction (utility) gained from consuming the commodity is greater than the asking price, i.e. the benefit of consumption to the consumer exceeds its cost.

For most goods, identifying the price presents no problems. For a sporting activity, data on price is not easily obtainable since the cost of participation is a composite item involving entrance charges, the rental value of any equipment used, travel costs, and time costs. Much of the recreational demand analysis has concerned itself with recreational activities with zero entrance charges and the underlying assumption has been that travel costs, or a combination of travel and time costs (which are normally closely related anyway), are the major elements of cost. This is often the case for resource-based outdoor recreation activities but is certainly not the case for indoor activities, where entrance charges and equipment costs are often dominant. Also, for outdoor activities such as skiing, equipment costs and entry charges are by no means negligible.

In the same way as we talk about the composite commodity of sport, we can also refer to the composite price. The composite price paid for a sport can be categorised into two types of cost for the participant – variable costs and fixed costs. The variable costs are:

1   entrance charges to sports facilities
2   travel costs

3   costs of participation-related food and drink consumption, equipment hire, and so on
4   time costs.

These costs are incurred every time the individual participates in sport. Other costs, fixed costs, occur irregularly and are not necessarily related to specific acts of participation. They are:

1   membership and subscription fees
2   cost of equipment, clothing, and footwear.

The division into variable and fixed costs of participation is an appropriate consideration because different costs will affect different demand decisions. The relevant price influencing the overall participation/non-participation decision is likely to be the total cost, i.e. both the fixed and variable costs of participation. For the person who has already made the decision to be a participant, the frequency of participation is likely to depend on the variable costs alone.

The ratio of fixed to variable costs of participation will vary from sport to sport. Golf, for instance, has a relatively high total cost because membership and equipment costs are relatively high. However, once a golfer has paid the membership fees and has bought golf equipment, clothing and footwear, the monetary variable cost of playing additional games is relatively low. In fact, the time cost is likely to be the single most important element in restricting the frequency of participation.

In general, other things being equal, the lower the variable cost of participation, the greater will be the frequency of participation. Having said this, it must be remembered that there are few or no degrees of freedom attached to the frequency decision for some recreational activities. This is particularly the case with team sports, where fairly rigid time-dating is the norm. Where other things are not equal, in particular where one sport has much lower time costs than another, the sport with the lower time costs would be expected to have a higher frequency of participation.

The relationship between quantity demanded of a commodity and its price is normally measured by the price elasticity of demand. Price elasticity of demand measures the responsiveness of quantity demanded of a good to a change in the price of that good. The numerical value of the price elasticity shows the percentage change in the quantity demanded of a good for a 1 per cent change in price. Price elasticities are normally negative since quantity demanded falls as price rises and vice versa; elasticities numerically above 1 indicate elastic (i.e. responsive) demand; elasticities numerically below 1 indicate inelastic (i.e. unresponsive) demand.

Overall estimates of the price elasticity of demand for specific sports are not available, mainly because of the problems of estimating the true composite price. There is evidence of the price elasticity of demand for components of the overall price, such as entry charges for specific facilities, and we will discuss this in the next chapter.

Income

We have seen that what distinguishes want from effective demand is the willingness and ability to pay the price asked. Consumers may be willing to pay the asking price but not able to do so because of lack of income. Thus income is a major determinant of the demand for a product.

The relationship between changes in income and changes in the quantity demanded of a specific commodity is referred to as the income elasticity of demand. The numerical value of the income elasticity shows the percentage change in the quantity demanded of a good for a 1 per cent change in income. Negative income elasticities indicate 'inferior' goods (since consumers reduce demand as incomes rise and they change to better, normally higher quality substitutes); positive income elasticities indicate 'normal' goods; and positive income elasticities above 1 indicate 'luxury' goods.

It is generally assumed that sports are normal or luxury goods, since cross-section survey data show that participation rates for nearly all sports rise with levels of income.

Prices of other goods

The quantity demanded of any good is affected by changes in the price of closely related goods. Such 'closely related' goods may be substitutes or complements. Two goods are said to be substitutes when an increase in the price of one results in an increase in the demand for the other. Two goods are said to be complements when an increase in the price of one results in a decrease in the demand for the other. Complements are goods that tend to be bought together (e.g. tennis rackets and tennis balls) so that when the price of one of them increases, this tends to reduce the demand for both.

The responsiveness of the quantity demanded of one good to the price of another good is referred to as the cross-price elasticity of demand. This is the percentage change in the quantity demanded of one good as a result of a 1 per cent change in the price of another. For complements, cross-price elasticities will be negative; for substitutes, they will be positive. If the cross-price elasticity is zero, no demand relationship exists between the two goods.

Probably the most interesting question when looking at the demand for a particular sport is which activity would be a substitute for, and which complementary to, the given sport. Unfortunately, we have virtually no information on the cross-price elasticities of demand for recreation activities which would allow us to answer such a question. Skjei (1977) suggests that the most serious problem in recreational demand analysis is the bias that arises from the inability to include information on the prices of substitute and complementary activities in the specification of the demand function. This specification problem arises because of the difficulties, discussed above, in constructing a price variable for an activity. Cicchetti *et al.* (1969) tried to identify substitutes and complements by including participation terms for other activities on the right-hand side of their regression equation for participation in a given activity. The results of this exercise proved difficult to interpret.

There are approaches, though, that might enable substitutes and complements to be identified. Lancaster (1966) views the consumer as maximising a utility function which has, as its determinants, commodity attributes rather than the quantities of the goods consumed. If we find 'product characteristics' for recreation activities we may be able to find substitute and complement relationships between activities on the basis of these characteristics. For instance, we would identify level of physical activity or degree of competitiveness as specific characteristics of sports. For those sports possessing a similar collection of characteristics we would expect to have substitute relationships. The problems with Lancaster's approach are first in identifying the relevant attributes of recreation activities, and second in obtaining objective measurements of such attributes for any given activity. These problems have tended to discourage any empirical work within Lancaster's framework, and recreation researchers have instead looked to various multivariate techniques as a means of identifying activities that 'go together'. We will look at the results of such approaches in the next chapter.

Tastes and preferences

The simple consumer demand model analysed so far assumes that all consumers have the same preferences and differ only in levels of income. In fact the most variable factor in the study of consumer demand for recreation is the tastes of the consumers. Early studies of participation patterns identified certain key socio-economic variables that were important in determining people's preferences for active recreation. These were age, sex, educational background, and occupation. The most significant relationship is between participation and age and sex.

Numerous studies have shown a consistent negative correlation between age and participation in virtually every sporting activity. Age is probably the most important variable in explaining variation in those sports that require physical contact and strength. But even in many less strenuous sports, participation normally declines steadily with age (golf is a notable exception to this rule).

Rodgers (1977) offers an interesting hypothesis concerning the relationship between age and sports participation. Rather than accepting the conventional view that people 'drop out' of active participation as they get older, he suggests that many people in the older age categories were never participants, even when young. He introduces the concept of 'sports literacy': the extent to which sections of the population are exposed and conditioned to active recreation. The older generation, he suggests, reveals a much higher proportion of 'illiteracy' than the younger generation. He presents some evidence to support this view. His 'index of sports penetration' measures the number of adults who have ever played at least one sport as a proportion of all adults. All the evidence shows that this declines steadily with increasing age.

This view of the causes of lower participation of older people has important implications for sports policy. If the aim of the government is to increase participation, then for many older people this means taking up an activity for the first time and not re-adopting one they have given up.

A similar argument relates to sex differences in recreation participation. Many surveys have shown that men have higher participation rates than women. Studies documenting the lower participation rates in many activities among girls explained these differences as due to the fact that, during childhood and adolescence, females are more constrained in exposure to, and opportunities for, active sport: in Rodgers' terms they are more 'sports illiterate' than boys. However, recent evidence discussed in Chapter 5 shows that these gender-related differences are diminishing rapidly.

Roberts and Brodie (1992) gave a more elaborate explanation of the relationship between sports participation and age and sex in their development of the concept of 'sports careers'. Roberts and Brodie discovered that the main reason why 'some sports careers became long-running' (that is, sports participation continued into later life) was the laying of secure foundations in sport during childhood and youth, similar to Rodgers' 'sports literacy' hypothesis. However, Roberts and Brodie identified a new, crucial variable in this early experience of sport:

> What did laying secure foundations mean? It could not be just a question of playing sport when young because virtually everyone had done this. Nor could it be a matter of simply enjoying or being particularly good at sport. Most children enjoy games, and there are thousands of inactive adults who can recall being quite good at particular sports when at school. Nor, according to our evidence, had the sheer quantity of sport played when young made the crucial difference. Rather, the characteristic that distinguished the early sport socialisation of the adults in our panel who persisted was the number of different sports that they had played regularly and in which they became proficient during childhood and youth.
>
> Among the adults in our panel with unbroken careers, 64 per cent had played three or more sports regularly, between ages and 16 and 19. Among those with interrupted sports careers, meaning that they had played at some time since age 20 but not during every year since then, only 20 per cent had played regularly in three or more sports in their late teens. Needless to say, the individuals that had never played any sport since age 20 reported less exposure earlier-on than all other groups of respondents. . . .
>
> At age 10 the individuals who were to build uninterrupted careers extending into adulthood were already playing the largest number of sports on average. Thereafter, up to age 15, they enlarged their ranges of sports more strongly than either of the other groups. By age 16 they were playing roughly three times as many sports on average compared with individuals whose post-16 participation was interrupted.

Roberts and Brodie's pioneering work on sports careers gives us a crucial insight into the formation of preferences for sports participation.

Household production and investment demand: sport as a means for health

Becker (1965) introduced a novel approach to consumer demand that is particularly relevant to the demand for sport. His approach uses a household production function, which demonstrates that any activity Q undertaken by an individual or household, even a pure leisure activity, involves inputs of market goods M and time T, as in:

$$Q = f(M, T)$$

Becker terms these activities 'composite commodities'. Each composite commodity involves different inputs of market goods and time, so that when the price of time or market goods alters, the effect on consumption of different activities will be varied.

In the long run, as real wage rates increase, the price of time rises relative to the price of market goods. Time is a finite input to household production, whereas market goods can be continually expanded. The change in relative prices causes consumption patterns to alter. Once again substitution and income effects operate to give a change in the optimum consumption pattern.

As the relative price of time and market goods changes, household production and consumption also alter to a different package of time-intensive and goods-intensive commodities. As wage rates rise, if the substitution effect dominates, the end result is falling consumption of time-intensive commodities. In practice the household and individual face not just the two-dimensional choice represented, but a multidimensional choice between composite commodities of varying degrees of time-intensity and goods-intensity. What the individual chooses depends on the relative strengths of the substitution and income effects, as in the conventional analysis.

The sophistication of this approach is to show that the demand for leisure time is, in fact, composed of many demands for different types of commodities with differing degrees of time-intensity and goods-intensity. As time becomes relatively scarcer and more expensive, household production and consumption of goods-intensive activities will increase relative to more time-intensive activities. It is still possible for consumption of time-intensive activities to rise, however, since the conventional income effect may ensure that it does. However, the dominant pressure is for goods-intensive activities to increase, i.e. the substitution effect. This can be seen in the increasing goods inputs and reduced time input in many so-called 'leisure' activities which may be seen as inferior, e.g. cooking, shopping, washing and cleaning, contrasted with the maintained, and often increased, time input in more enjoyable leisure activities, like sport.

Even in such areas as sport it has been noted by Vickerman (1980) that:

> Pure leisure activities are also becoming more capital-intensive, ranging from passive activities such as air travel based holidays in the sun to the main growth sports, e.g. squash, all water sports and the UK television-induced boom in snooker.

Whereas Vickerman sees this greater capital (or goods) intensity as being 'at odds with a society in which leisure time is likely to become a cheaper and cheaper commodity', the household production function approach suggests that the greater goods-intensity in activities is a rational household decision, because rising wage rates make time more expensive relative to market goods. Vickerman is making the assumption that the growth in leisure time is going to have a bigger influence than the effects of increasing wages on the relative scarcity of time. However, according to the indicators discussed earlier, leisure time in Britain is not expanding rapidly.

The time-intensity of sporting activities is often not reducible, e.g. soccer and squash. So marginal changes in time allocation to sport may be difficult. In addition, evidence suggests that sport is a superior activity, i.e. as incomes rise, participation rises more than proportionately. It seems logical to suggest, therefore, that the income effect will continue to outweigh the substitution effect. In other words, participation in sport, even time-intensive sport, will continue to increase despite the rising relative scarcity and relative value of time.

Linder (1970) also explores the changing value of time and concludes that leisure is becoming less self-determined and less 'leisurely'. The dominant tendency of increased affluence causes increased consumption of goods-intensive activities, and this traps the consumer into maintenance of this increased goods input in the household production process. Furthermore, the same affluence encourages an increased array of leisure time activity choices. These pressures result in time becoming even more scarce, and this brings about the 'harried leisure class'. Other writers bemoan the decreasing leisureliness of leisure time – in particular the emergence of an 'anti-leisure' attitude, filling non-work time with greater amounts of compulsive activities, complete with such work-related traits as anxiety, externally imposed conditions and time-consciousness.

Becker's household production approach provides an alternative model of consumer demand for sport and recreation activities. It is a more useful framework than the classical utility-maximising model, since it not only gives us demand functions for the activities but also generates derived demand for facilities, travel and recreation goods. It is a hierarchical demand model with the demand for activity playing the role of the parent demand function, and the time input plays a crucial role in the analysis. Perhaps the most novel application of the household production approach that is relevant for the demand for sport is that by Grossman (1972), whose demand for health model has direct implications for the demand for sport.

There is no doubt that a large proportion of sport participants, particularly those over 30, use sport as a means to maintain or increase health status. This makes sporting activity not purely a consumption good yielding utility, either now or in the future, but also an investment good, where people sacrifice present satisfaction in order to reap future returns. The returns will be of the form of higher health status in future years, which is really an investment in human capital, which will yield a return in higher incomes.

Grossman characterises the 'health production function' as being dependent on several inputs, one of which is exercise (the others being diet, housing conditions, work conditions, and the health services of doctors and hospitals). The amount of exercise demanded will be related to the rate of return on health capital, which in turn depends on two variables: the wage rate and the number of healthy days generated by increased exercise.

The effect of wage rates is a result of two conflicting elements. The higher the level of the consumer's income, the higher will be the marginal product of health capital; on the other hand, the higher the level of income, the more valuable is the consumer's time, and so the cost of generating health capital through exercise is higher. The relationship between investment demand for exercise and income is therefore not unambiguous. We might expect higher income individuals to have a greater investment demand (because of the high rate of return), but to economise on the time input by choosing the form of exercise that yields the highest health benefits per unit of time.

The second major influence on investment demand is age. This works through two channels. First, as a person gets older the rate of depreciation of health capital increases and so more investment is required each year to maintain a given stock of health capital. That is, the costs of producing health capital increase. At the same time the rate of return on health capital is lower, since with advancing years and an assumed fixed age of retirement there are fewer and fewer years to reap the benefit of health capital in the labour market. If we define the total product of health capital as the discounted sum of future earnings, then with each year of age the number of years we consider is decreased by one. Thus Grossman's model leads to the rather surprising result that an individual will choose a lower health state in each successive year. This will eventually lead him to choose his length of life, as the optimal health stock will ultimately decline below some necessary life-supporting minimum.

Although Grossman's model is a general model of the demand for health, the importance of exercise in the health production function allows us to use the model to add another dimension to the overall demand function for recreation. The analysis of the investment aspect of demand is useful for three reasons.

First, it gives us an insight into why income is an important determinant of demand. Classical demand theory regards income as a constraint on consumer choice, but the implication of this is that the constraint would be binding for some expensive activities such as skiing or sailing, but not binding for, say, walking or jogging. Yet even for inexpensive recreation pursuits we still find a strong positive correlation of participation with income. We can explain this by saying that tastes are correlated with income, but this is untestable. Grossman's analysis offers a more analytical treatment of why rational economic behaviour would require higher participation by higher income groups.

Second, the analysis allows some insight into which activities will be substitutes for one another, and which will be complements. If the prime motivation of the participation decision is the investment one, then a close substitute to a particular sport will be another activity that produced a similar quantity of health capital for a similar input of time and money. Thus a person who takes up jogging for health reasons may regard aerobic fitness classes or cycling as a good substitute. Complementary activities are likely to be outside the recreation field and include such behaviour as a high-fibre diet, adequate sleep and non-smoking.

Finally, Grossman's analysis indicates that people will respond differently to changes in certain variables depending on whether their motivation for parti-cipation is consumption rather than investment. For instance, let us take two joggers: one (Jogger A) participates primarily for the utility aspects; the other (Jogger B) primarily for health reasons. Both are promoted to higher-paid but more demanding jobs involving greater time commitment and more stress and anxiety. We would expect Jogger A to respond by reducing the hours spent jogging since these changes are unlikely to change the marginal utility of an hour's jogging, but the time costs have increased considerably. On the other hand, Jogger B is likely to maintain or increase exercise activity since the extra stress will accelerate the rate of depreciation of health capital and at the same time the increased income has increased the marginal product of health capital.

However, there are problems in applying Grossman's model to the demand for sport and recreation. The model assumes that the individual has perfect knowledge of the health production function and the rate of return on health capital. In reality, people are uncertain of the impact of exercise on their health capital, but even more uncertain as to the rate of return on health capital. But probably the biggest weakness of applying Grossman's theory to recreation relates to the categorisation of sport and recreation as an economic good in Chapter 1. There we specified that sport had aspects of both pecuniary and non-pecuniary investment goods. Grossman assumes that the only benefit to increased health status is in income returns in the labour market. The non-pecuniary investment good aspect of exercise relates to the fact that many participants report that increased exercise gives them the energy and motivation to take part in many more 'household production' activities, outside the labour market. That is, the exercise yields a future utility stream by raising the level of consumption activities. These returns are likely to be greater the older the individual, and therefore demand from this source may be positively related to age. The general point is that Grossman has been too restrictive by limiting returns to health capital purely to those realised in the labour market.

Perhaps the biggest problem with Grossman's model is that, despite the incorp-oration of the household production framework, it is still basically a neoclassical demand model.

The basic neoclassical approach to demand has received substantial criticism even within the economics profession. Hosseini (1990) argues:

> Neoclassical economic theory has been founded on the assumptions that economic agents are omnisciently rational and that they are always optimising. ... That is to say that the standard neoclassical theory, at least implicitly, assumes that economic agents should do what they believe right and believe

that what they do is right. In this body of thought, values and actions are always consistent. . . .

The optimisation hypothesis is based on what should be well-established preferences. For example, we assume that future preferences are exogenous, stable and known with adequate precision to make decisions unambiguous. These assumptions are questionable. When dealing with collective decision-making, individual objectives might be in conflict, or individual preferences might very often be inconsistent, fuzzy and changing over time. It can also be argued that as human beings, while engaged in decision-making, we often ignore our fully conscious preferences. Instead of maximising rationally, we follow rules, traditions, hunches, and advice and actions of others.

Fine (1990) points out how the neo-classical economic approach prevents broader analysis of consumer behaviour and shifts the emphasis away from the individual and on to the commodity markets:

> By homogenising and setting aside non-utility maximising behaviour as 'irrational', economics precludes the possibility of an *inter-disciplinary* theory of consumer behaviour and heavily discourages even a *multi-disciplinary* approach. In addition, the economic theory of consumer behaviour focuses attention away from individual acts of exchange. These become of no interest in their own right, since each is meaningless in isolation from the others. Only bundles of commodities yield utility, so that the individual acts of obtaining and enjoying them become irrelevant.

Similarly, Kenneth Boulding (1956) has argued that: 'it is the behaviour of commodities not the behaviour of men which is of prime interest in economic studies'. He goes on to emphasise that the economist 'is not really interested in the behaviour of men' (quoted in Hosseini, 1990).

Some economists, however, have attempted to make demand analysis more targeted at individual behaviour rather than market behaviour by making motivational aspects more explicit. This involves using psychological theory, as well as economics, in the analysis of demand.

Economic psychology and consumer behaviour in sport

Scitovsky (1976) criticises the neo-classical theory of consumer demand, indicating that at best it can contribute only to a partial analysis of consumer behaviour. He particularly criticises the assumption of a given set of preferences, the model of a rational consumer who knows what he wants and fails to achieve it only for lack of means. For Scitovsky, to understand demand one has to understand the motivational force behind behaviour, i.e. one needs to investigate how preferences are formed. To do this his starting point is psychology, and in particular the theory and concept of arousal.

The level of arousal has a lot to do with general feelings of satisfaction or dissatisfaction. Too much arousal and too little arousal are both unpleasant. Scitovsky uses the example of solitary confinement of prisoners as a case of low arousal and stimulus deprivation leading to pain, nausea, confusion and a general feeling of unpleasantness. Similarly, over-arousal felt by an executive faced with too much extremely demanding work can lead to stress, fatigue, anxiety and physical illness.

Psychologists argue that there exists an optimum level of total stimulation and arousal which, when reached, gives rise to a sense of comfort and well-being. Below this optimum, a person is likely to feel boredom; above it, they are likely to feel anxiety and tension. If the arousal level falls below the optimum level, or rises above it, these feelings provide an inducement to attempt to bring the arousal level back to the optimum. The greater the divergence of the present position from the optimum, and the longer the duration of this divergence, the greater is the inducement to attempt to return to the optimum level. Thus this theory of optimal arousal provides the motivation for human behaviour.

The theory of optimal arousal as a basis for analysis of behaviour is broader than the economic approach, although there is a considerable overlap. Economists see consumer demand as want satisfaction. If an individual is deprived of food, he experiences discomfort in hunger (i.e. he becomes over-aroused). Consumption of food relieves the discomfort and lowers his arousal level back towards its optimum level. Pleasure (utility) results from the comfort of returning to an optimum level of arousal from the heightened level caused by hunger. Comfort is the feeling that results from being at the optimal level of arousal; pleasure, on the other hand, results from moving towards the optimal level from a non-optimal level. Scitovsky uses the analogy between speed and acceleration (or deceleration) to explain the difference between comfort and pleasure.

When we are deprived of the essential elements of human existence (food, clothing, shelter) then we 'demand' these essentials and receive pleasure from the satisfaction of these demands. However, this is not the only source of pleasure. Pleasure flows from the change in arousal level rather than the state of being at a particular level. Pleasure will also follow from moving from a low level to a higher one: the relieving of boredom. Some activities are so stimulating that they raise arousal levels too high (i.e. beyond the optimum level), causing anxiety and tension, but pleasure still follows when the activity finishes and arousal levels fall back towards the optimum.

Scitovsky (1976) criticises economists for only considering the want satisfaction (lowering excessively high arousal) aspects of demand and completely ignoring stimulation-seeking behaviour (raising excessively low arousal). It is this latter aspect that relates his theory to demand for sport:

> The simplest remedy for too low arousal is bodily exercise. Not only is bodily exercise a good weapon against boredom, it is also pleasant. It seems most pleasant when it fully engages our skill and powers. . . . Competitive sports and games are popular because the pleasantness of exercise is maximised

by the full exertion of our strength and skills called forth by competition. Higher animals also engage in playful combat and other forms of competitive behaviour.

The basic source of stimulation is experience that is new, unexpected, or surprising. New and surprising experience is always stimulating, but if it is completely outside the bounds of our previous experience it can be so stimulating as to be disturbing. As Scitovsky indicates, 'what is not new enough and surprising enough is boring: what is too new is bewildering. An intermediate degree of newness seems the most pleasing.' What an individual considers 'new' obviously depends on his previous experience. What is stimulating to one person may be boring to another, not because of differences in tastes but because of differences of experience. The nursery slope can be terrifying to the person on skis for the first time, and yet boring to the expert.

Danger or threat is the most obvious source of stimulation, but we need to broaden our view of what we mean by a threat, as Scitovsky (1976) explains:

> Each of us, through the accumulation of personal experience, develops a view of the world, starting from day one. And that view is the basis of the strategy we use for living – for surviving. Which would be fine if it were not for the fact that the world changes all the time and so threatens to render our strategy obsolete. For that reason we must continually update our world view, by perceiving new information, processing it, and relating it to our previously accumulated fund of knowledge which it will complete and modify. By doing this we update our strategy of survival.

In this quote, Scitovsky is introducing the concept of 'skilled consumption'. The perceiving and processing of new information is 'skill acquisition' and the more skills acquired, the greater is the opportunity for pleasure through stimulation. Enjoyment of novelty requires learning.

The main question Scitovsky addresses in *The Joyless Economy* is why, in the USA, increasing affluence does not seem to have led to increasing happiness. He argues that a major reason for this is that there has been too much emphasis on the acquisition of production skills and not enough on the acquisition of consumption skills. Consequently, American consumers seek pleasure through want satisfaction rather than stimulation-seeking, since they do not possess the skills to 'enjoy' the stimulation. However, once the basic demands for material goods have been met, there is less and less opportunity for pleasure through want satisfaction. Hence the overall picture of an affluent, but bored, joyless society.

The overall point of Scitovsky's analysis is that stimulation-seeking is the motivator behind many if not most leisure demands, and is certainly the main motivation for participation in sport. Not all leisure activities require a high degree of consumption skill. Scitovsky makes the point that America's three most popular leisure-time activities – watching television, shopping and driving for pleasure – are low-skill activities.

Thus Scitovsky's approach can be adopted to provide the basis of a theory of demand for sport. As a society becomes more affluent, there is less and less potential for pleasure through want satisfaction (i.e. wishing to earn money to purchase goods and services that by themselves give pleasure) and a major avenue to pleasure comes through stimulation-seeking. Such stimulation can be obtained through interesting and challenging work, again conflicting with the economists' categorisation of work as disutility. However, for many it is through their leisure activities that we would expect to see stimulation-seeking behaviour.

Low-skill leisure activities can be stimulating when tried for the first time, but repetition can quickly make the experience boring. Hence the tendency for the demand for leisure activities in general to be volatile as consumers move in and out of the market. We often see rapid growth in demand for a new leisure activity (e.g. the cinema in the 1930s) only to see equally rapid decline in demand as the novelty effect wears off and other new leisure experiences emerge (e.g. television) to widen the spectrum of leisure-time choices facing the consumer.

Activities that provide the potential for skilled consumption can continue to be stimulating since, as the consumer's skills develop, the nature of his or her enjoyment also changes. The competitive sportsperson may move to higher and higher levels of competition and even find that excitement and stimulation increase the more skilled he becomes and the higher the level of competition he enters. Within the broad field of sport, however, demand will be heterogeneous since participants will have different backgrounds, experiences, interests, and skills. What is stimulating to a football participant may be boring or uninteresting to a golfer. The demand for sport is not a homogeneous demand.

A more detailed analysis of the way in which sport generates satisfaction and happiness is given in Csikszentmihalyi's (1975) fascinating study into humans at play entitled *Beyond Boredom and Anxiety*. The aim of his study was to explore why people took part in activities that yielded no extrinsic rewards. He referred to such activities as autotelic, which he defined as an activity that required formal and extensive energy output on the part of the actor yet provided few, if any, conventional rewards. Thus, he was interested in why people spent a lot of their time in activities that an industrial society would regard as unproductive.

He attempts to describe the nature of autotelic experience:

> It is easier, at first, to say what the experience is not like. It is not boring, as life outside the activity often is. At the same time, it does not produce anxiety, which often intrudes itself on awareness in 'normal' life. Poised between boredom and worry, the autotelic experience is one of complete involvement of the actor with his activity. There is no time to get bored or to worry about what may or may not happen. A person in such a situation can make full use of whatever skills are required and receives clear feedback to his actions; hence, he belongs to a rational cause-and-effect system in which what he does has realistic and predictable consequences.

Csikszentmihalyi refers to this 'holistic sensation that people feel when they act with total involvement' as flow. He describes the relationship between flow and skills:

> . . . at any given moment in time, people are aware of a finite number of opportunities which challenge them to act, at the same time, they are aware also of their skills – that is, of their capacity to cope with demands imposed by the environment. When a person is bombarded with demands which he or she feels unable to meet, a state of anxiety ensues. When the demands for action are fewer, but still more than what the person feels capable of handling, the state of experience is one of worry. Flow is experienced when people perceive opportunities for action being evenly matched by their capabilities. If, however, skills are greater than the opportunities for using them, boredom will follow. And finally, a person with great skills and few opportunities for applying them will pass from the state of boredom again into that of anxiety. It follows that a flow activity is one which provides optimal challenges in relation to the actor's skills.

This quote adds a greater insight into Scitovsky's concept of skilled consumption, and it also explains why such skilled consumption can generate high levels of consumer satisfaction. Moreover, whereas sport has the potential for providing such flow experiences, Csikszentmihalyi argues that normal life experiences rarely have the ability to provide such enjoyment. This is because in many everyday experiences we do not have the control to make sure that challenges match our skills. Also, most activities in life are not experiences in the sense of being 'interactive sequences with a beginning, a middle and an end, which provide a clear cognitive or emotional resolution'. Sport provides both of these characteristics: the ability to equate the degree of challenge with one's skills and clearly an experience in the sense defined above. Csikszentmihalyi summarises the nature of enjoyment for consumers during a flow experience:

> they concentrate their attention on a limited stimulus field, forget personal problems, lose their sense of time and of themselves, feel competent and in control, and have a sense of harmony and union with their surroundings.

Sport is not the only route to flow experiences. However, we would argue that all sport has the potential to provide such experiences. It is this potential that makes sport different from many other types of consumer behaviour.

Thus Csikszentmihalyi's work complements that of Scitovsky in its attempt to investigate the nature of consumer satisfaction, and provides a further building block in our analysis of consumer behaviour in sport.

Conclusion

In this chapter we have looked at three different theoretical approaches to the demand for sport. The neo-classical demand model identifies the main variables that influence consumer choice in sport as the price of taking part, the income of the consumer, and the prices of related goods and services (complements and substitutes). The household production approach extends the neo-classical framework to incorporate the time input into consumption. We have shown how this approach can be used to model the investment demand for sport, i.e. the demand for sport as a contributor to health status.

Finally, we have looked at a broader approach to the demand for sport that concentrates more on the way in which sport gives satisfaction to the consumer. This economic psychology approach takes on the job of attempting to explain what economists assume away: the formation of tastes and preferences.

We have concentrated in this chapter on theoretical approaches to the demand for sport. In order to test these theories two further stages are required. We must first move from the theory to an empirically testable model. Second, we must obtain the data that is required to test that model. We will see in the next chapter that neither of these stages can be accomplished easily in the case of the demand for sport.

5 The demand for sport

Evidence

Introduction

We are still some way from having a rigorous testing of the theoretical approaches to the demand for sport put forward in the previous chapter. One of the reasons for this is the limited number of empirical economists working in the field of the demand for sport. Another is the difficulty of moving from the theoretical discussion to the specification and testing of an empirical model. Finally, the data available is often inadequate to test fully the theories put forward.

This chapter therefore cannot exactly match the structure of the previous one in the presentation of evidence on the demand for sport and recreation activities. By necessity it is limited to empirical studies that have been carried out in this field. The biggest constraint, however, on the ability to carry out empirical studies on the demand for sport is the availability of data.

We spend the first part of the chapter discussing the availability of data on sports participation and the difficulties of using the data that is available to establish patterns of sports participation, trends in sports participation, and international comparisons of sports participation. We then move on to consider in detail two studies of the demand for sport that have been carried out in Britain.

Data on sports participation

The data on sports participation typically comes from large nationwide surveys of people's sport and recreation activities which are often part of the broader multi-purpose surveys where sports participation questions are included on a regular basis. In Britain, the main source of sports participation data has been the General Household Survey (GHS).

The GHS began in Britain in 1972 as an annual broad, multi-purpose social survey. Questions on sports participation have been included, normally at 3-year intervals.

Sports participation data was first collected in 1973 and then in 1977, 1980, 1983, 1986, 1987, 1990, 1993 and 1996. Methodological changes were made in 1977 and 1987, so that time series data are broadly comparable over the 1977–1986 period and 1987–1996 period. Substantial changes were also made to the questionnaire in 1996 when data on club membership, facility usage, whether participation was competitive or not, and whether coaching was received were collected for the first time. However, the main questions on participation remained the same, so that the 1996 data should be comparable with the 1987–1993 data although allowing more detailed analysis.

In the 1970s and early 1980s the sample size was above 20,000, but more recent surveys have been in the 15,000 to 18,000 range. A random sample of households is chosen and every individual 16 years of age and older is interviewed. Respondents are asked about their sports participation behaviour over the past four weeks and over the past twelve months. Forty separate sporting activities are prompted and the frequency of participation in each activity over the past 4 weeks is recorded. The survey takes place over a 12-month period beginning in April and finishing in March.

Data on young people's sports participation was collected for the first time for England in 1994. The age range studied was 6 to 16 years. The field work was carried out in June and July and referred to sports participation over the previous 12 months. The sample size was 4,400. The survey was a sports-specific survey and therefore included more detailed questions about sports behaviour than the GHS adult survey. Questions about sport done in school and out of school were included, as well as sport done in sports clubs, youth clubs and other organisations. Questions about young people's attitudes to sport were also included.

In addition to this regular collection of data on sports participation there are specific one-off surveys looking at more targeted aspects of sports participation. The two most important of these have been the Health and Lifestyle Survey, designed to include all elements of Grossman's health production function, carried out first in 1985 and then again in a 1991 follow-up, and the Allied Dunbar National Fitness Survey in 1994.

Both these surveys incorporated data on physiological fitness tests as well as similar (though not identical) measures of sports participation to those recorded in the GHS.

At the outset we should be aware of the problems of using this type of information. This survey data is cross-section data taken from a sample of households at a particular point in time. It seems that one of the most important aspects of demand, the relationship of quantity demanded to price (the demand curve) is excluded from analysis on the basis of this data, as price is not a variable and some aspects of price (e.g. travel cost) vary from household to household at a particular point in time. Unfortunately, these national surveys do not usually collect this type of information.

A second problem with this type of data relates to attempts to use successive surveys, taken at different times, to establish time trends. The most serious problem arises when one attempts to compare surveys carried out by different organizations. Veal (1976) indicates the problem by comparing the results of the GHS (1973) with those of the Pilot National Recreation Survey (British Travel Association/University of Keele, 1967) and *Planning for Leisure* (Sillitoe, 1969), two earlier surveys carried out in 1965. We would have expected participation to

Table 5.1 General Household Survey (GHS, 1973) compared with Pilot National Recreation Survey (PNRS, 1965) and *Planning for Leisure* (PFL, 1965)

Sport	GHS (1973) Percentage participating in 4 weeks prior to interview	PNRS/PFL (1965) Percentage participating in year prior to interview
Golf	2.7	3.5
Long-distance walking	3.3	5.0
Football	3.0	5.0
Cricket	1.4	4.0
Tennis	2.4	4.5
Bowls	1.0	3.0
Fishing	3.2	5.0
Badminton/squash	1.8	3.0
Table tennis	0.9	6.0
Swimming (indoor)	3.7	} 11.5
Swimming (outdoor)	4.6	

From: Veal (1976).

have increased over this 8-year period, yet the 1965 results clearly suggest much higher participation, as Table 5.1 indicates.

There are several reasons for these differences. First, the questions asked in the surveys related to behaviour over different time periods. The 1973 GHS asked respondents what activities they participated in 4 weeks prior to interview. The 1965 surveys asked for activities participated in over the past 12 months. The latter question will yield a higher participation rate than the former, since it picks up infrequent participation. It is also much more affected by poor memory and exaggeration. In 1987, for the first time, the GHS recorded participation over the past 4 weeks and the past 12 months.

Also, the sampling frames were different for the surveys, with the major difference being between the GHS, where only persons of 16 years of age and over were sampled, and the Pilot National Recreation Survey, where persons aged 12 and over were sampled. As we saw in Chapter 4, age is a major influence on participation.

Some of these problems should be solved by having results from the same survey over different time periods. For instance, we have GHS results every three or four years. However, there have been problems in comparing GHS results from one survey to another because of differences in the questions asked and, in particular, because changes in the prompt card made substantial differences to recorded participation rates in some activities between 1973 and 1977, and between 1986 and 1987.

Finally, in relation to data availability, there are specific research studies that have involved primary data collection on sports participation and expenditure on sports that have specific relevance to demand modelling. We will consider two such studies in detail during the course of this chapter. However, before we move on to discuss models of sports participation we consider the information on characteristics of sports participation that the GHS data have provided.

Great Britain: levels and frequency of sports participation

Table 5.2 gives the pattern of sports/physical recreation participation (4-week and 12-month) and the frequency of participation (over 4 weeks) for 1996. Fifty-six per cent of adults (16+) took part in at least one sporting activity in the four weeks before interview in 1996, and 81 per cent took part in at least one activity in the previous 12 months. If we exclude walking (i.e. those participants who only go walking and do no other sport or recreation activity), then the 4-week and 12-month participation rates fall to 46 and 66 per cent respectively.

The activity with by far the highest participation rate was walking, with a 4-week rate of 45 per cent and a 12-month rate of 68 per cent. The next most popular activity was indoor swimming, with a 4-week rate of 13 per cent and a 12-month rate of 35 per cent.

Only three other activities had 4-week rates into double figures: keep fit/yoga (including aerobics) (12 per cent), snooker/pool/billiards (11 per cent), and cycling (11 per cent).

An important feature of Table 5.2 is the relationship between 4-week and annual participation rates. The latter measure, obtained by asking respondents if they had participated in the previous 12 months, includes less frequent participants. It also takes some account of seasonality, since the 4-week rate is an average of four quarterly, or seasonal, sets of data. If there is substantial seasonal variation, as there is in many outdoor sports, the average 4-week rate is reduced by the averaging procedure. Thus, for example, in the case of tennis, the 4-week participation rate in the third quarter (summer) is 4 per cent, in the first quarter (winter) it is 1 per cent and the average over four seasons is 2 per cent. The 12-monthly, or annual rate is 7 per cent, and therefore the ratio of annual to 4-week rates is 3.5 (7:2). Seasonal sports tend to have a high ratio of annual to average 4-week participation rates.

Table 5.2 gives the frequency of participation over the 4 weeks before interview. Sports participants have much higher frequencies of participation than do participants in other leisure activities such as the arts. The highest frequencies occur in cycling (eight occasions per 4-week period) and keep fit/yoga (seven occasions per 4-week period). Thus participation occurs in these sports on average once every 4 days. Since these figures represent averages over all participants, some participants will have considerably higher frequencies than this. This high frequency of participation across a large number of sports is an important characteristic of sports participation.

Trends in sports participation

Conventional analysis of the type carried out by the Office of National Statistics in its analysis of the GHS sports participation data has indicated a relatively

Table 5.2 Sports, games and physical activities: all persons aged 16 and over, Great Britain, 1996

Active sports, games and physical activities*	Participation rates in the 4 weeks before the interview	Participation rates in the 12 months before the interview	Average frequency of participation per participant in the 4 weeks before the interview
Walking[†]	44.5	68.2	..
Any swimming	14.8	39.6	4
Swimming: indoor	12.8	35.1	4
Swimming: outdoor	2.9	14.9	5
Keep fit/yoga	12.3	20.7	7
Snooker/pool/billiards	11.3	19.2	4
Cycling	11.0	21.4	8
Weight-training	5.6	9.8	7
Any soccer	4.8	8.5	5
Soccer: outdoor	3.8	6.9	5
Soccer: indoor	2.1	4.8	4
Golf	4.7	11.0	4
Running (jogging etc.)	4.5	8.0	6
Darts[‡]	..	8.6	..
Tenpin bowls/skittles	3.4	15.5	2
Badminton	2.4	7.0	3
Tennis	2.0	7.1	4
Any bowls	1.9	4.6	6
Carpet bowls	1.1	3.0	5
Lawn bowls	0.9	2.8	6
Fishing	1.7	5.3	3
Table tennis	1.5	5.3	3
Squash	1.3	4.1	4
Weight-lifting	1.3	2.6	8
Horse riding	1.0	3.0	8
Cricket	0.9	3.3	3
Shooting	0.8	2.8	4
Self-defence	0.7	1.7	6
Climbing	0.7	2.5	2
Basketball	0.7	2.0	3
Rugby	0.6	1.3	4
Ice skating	0.6	3.2	1
Netball	0.5	1.4	3
Sailing	0.4	2.3	4
Motor sports	0.4	1.6	3
Canoeing	0.4	1.6	2
Hockey	0.3	1.1	4
Skiing	0.3	2.6	4
Athletics – track and field	0.2	1.2	5
Gymnastics	0.2	0.7	6
Windsurfing, boardsailing	0.2	1.1	2
At least one activity (excluding walking) §	45.6	65.9	
At least one activity §	63.6	81.4	
Base = 100%	*15,696*	*15,696*	

Source: General Household Survey (1996)

*Includes only activities in which more than 0.5% of men or of women participated in the 12 months before interview.
[†] In 1996 respondents were not asked how often they went walking.
[‡] In 1996 respondents were asked about darts only in relation to the past twelve months and not the past four weeks.
§ Total includes those activities not separately listed.

static position as regards overall levels of sports participation in the 1990s, with rises in activities such as cycling and weight-training matched by declines in squash and snooker/pool/billiards. Prior to the 1990s the picture was one of very gradual growth in sports participation in the 1977–1986 period, with the most significant feature being the growth in the participation of women in indoor sport (rising from 13 per cent in 1977 to 21 per cent in 1986).

With this exception, the conventional analysis of the GHS data has indicated a fairly static pattern of association between sports participation and the standard classification variables of age, gender, and socio-economic group. For instance, in the report on the 1983 GHS it was stated that:

> The pattern of participation rates among the different age groups is similar to that found in the 1977 and 1980 surveys. Participation generally tends to be highest among those aged 16–19 and to decline with age.
>
> (OPCS, 1985)

Similarly, the report on the 1986 GHS stated that:

> The pattern of participation rates among the different age groups in 1986 is similar to that found in the 1983 survey.
>
> (OPCS,1989)

The conventional approach has been very successful in identifying the basic pattern of sports participation. We now know what the most popular participation sports are, how frequently participants take part, and how participation is related to major classification variables such as age, gender and socio-economic group. Less attention has been paid, however, to trends in participation. In fact, there are two aspects of the conventional approach that may make it difficult to pick out major trends.

The first relates to the activities included in the definition of sport. Camping/ caravanning is included in the outdoor sport category of the GHS throughout the 1977 to 1986 period. There is little logic to this. This activity has a participation rate of 2 per cent in the most popular (third) quarter, a significant amount for an activity with little or nothing to do with active sport. More seriously, two indoor activities dominate the indoor sport category for men: snooker, with a male participation rate of 17 per cent in 1986; and darts, with a male participation rate of 9 per cent in 1986 (but 15 per cent in 1977). There is perhaps more of an argument for including these activities as sports than there is for camping/ caravanning, and they may be important activities for indicating the overall pattern of leisure participation. However, if the main interest is to indicate the trends in sports participation in order to assess the success of publicly financed policies aimed at encouraging people into active sport, then it is much better to exclude these activities for two reasons.

First, because public subsidy to sport is based to some extent on the sports participation/health relationship, the definition of sport in the statistical indicators used to measure the effectiveness of such subsidy policies should include those sports involving some positive aspect of health promotion. Similarly, excellence arguments relating to the promotion of international sporting success have little relevance in these activities.

The second reason is more important. Any statistical indicator of sports participation will be influenced to a major extent by these two categories because of their size. Since one of them, snooker, has grown considerably over the 1977 to 1986 period, but the other, darts, has declined to almost an equal extent, statistical indicators containing them will show little or no change. This may be one of the reasons there has apparently been more change in the indoor participation of women than of men, since darts and snooker are dominated by male participants.

Another major problem with the conventional analysis probably results from the initial interest in the data for the investigation of the pattern of participation. This initial interest led to the reporting of results for a large number of sports categories, some of which have very small sample sizes and hence are prone to large sampling errors. As a result only a few aggregate indicators of sports participation have been derived, and all of these suffer from the problems raised in the previous paragraphs (i.e. they include camping, snooker, and darts). There is a need for a series of participation indicators which represent the major features of the GHS data. These indicators should be capable of providing an adequate summary of the data in a relatively small set of statistics. By analysing the path of these indicators over time, it would then become possible to analyse the major trends in the data. This is exactly what is attempted in the next section.

Trends in sports participation 1977–1986: an alternative approach

In this section an attempt is made at an alternative approach to the analysis of trends in sports participation as revealed by the GHS data. Some of the results of a research programme, funded by the Health Promotion Research Trust, that was carried out at Manchester Metropolitan University from 1988 to 1991 are summarised. The full results are available in Gratton and Tice (1994). The time period chosen for the trend analysis was 1977 to 1986, because the only data available prior to 1977 was the 1973 data which is not comparable with 1977 and later, and the data collected from 1987 onwards was not directly comparable with the earlier data.

The basis of this alternative approach is to extend the use of aggregate participation groups from the four that have been used since 1983 (i.e. at least one outdoor activity, both including and excluding walking, at least one indoor activity, and at least one indoor and/or outdoor activity) to a wider range of participation indicators that together represent the major dimensions of sports participation behaviour. Altogether 14 different participation groupings were used, we report here on only six groups and for clarity of exposition we include walking as a sport in all six groups. In addition, we have excluded darts, billiards/snooker, and camping and caravanning from our definition of sport for the reasons given in the last section.

Table 5.3 Sports participation groups

Name	Description: respondents included in this group if they take part in
1. Sport	at least one sport
2. Outdoor	at least one outdoor sport (including walking)
3. Indoor	at least one indoor sport
4. Outdoor only	outdoor sport only (including walking)
5. Indoor only	indoor sport only
6. Indoor and outdoor	both indoor and outdoor sport

Table 5.4 Sports participation rates, Great Britain, 1977–1986

Group	% participation in 4 weeks before interview*				% change
	1977	1980	1983	1986	1977–1986
1. Sport	33.3	36.4	38.2	40.7	22.2
2. Outdoor	27.6	29.7	30.7	31.4	13.8
3. Indoor	11.8	14.3	15.8	18.6	57.6
4. Outdoor only	21.5	22.1	22.5	22.1	2.8
5. Indoor only	5.8	6.7	7.5	9.3	60.3
6. Indoor and outdoor	6.1	7.6	8.2	9.3	52.5

* Annual average of four quarterly surveys.

The six participation groups that provide the structure of the analysis are defined in Table 5.3. Table 5.4 reports the participation rates for these six sports groups, as well as the percentage changes in participation for the period as a whole.

Table 5.4 shows how the various indicators of participation have changed from 1977 to 1986. The first group, SPORT, shows a rise in participation from 33.3 per cent to 40.7 per cent from 1977 to 1986, i.e. a rise of 22 per cent. Thus participation in sport is increasing due to a higher proportion of the adult population taking part in at least one activity.

Looking at the categories relating to aspects of outdoor sports participation, the general characteristic is that there has been very little growth in these categories over the 1977–1986 period. OUTDOOR refers to those that took part in at least one outdoor sport over the 4-week reference period. By 1986 this category had a participation rate of 31.4 per cent, but the rate of growth from 1977 to 1986 was only 14 per cent. OUTDOOR ONLY picks out a different aspect of outdoor sport: it looks at those that participate only in outdoor sport. This group shows virtually no growth between 1977 and 1986. This highlights a major feature of the participation data for this period: outdoor sports were not attracting a significantly greater number of participants in 1986 than in 1977. In particular, those people that take part only in outdoor sport represented the same share of the adult population in 1986 as they did in 1977.

The picture for indoor sports is remarkably different. INDOOR (i.e. participants in at least one indoor sport) has a growth rate of 58 per cent between 1977 and 1986. The equivalent figure from the conventional GHS analysis is 29 per cent, indicating how the inclusion of darts and snooker has effectively halved the growth rate in indoor sports participation. INDOOR ONLY has a growth rate of 60 per cent. Thus we see a clear difference in the growth of participation between indoor and outdoor. Gratton and Taylor (1991) analysed the relationship between growth of public indoor swimming pools and sports centres over the 1970s and 1980s, and concluded that it was the massive public investment in new indoor facilities that had led to the large increase in participation in indoor sport. What the current analysis indicates is that the increase was under-recorded by the conventional measure of indoor sports participation.

The final group, INDOOR AND OUTDOOR, represents those taking part in both indoor and outdoor sport. INDOOR AND OUTDOOR is a core group of sports participants that is represented in many other groups. It was a small group in 1977 at only 6.1 per cent, but grew rapidly with a 52.5 per cent growth rate between 1977 and 1986.

The definition of the participation groups in Table 5.3 has enabled us to pick out clear patterns of participation and changes in participation that conventional analysis of the GHS data has not fully revealed. The major feature of the period 1977 to 1986 is the contrasting growth rates in participation between indoor and outdoor sports, with the former far outstripping the latter. Such clear trends are much easier to identify by first using a more meaningful definition of sport, and second using a wider number of indicators covering different aspects of the types of sports participation.

Frequency of participation

Table 5.5 gives frequency of participation for the various groups. There is an increase in frequency of participation over the period 1977 to 1986 in all groups. The pattern of growth in frequency is not as steady, though, as for participation.

Table 5.5 Frequency of participation in sport, Great Britain, 1977–1986

Activity group	Participants' frequency of participation in 4 weeks before interview*			
	1977	*1980*	*1983*	*1986*
1. Sport	8.2	8.9	9.7	9.3
2. Outdoor	9.0	9.7	10.8	10.5
3. Indoor	8.7	9.4	10.0	10.1
4. Outdoor only	7.9	8.5	9.5	8.7
5. Indoor only	4.5	4.9	5.2	5.3
6. Indoor and outdoor	12.7	13.3	14.5	14.9

* Annual average of four quarterly surveys.

Whereas the largest growth in participation in indoor sports occurred in the 1977–1980 and 1983–1986 periods, the largest growth in frequency of participation occurred in the 1980–1983 period. In fact frequency actually decreased in the 1983–1986 period in most groups.

In general, frequency of participation in outdoor sports is higher than that for indoor sports. The lowest frequency is in the INDOOR ONLY group. By far the highest frequency is for the INDOOR AND OUTDOOR group. Although the participation rate for this category was only 9.3 per cent in 1986, these participants took part in sport on average 15 times per 28 day period, i.e. more often than every other day. This group therefore represents the most committed sports participants.

Characteristics of participants

In this section we analyse the characteristics of participants in the fourteen participation groups with regard to the standard classification variables conventionally associated with sports participation.

Age

Table 5.6 records the average age of participants for the different participation groups for the four GHS surveys in the 1977–1986 period. The pattern is remarkably consistent from year to year and across groups, with a gradual increase in the average age of participants over time.

For most of the groups the average age is in the thirties, with indoor sports groups having a lower average age (normally in the early thirties) than outdoor groups (normally in the late thirties). In 1986 the average age across all sports participants was 39 years.

The consistency in the way average age of participation has changed over time is quite remarkable. All groups have shown a steady rise over the 1977 to 1986 period. For all participants (SPORT) the average age rose from 38.2 years

Table 5.6 Age of sports participants, Great Britain, 1977–1986

Activity group	Average age in years			
	1977	1980	1983	1986
1. Sport	38.2	38.3	38.9	39.0
2. Outdoor	39.3	39.5	39.9	40.4
3. Indoor	32.2	32.0	33.4	33.9
4. Outdoor only	41.5	42.4	42.7	43.3
5. Indoor only	33.2	33.0	34.5	34.2
6. Indoor and outdoor	31.3	31.2	32.3	33.7
Average (whole sample)	45.4	45.3	45.7	45.5

to 39 years over this period. In general, groups relating to indoor participation have shown larger increases in average age of participants than groups relating to outdoor participation, although on average participants in indoor sport are still younger than participants in outdoor sport. The largest rise in average age is in the core group of most committed sports participants, the INDOOR AND OUTDOOR group, whose average rose from 31.3 in 1977 to 33.7 in 1986.

This provides some evidence in support of Rodgers' (1977) hypotheses concerning the relationship between age and sports participation. Rather than accepting the conventional view that people 'drop out' of active participation as they get older, he suggested that many people in the older age categories were never participants, even when young. He introduced the concept of 'sports literacy', the extent to which sections of the population are exposed and conditioned to active recreation. The older generation, he suggested, reveals a much higher proportion of sports illiteracy than the younger generation. Table 5.6 suggests that between 1977 and 1986, as a more 'sports literate' generation got older, they continued to be involved in sport, so that many more older people were regular sports participants in 1986 than ten years earlier. If this interpretation is correct, the implication is that the average age of participants would have continued to rise gradually after 1986.

Gender

Table 5.7 gives the percentage of female participants in each of the six groups. In 1977 just over 42 per cent of all sports participants were women. By 1986 this had risen to nearly 46 per cent. The table shows, however, that this rise conceals a varied pattern of change among the different groups. There was little change in the proportion of female participants in the outdoor sport groups.

In contrast with these outdoor groups, the proportion of women in the indoor sports participation groups has increased dramatically, so that in INDOOR (those taking part in at least one indoor sport) female participants outnumbered male participants in 1986, the reverse having been true in 1977. For INDOOR

Table 5.7 Percentage of female sports participants, Great Britain, 1977–1986

Activity group	% of participants who are female				% change
	1977	*1980*	*1983*	*1986*	*1977–1986*
1. Sport	42.4	44.5	45.7	45.6	7.6
2. Outdoor	40.7	42.5	42.6	41.1	1.0
3. Indoor	42.4	45.8	50.1	51.4	21.2
4. Outdoor only	42.4	43.6	42.6	40.6	−4.3
5. Indoor only	50.5	53.5	58.6	60.5	19.8
6. Indoor and outdoor	34.7	39.1	42.4	42.3	21.9
Whole sample	53.4	53.6	54.1	53.7	

ONLY, females were about equal to males in 1977 but by 1986 females accounted for over 60 per cent of the participants in this group.

Probably the most interesting aspect of Table 5.7 relates to the percentage of females in the core category, INDOOR AND OUTDOOR, over the period 1977 to 1986. The proportion of females in this most committed group of sports participants rose from over 34 per cent of the total in 1977 to over 42 per cent by 1986, the biggest proportionate rise of any of the groups.

The 'sports literacy' argument discussed in the last section in relation to age could also be part of the explanation for the rising level of female participation in sport. Historically women have been less sports literate than men. However, this was less and less true in the last quarter of the twentieth century. Women increasingly have had similar exposure and opportunities for sport to men. This is starting to be expressed in the statistics, but more for indoor sport than outdoor. There is interaction here, however, between age and gender. It is younger women that are showing similar patterns of participation with men. The difference in sports literacy between men and women in older age groups results in continuing disparities between male and female participation rates for these age groups.

International comparisons of sports participation

Rodgers (1978) attempted to compare the level of sports participation across six European countries. A recent study, COMPASS 1999, has attempted to develop this approach further.

COMPASS 1999 reports the results of an ambitious European project to investigate the availability of sports participation data in all European countries, to make cross-national comparisons of the level and structure of sports participation across seven of these countries, and to produce guidelines for greater harmonisation in sports survey methodology.

The results have been achieved through close co-operation of the major sports agencies and national statistical offices in these seven countries. There are considerable difficulties in making cross-national comparisons of sports participation when the surveys used to collect the data have used different methodologies. These are similar to the difficulties discussed above when making comparisons between different surveys over time in any one country. However, the exercise has revealed useful outcomes, not least in the development of an analytical framework, which adds to understanding in each of the seven countries of the nature and structure of sports participation. The analytical framework proposed in COMPASS is based on analysing the structure of sports participation across a spectrum ranging from no participation at all to high-intensity, frequent participation at a competitive level, being a member of a sports club.

Despite the difficulties in making cross-national comparisons in sports participation across European countries, the COMPASS 1999 report has shown that there is evidence of an emerging European profile of sports participation. One of the most important patterns to emerge is a north/south divide in the intensity of participation, as shown in Table 5.8.

Table 5.8 Sports participation across seven European countries (adults 16+, %)

	Spain	Finland	Ireland	Italy	Netherlands	Sweden	UK
Competitive, organised, intensive	2	6	7	2	8	12	5
Intensive	7	33	11	3	8	24	13
Regular, competitive and/or organised	2	5	7	2	10	5	4
Regular, recreational	4	28	3	3	6	17	6
Irregular	10	6	15	8	25	11	19
Occasional	6	2	21	5	6		20
Non-participant: participation in other physical activities	43	16	10	37	} 38	8	15
Non-participant: no physical activities	26	3	26	40		22	19

Finland and Sweden stand out as having the highest levels of participation and the highest percentage of participants in the high-frequency, intensive groups. Italy and Spain have lowest recorded levels of participation, although comparisons with these two countries are most affected by differences in survey methodology. The UK, the Netherlands and Ireland are similar in both the overall level of participation and the structure of participation over the various groups. These three countries differ from Finland and Sweden not so much in the overall level of participation but in the distribution of participation over the various participant groups, since they have a much higher proportion of participants in groups with lower frequency levels of participation than the Scandinavian countries.

Again, the Scandinavian countries seem to have been the most successful in overcoming traditional barriers to 'sport for all', in particular being elderly or female. However, all countries have higher participation rates for older people and women than was the case in a previous European cross-national comparative study carried out by Rodgers 20 years ago, so there do seem to be common European trends emerging in the pattern of participation. This study has provided evidence in support of the Rodgers hypothesis that these groups had low participation rates in his study because of high rates of 'sports illiteracy'. These rates of 'sports illiteracy' appear to have fallen considerably in European countries in the intervening 20 years.

This is illustrated in Figure 5.1, which shows the percentage of adults who either do not participate in sport or do so only occasionally (less than once a month). Again Finland, stands out as having the smallest percentage of the population in these two groups and, after the age of 25, no substantial increase in the percentage doing little or no sport. For all other countries, the percentage in these two groups steadily increases with age but at a much slower rate than previous results would have suggested.

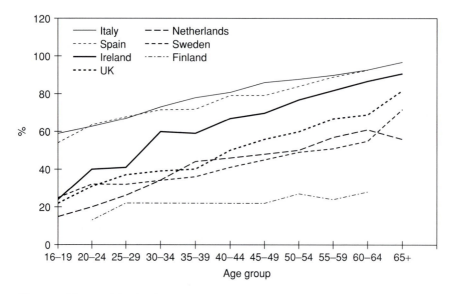

Figure 5.1 Non-participation/occasional participation in sport by age group.

COMPASS 1999 is just the beginning of the increase in our understanding of international comparisons of sport participation behaviour. Greater harmonisation of data and an increase in the number of countries participating in the project is likely to lead to much greater understanding in the coming years.

Demand models: the parent demand function

We now move on from the simple descriptive analysis of sports data to a more analytical approach based on the theoretical approach to demand developed in the previous chapter. In this section, we report the results of a demand study carried out by Gratton and Tice (1991). This study estimated a two-stage 'parent' demand function which, in the first stage, attempts to explain the decision to take part in sport and in the second stage attempts to explain the intensity of participation. A similar set of explanatory variables is used in both stages. The data used to test the model is the Health and Lifestyle Survey data, which provides some advantages over the GHS in the measurement of the intensity of participation.

Data

The Health and Lifestyle Survey (Cox *et al.*, 1987) is a survey of adults aged 18 years and over living in private households in England, Wales, and Scotland. It was funded by the Health Promotion Research Trust. Interviewing was carried out between autumn 1984 and summer 1985 with 9,003 individuals. The aim of the survey was to collect information on factors that contribute to a healthy, or unhealthy, lifestyle. The survey focused on four major factors: diet, exercise, smoking, and alcohol consumption.

The survey collected information about respondents' participation in sport and other energetic leisure activities 'in the last fortnight' before interview. The broad pattern of participation revealed was similar to that found in the GHS. In addition to this, questions were asked about time spent in participation over the 2-week period, sport by sport.

From this data we devised three indicators of sports participation. The first, represented by the variable PARTICIPATION, is a dichotomous variable taking the value 1 if the individual had taken part in any sport in the 2 weeks prior to interview, or 0 if the individual had taken part in no sport, and effectively divides the sample into participant and non-participant groups.

The other two indicators were derived only for the participant group, and aimed to identify the intensity of participation. The first of these, the variable SPORT-TIME, is the total time spent participating in all sports by the individual over the 2-week period recorded. Thus if an individual played squash for 90 minutes, went jogging for 60 minutes, and swam for 120 minutes over the 2-week period his or her SPORT-TIME would be 270 minutes.

However, some sports are much more energetic than others, and whereas it is quite possible to spend 3 or 4 hours over a game of golf, most games of squash last less than 1 hour. Thus the SPORT-TIME variable could be an inadequate measure of intensity of participation. We therefore derived a second measure of intensity, the variable ENERGYINDEX. This variable attempted to measure an index of energy expenditure for each participant. The index was constructed from the SPORT-TIME variable together with a classification of the energy expenditure (in kcals) associated with a typical time of participation for a sport, as given in Durnin and Passmore (1967). This ENERGYINDEX is calculated for each participant as a weighted average of times spent participating in all the sports done by that participant, the weights being the energy expenditure associated with each sport.

These three variables – PARTICIPATION, SPORT-TIME, and ENERGY-INDEX – became the dependent variables which the model set out to explain.

The model

There have been several attempts to estimate two-stage econometric models of participation in recreation. These, however, have been confined to North America, and to outdoor recreation (see Cicchetti *et al.*, 1969; Cicchetti, 1973; Kalter and Gosse, 1970). Our approach follows from these studies in that we adopt the same two-stage approach. The first stage estimates the conditional probability of participating in sport by regressing PARTICIPATION on the explanatory variable set. The second estimates the intensity of participation for those in the participant group. We have two variables to represent intensity: SPORT-TIME and ENERGYINDEX. The same explanatory variable set was used in the estimation.

The variables to be included in the explanatory variables set have to some extent been determined by the previous research into the determinants of sports participation. As we have seen, studies of sports participation patterns have identified certain key socio-economic variables that are important in determining people's preferences for active recreation. These were age, gender, and income. Sports participation is positively related to income and negatively related to age. Men participate more than women. We have shown earlier how these patterns have emerged from the GHS data and how they have been changing over time. These patterns are confirmed for the Health and Lifestyle Survey data.

Another variable recorded in the survey, and likely to be an important determinant of sports participation, is whether or not the individual suffers from a long-standing illness/disability. This is represented by a variable which takes the value 1 if the individual has a long-standing illness or disability and 0 otherwise. We expect this variable to have a negative coefficient, those with a long-standing illness being less likely to take part in sport.

Similar 0/1 variables (normally referred to as 'dummy variables') were included to represent ethnic background, marital status, and work status. In general we expect ethnic minority groups to participate less than average (again on the basis of previous studies of sports participation), and married people to participate less than single people (because of other demands on time). Another variable, household size, reinforces this effect. The work status variable is also included as an indicator of time availability. In general, other things being equal, we expect those with more time available to be more likely to participate in sport. However, the work status variable is more than an indicator of time availability since part-time employed, unemployed, permanently sick/disabled, retired, full-time students and housewives (keeping house) are identified separately as work status categories, and therefore the influence of income, age, and gender will also possibly be picked up in these categories.

The final variable included is the total number of different leisure activities that the individual respondent had participated in over the two weeks before the interview; this is included because of previous work carried out by Gratton and Tice (1989) on the Health and Lifestyle Survey. They discovered that sports participants have a very strong leisure orientation when compared with non-participants, i.e. they take part in many more non-sport leisure activities than non-participants. This is true across all age and income groups. To some extent, this variable is picking up levels of leisure consumption skills since it indicates the consumer's ability to obtain utility across a wide range of leisure activities.

Results

The results of the estimation of the three equations appear in Tables 5.9, 5.10, and 5.11. Because all the regressions include the variable, net weekly household income, the sample size is reduced because of missing values for this variable in the survey. Thus in Table 5.9, for instance, the total sample size is reduced from 9,003 to 7,151.

Table 5.9 The determinants of PARTICIPATION

Variable name	Parameter estimate	t-ratio
Intercept	−1.444	−8.56
Age (years)	−0.0297	−9.52
Respondent's gender	−0.0321	−4.13
Household size	0.010	0.377
Long-standing illness	−0.189	−2.57
Net weekly household income	0.00123	3.88
Number of activities last 2 weeks	0.529	33.11
Part-time employed	0.263	2.42
Unemployed	−0.125	−0.86
Permanently sick/disabled	−0.028	−0.10
Retired	0.243	1.77
Full-time student	0.340	0.91
Keeping house	0.201	1.88
Widowed	0.0626	0.35
Divorced	0.320	1.88
Separated	0.385	1.83
Married, living with spouse	−0.071	−0.679
Asian	−0.034	−0.12
Black	0.495	1.6
Other non-white	0.389	1.05

Table 5.9 reports the results of a logit model estimation procedure since PARTCIPATION is a dependent variable which only takes the value 1 (for a sports participant) or 0 (for a non-participant). Conventional regression analysis results in a model where the predicted dependent variable represents the probability of participation but gives predictions outside the range 0 to 1. The logit model remedies this problem.

Table 5.9 shows that many of the a priori expectations are confirmed by the estimated parameters. Age, gender, and long-standing illness are all significant, with the expected negative sign. Household income is significant and positive as expected. The only other variables to have significant coefficients are the number of activities (positive, as expected) and being part-time employed (also positive). As indicated earlier, the number of activities variable is an indicator of leisure orientation; the very high *t*-statistic of 33.11 is confirmation of the importance of this variable for predicting sports participation.

Perhaps the surprising aspect of the result for the part-time employed variable is the fact that it is the only other significant variable. Although it could be argued that it shows the importance of more leisure time in determining the demand for sport, we would have expected to see the influence of the time factor in the work status variables, in particular the unemployed, retired, full-time student, permanently sick/disabled and keeping house, all of which are not significant in determining sports participation in this model. One possible explanation for this result is that these last four categories have been represented adequately by other

Table 5.10 The determinants of SPORT-TIME

Variable name	Parameter estimate	t-ratio
Intercept	18.398	4.2
Age (years)	0.012	0.133
Respondent's gender	−14.428	−7.1
Household size	−0.241	−0.34
Long-standing illness	−0.776	−0.38
Net weekly household income	−0.000035	−0.45
Number of activities last 2 weeks	3.333	9.9
Part-time employed	4.893	1.67
Unemployed	21.470	5.6
Permanently sick/disabled	7.620	0.82
Retired	8.972	2.15
Full-time student	10.303	1.84
Keeping house	3.090	1.03
Widowed	−2.142	−0.37
Divorced	−0.210	−0.046
Separated	−5.224	0.93
Married, living with spouse	−1.237	−0.50
Asian	−4.885	−0.65
Black	4.494	0.62
Other non-white	−11.994	−1.35

variables in the model, in particular income (for retired and unemployed), age (for student and retired), and gender (for keeping house). Similarly, the lack of influence for the permanently sick/disabled variable could be explained by the fact that it would have been picked up by the long-standing illness variable, although the latter variable covers many more respondents than the former, which only relates to reasons for not being in full-time employment. The significance of the results for these work status variables is that students participate more in sport not because they are students, but because they are young. Similarly, the unemployed do not participate less because they are unemployed, but because they have low incomes.

Household size, marital status, and ethnicity all failed to show a significant influence in the participation model.

The most interesting aspect of the results is the contrast between estimation of the participation model in Table 5.9 and the regressions for the intensity measures in Tables 5.10 and 5.11. Looking first of all at Table 5.10, the regression model for the time spent participating in sport (SPORT-TIME), the major change is the lack of significance for age, long-standing illness, and income. It appears that being older, having a long-standing illness and low income all act as barriers to sports participation, but if that barrier is overcome and an individual does become a participant then these variables are no longer important features in determining the extent or intensity of participation.

Table 5.11 The determinants of ENERGYINDEX

Variable name	Parameter estimate	t-ratio
Intercept	109.467	5.84
Age (years)	−0.556	−1.41
Respondent's gender	−84.194	−9.81
Household size	0.588	0.20
Long-standing illness	−5.687	−0.66
Net weekly household income	−0.00040	−1.26
Number of activities last 2 weeks	15.946	11.18
Part-time employed	21.770	2.0
Unemployed	97.081	5.98
Permanently sick/disabled	33.410	0.85
Retired	40.082	2.26
Full-time student	31.810	1.34
Keeping house	12.957	1.02
Widowed	−10.985	−0.45
Divorced	−3.490	−0.18
Separated	−24.931	−1.04
Married, living with spouse	−9.233	−0.87
Asian	−11.981	−0.38
Black	32.312	1.04
Other non-white	−55.958	−1.48

Two variables that were not significant in the participation model became significant for SPORT-TIME. These were the dummy variables representing the unemployed and the retired. The positive signs on both indicate that these variables were probably indicating availability of leisure time. Thus, again, if the initial barriers to participation of low income and/or age are overcome, then time availability becomes a major factor in sports participation over a given time period. This time effect is not evident for the part-time employed dummy variable which is not significant, though still having a positive sign, in the SPORT-TIME model.

Gender continues to be significant and negative in the SPORT-TIME model, as for PARTICIPATION. Not only do women participate in sport less than men, but also among sports participants they spend less time participating.

Similarly, the leisure orientation variable, number of activities, continues to be an important indicator of intensity of sports participation as it is of sports participation. Again there is no effect in Table 5.10 for marital status or ethnicity.

Table 5.11 reports the results for the ENERGYINDEX variable. Whereas Table 5.10 attempts to explain the time spent participating, Table 5.11 attempts to explain how much energy is used up in participation over a given time period. Given that the ENERGYINDEX is partly based on SPORT-TIME, it is perhaps not surprising that the pattern of results (though not of course the sizes of the estimated coefficients) remains broadly the same. The only substantial difference is that the part-time employed variable is significant for the ENERGYINDEX model.

Table 5.12 The relationship between time spent participating, energy index, and age for low-activity, medium-activity, and high-activity sports

	Low-activity sports only	Medium-activity sports only	High-activity sports only
SPORT-TIME	42.1	22.5	13.7
ENERGYINDEX	100.9	100.0	100.8
AVERAGE AGE OF PARTICIPANTS	47.1	38.5	31.5
NUMBER OF ACTIVITIES	4.2	4.8	5.0

The relationship between SPORT-TIME and ENERGYINDEX is indicated in Table 5.12. Durnin and Passmore (1967) picked out three levels of activity in sports participation (in energy terms) and grouped sports into low, medium, and high groups depending on the level of energy used. Gratton and Tice (1991) selected those respondents who participated *only* in one of these three categories. They then averaged the time they spent on these sports (SPORT-TIME), the energy index (ENERGYINDEX), their age, and the number of leisure activities in which they participated. These are the results that appear in Table 5.12.

As we might expect, there is a steady drop in the average age of participants as we move from low-activity sports through medium-activity sports to high-activity sports. More surprisingly, though, the average time spent on low-activity sports is higher than for medium-activity sports, which itself is higher than for high-activity sports. The net result is that the average energy index is virtually the same for the three categories of activities. One scenario that is consistent with this evidence is that sports participants, as they get older, switch to less demanding activities but at the same time spend more time on these activities. That is, there is a trade-off between the energy demands of particular sports and the time spent in participation. Younger people economise on time, but choose demanding sports; older people choose less demanding activities but spend more time on them. Of course, Table 5.12 looks at participants who only choose sports in one energy category. Many participants are excluded from the table because they engage in low-, medium-, and high-energy expenditure category sports, or at least two of the categories. However, the fact that this trade-off effect is present to some extent may explain the similarity of the results between Tables 5.10 and 5.11.

The Gratton and Tice (1991) study is an attempt to estimate a demand model for sport in Britain using a large-scale social survey, the Health and Lifestyle Survey (HALS). They used a two-stage approach similar to that carried out in North America, particularly in the analysis of the USA's National Recreation Survey data.

The demand model used is significantly different from conventional economic demand models since there is no expenditure data and no price data. Also, the data is cross-sectional rather than time-series, hence price variation over time is not relevant. It is possible, however, to obtain demand indicators which do represent different consumer behaviour patterns with respect to sport.

The results show that the factors that determine participation in sport are not the ones that determine time spent participating or energy expenditure in participation. The evidence indicates that time availability is more important in explaining intensity of participation than it is in explaining the participation decision.

A major factor with significant explanatory power for both participation and intensity is the leisure orientation of the consumer. Those consumers with a wide variety of different leisure pursuits are likely to be sports participants and to have high intensity of participation. Consumption skills are an important determinant of leisure behaviour.

The HALS data is of a form that offers opportunities for analysis that do not exist in GHS. In particular, there is no data on time spent participating in GHS, and consequently we cannot construct either a SPORT-TIME variable or an ENERGYINDEX variable, which depends on the availability of SPORT-TIME. Although HALS is not a continual data survey in the same way as GHS has been, the analysis above shows its usefulness in giving insights into the demand of sport.

Facility demand

As indicated in the previous section, one of the difficulties of using large-scale data-sets for demand estimation in sport is the lack of expenditure and price information. One study in Scotland (Centre for Leisure Research, 1993; Coalter, 1993; Gratton and Taylor, 1994) attempted to deal with this problem by looking at the role of price in the demand for public sector sports facilities.

The influence of price on a consumer's decision to use a particular sports facility is more complicated than our rather simplistic analysis of the price elasticity of demand might indicate. In particular, as McCarville and Crompton (1987) and McCarville *et al.* (1993) have explored, reactions to price levels and changes in prices are conditioned by a set of expectations or 'reference prices'. Reference prices are levels of prices felt to be appropriate by consumers. These reference prices result from a variety of stimuli, including psychological determinants such as values held by the consumer; contextual determinants such as other prices and information on current subsidy or cost levels; and immediate determinants such as the physical quality of the facility. Information, experiences and perceptions servicing the reference prices are in a continual state of change, such that the reference prices fluctuate.

McCarville and Crompton (1987) found that there was a significant, positive impact of contextual information on reference prices for public sector swimming pools. If users were informed about the cost of providing the facilities, price increases were likely to have a less elastic effect on demand. McCarville *et al.* (1993) endorsed the positive influence of total cost information on reference prices and also reported a similar positive effect from informing users that any shortfall in income for the facility would have to be made up by funds from other public recreation services.

Table 5.13 Changes in prices, usage, and revenues

	Average % price change	% change in usage (in year following price change)	Crude measure of price elasticity	% change in revenue (in year following price change)
Centre 1				
Older fitness centre	+13	−3	−0.2	+19
Newer fitness centre	+15	+134	+8.9	+120
Centre 2	+70	−37	−0.5	+11
Centre 3	+31	n.a.		n.a.
Centre 4	+71	+9	+0.1	+39
Centre 5	−100	+51	−0.51	−54

Note: The crude measure of price elasticity of demand is % change in use divided by % change in price. n.a. = not available.

The main implication of analysis of reference prices for practitioners is that the effect of price increases on demand, i.e. the price elasticity of demand, might be a variable which can be influenced by appropriate management action.

The Scottish study (Centre for Leisure Research, 1993; Coalter, 1993; Gratton and Taylor, 1994) was conducted with the express purpose of complementing normally recorded management information on prices and usage with a substantial amount of market research. This market research was designed to provide evidence relevant to many of the theoretical complications discussed in the previous sections. Local authorities agreed to implement deliberately radical adjustments (typically upwards) to prices in five case study facilities. User surveys were conducted in these facilities several months before and after the price changes, with a total of just under 2,500 respondents. Also, household surveys were conducted in the surrounding catchment areas, again before and after the price changes, with just over 5,300 respondents.

Conventional economic analysis would examine the quantitative evidence of price changes and consequent changes in the quantity demanded, allowing as far as possible for other changes affecting demand in the same period. Unfortunately, in the Scottish study specific details of demand changes relating to precise price changes for specific activities or types of user were not available for the five centres used as case studies.

Nevertheless, an aggregate picture is possible, using normally recorded data on prices and usage: it is presented in Table 5.13. This demonstrates different degrees of price elasticity of demand, not only by comparing the percentage change in quantity demanded with the percentage change in price, but also by examining the effect of the price changes on revenue at the centres. The measures of price elasticity of demand in Table 5.13 are crude because they are estimated over widely different price changes in the different facilities and because they do not statistically allow for changes in non-price influences, although these are not felt to be significant over the short period over which the effects of the price changes were measured.

The general picture that emerges from the Scottish study, as reported by Coalter (1993), is of price inelastic demand, such that higher prices lead to increases in revenue. In the case of the newer fitness facility in centre 1 and also for centre 4, the price elasticities are positive rather than the conventionally expected negative. In these cases, either price increases have had no deterrent effect on usage or such an effect has been completely outweighed by other factors encouraging use.

Further detailed analysis of the evidence in Table 5.13 is prevented by data constraints. In the absence of reliable and accurate time series data for demand and prices in the facilities being investigated, the Scottish study used market research to identify many of the aspects of the price–demand relationships.

Facility price in relation to total price

As Coalter (1993) has described, the average weekly expenditure on entrance charges of £1.10, paid by user survey respondents for facilities, amounted to just under a third of their average weekly cost of participation, £3.42. This calculation excludes any consideration of time costs, which evidence suggests are considerable. It is therefore unlikely that entrance charges, or even significant changes in them, will have a large impact on the number of participants. Doubling the expenditure on entrance charges to £2.20 would lead to total participation cost rising by less than a third, to £4.52 a week.

Expenditure on entrance charges of £1.10 a week represents less than half of the variable cost of participation, which in the Scottish study is £2.53 per week. So the impact of changes in entrance charges on the frequency decision by participants is diluted by the other variable costs. Table 5.14 demonstrates that there is a high degree of ignorance among consumers in the Scottish study, both of the previous price level and of the changes to prices. This is not surprising given that entrance charge is only a part of the relevant composite price. The ignorance over prices helps to explain the price inelastic demand, especially considering that most users in the research were regular users.

Table 5.14 Attitudes to price increases

| | Average price increase (%) | % of respondents | | | |
| | | Were not aware of previous price | Attitudes | | |
			Reasonable	Did not notice price increase	Excessive
Centre 1					
All activities	10	27	36	29	9
Older fitness centre	13	33	40	20	7
Newer fitness centre	15	44	34	14	9
Centre 2	70	35	28	20	17
Centre 3	31	44	(not asked question)		
Centre 4	71	18	38	14	36

This finding is somewhat dependent on the highly subsidised nature of most entrance charges in the Scottish sample of facilities. However, such subsidies are still common in UK local authority leisure centres and swimming pools. The finding implies that any facility operating under similar circumstances has a licence to consider significant price increases, because the impact on consumer participation costs, i.e. the composite price, is likely to be proportionately much lower than the percentage increase in charges. Local authorities may wish to explore this possibility because of an increasing financial imperative to reduce net expenditure. Taylor and Page (1994) present evidence that in the early 1990s financial cuts were the norm for local authority recreation services.

Elasticity of substitution

The Scottish study did not contain any direct questioning of the degree to which participants altered their relative expenditures on the components of the composite commodity necessary to participate, in response to changing relative prices for these components. The main components identified and valued in the study were facilities (entrance charges); transport; team/club organisation fees (membership and match fees); and kit/equipment. The main trigger for any substitution between these components was likely to have been the large proportionate increases in facility entrance charges: the reason for the study.

Indirect evidence indicates that there is a fairly stable relationship between the different components making up the overall composite commodity of which demand for facilities is a part. In particular, the main reaction identified in the research on the increases in facility entrance charges was a small percentage of users (3 per cent or less) who had reduced the frequency of their participation. No participants in either the user surveys or the household surveys suggested that they substituted the use of facilities with other components in order to maintain their participation levels.

This finding is not surprising. First, the cost of sports participation for those surveyed is identified as being comparatively low:

> Compared to a wide range of other leisure activities sport is cheap. Despite the large percentage increases in admission charges, the actual cost of admission to the centres could not be considered expensive when compared to most other regular items of leisure expenditure.
>
> (Centre for Leisure Research, 1993)

This suggests that there is little financial incentive for participants to seek to substitute facilities with other components in the composite commodity which their participation comprises.

Second, in principle there are only a few activities where substitution of facilities with other inputs is feasible. The most obvious of these are aerobics/keep fit and weight-training, where use of a purchased facility can be substituted by expenditure on appropriate equipment (steps, video, weights, etc.) for participation at home. However, for activities such as badminton, soccer, swimming and squash, it is not easy to conceive of substituting appropriate facilities with other components in the composite commodity.

This consideration of elasticity of substitution qualifies the implication of price inelastic demand of raising facility charges to accommodate financial objectives. A facility manager needs to be sure that either the activities for which increasing prices are being considered are not easily substituted by other composite commodity components, such as equipment for participation at home, or that the activities are marketed in such a way that the facility is providing a qualitatively superior participation experience to that available by using the substitute component.

Cross-price elasticity

In the Scottish study, this concerns the likelihood of responding to changes in facility entrance charges by substituting use of the higher priced facility with use of a lower priced facility, i.e. diverted demand from the former to the latter. In the Scottish study there were two *potential* cases of such positive cross-price elasticity.

The first case involved two competing fitness facilities within the same leisure centre, one of these being newer, higher quality and 77 per cent more expensive than the other. In the year following similar price increases in both facilities, in the higher priced facility usage more than doubled, while in the lower priced facility usage fell very slightly.

Crude estimates of cross-price elasticity (percentage change in the quantity demanded of one facility divided by percentage change in the price of the other facility) yield figures of over 10 for demand for the newer, higher priced facility and −0.2 for demand for the lower priced facility. Positive cross-price elasticities normally indicate a substitute or competitive relationship in demand for the two facilities. However, the market research reveals that there was not a significant switching of demand from one facility to the other in response to price increases. The reason for the high cross-price elasticity in the case of demand for the newer, higher priced facility is simply growth in new markets for this facility – regardless of changing relative prices, the demand for the facility is likely to have increased.

The market research results confirm that the two facilities serve different markets, rather than being substitutes – a desirable outcome for management. Most of the users of the newer fitness centre had not used the older fitness room; the newer facility attracted many more females from non-manual occupations, while the older facility attracted many more males from manual occupations.

The second case of potential diverted demand concerned a pool which experimented with free use for casual swimmers. Another swimming pool is situated 4 miles away from the free use pool, this other pool being of higher quality and offering a greater range of activities. The other pool is near enough for the free use to have had a possible effect on its demand, given the radical nature of this experiment. However, it must be emphasised that the catchment area of an urban, conventional swimming pool, simplistically represented by a circular area around the facility, is typically of about 3 miles radius. Thus distance is always a likely constraint to diverted demand, even when, as in this case, the facilities are fairly close to each other.

The free use experiment had a negligible effect on the demand for the other pool, which had constant visit numbers despite the free entry competition. Formally, the crude cross-price elasticity in this case is zero (zero change in demand for the other pool in response to the 100 per cent reduction in price of the free use pool). The market research revealed the reasons for the zero cross-price elasticity: half of the survey respondents at the other pool were unaware of the free use offer; two-thirds of them travelled 2 miles or less to swim and most of these considered a trip to the free use pool to be too far to travel.

In neither of these 'tests' of cross-price elasticity, therefore, was a substitute relationship found, even when positive cross-price elasticities were estimated. Instead it is apparent from the market research that product differentiation can eliminate the danger of diverted demand, particularly if it uses quality differentiation. Also, distance can be a crucial separator of markets even when the distance is not large and the price difference is considerable.

Once again, an important consideration influencing the likely elasticity of derived demand for facilities has, in this particular research study, signalled price inelastic demand, giving licence to raise entrance charges if financial objectives require higher revenue.

Non-price influences

The findings of price inelastic demand and a lack of diverted demand need to be qualified by the extent to which the research tested for changes in other important variables in the research period, apart from price. It is possible in principle that changes in other variables were masking the true effect of price changes.

One set of non-price variables which could have affected demand is supply generated. Examples include higher promotion, refurbishment of facilities, improvements in programming and new, non-price attractions to customers. However, to the authors' knowledge no significant supply changes occurred in the research period, beyond the obvious provision of a new fitness suite at one of the facilities.

Non-price influences were also tested by the market research. The questionnaires were administered in two phases, 'before' and 'after' the price changes. In each case questions investigated other variables which might have affected demand, namely employment status, socio-economic status, age, gender, education, access to personal transport, and a prompt list of constraints to participation which included family and work commitments, weather, and time. There were no cases where significant differences occurred between the responses to these non-price questions before and after the price changes. Thus it is considered valid to use the price-inelastic demand findings.

Table 5.15 Attitudes to higher price levels

	Average new price level (£)	Attitudes*	
		Reasonable	Too high
		(% of respondents)	
Centre 1			
All activities	1.46	89	11
Older fitness centre	1.30	88	8
Newer fitness centre	2.30	71	29
Centre 2	1.73	85	13
Centre 3	1.93	86	12
Centre 4	1.11	87	12

* The attitude responses do not always sum to 100%. The residual 1–4% in such cases comprises the respondents who answered that the prices were 'too low'.

Table 5.16 Perceptions of value for money after price changes

	Value for money perception			
	Excellent	Good	OK	Poor
		(% of respondents)		
Centre 1				
All activities	24	57	17	2
Older fitness centre	18	64	10	8
Newer fitness centre	37	46	17	0
Centre 2	27	52	18	3
Centre 3	26	52	21	1
Centre 4	18	63	18	1
Centre 5 (free use)	50	36	12	2

Behavioural considerations

To explain the reactions to price changes in the Scottish study, four attitudinal considerations were measured through the market research. These help to define how consumers' participation decisions relate to price changes. They are: attitudes to the price changes imposed; attitudes to the new price levels after the changes; perceptions of value for money in the facilities before and after the price changes; and perceptions of 'reasonable' highest and lowest admission charges for the activities in which the respondents participated – their reference prices.

The results, summarised in Tables 5.15 to 5.17, add qualitative detail to the more conventional economics findings above. Attitudes to price increases were mixed, depending on the centre, as shown in Table 5.14. In only two centres, 2 and 4, can the attitudes be said to be indicative of serious concern, with 17 and

Table 5.17 Reference price boundaries

	Highest acceptable price	Lowest acceptable price
	(in relation to actual price paid)	
Centre 1		
(newer fitness facility)		
before 15% price increase	3% higher	23% lower
after 15% price increase	6% higher	25% lower
Centre 2		
(average across five activities)		
before 83% price increase	102% higher	27% higher
after 83% price increase	75% higher	19% lower
Centre 3		
(average across four activities)		
before 6% price increase	42% higher	13% lower
after 6% price increase	60% higher	30% lower
Centre 4		
(average across all activities)		
before 71% price increase	32% higher	8% higher
after 71% price increase	56% higher	24% lower
Centre 5		
(swimming only)		
before 100% price decrease	41% higher	21% lower

36 per cent of users respectively claiming that price increases of 70 per cent were excessive. However, it must be pointed out that the evidence of Table 5.13 suggests that in both centres there is a low level of price elasticity of demand: indeed, in centre 4 the 70 per cent price increase was followed by a 9 per cent rise in usage in the subsequent year. This tends to support the hypothesis that although customers will complain about price increases it does not necessarily alter their visiting behaviour. An obvious implication is that complaints do not always merit action, even when they are well-founded.

Another finding of importance in Table 5.14 is the high proportion of users who were unaware of either the previous prices or the price increases, such that they could not offer a judgement on the price increases. This degree of ignorance was nearly a third of respondents in centre 4 and over half of respondents in centres 1 and 2. It is another indication of the relative unimportance of price in many customers' participation decisions, perhaps because entrance prices are highly subsidised and not a major part of participation costs. The lack of awareness of price levels and price increases was not influenced by newness to the facilities – in all facilities surveyed the level of regular usage was high and the number of new users was low.

Attitudes to the new, higher price levels, as reported in Table 5.15, demonstrate a potentially serious constraint to participation only in the case of the newer fitness facility in centre 1, where 29 per cent of respondents thought the new price to be too high. However, again it is important to cross-refer to Table 5.13, which shows this facility to be the most extreme example of price inelasticity, a 15 per cent price increase being followed by a 134 per cent increase in demand in the subsequent year. Again, what appears to be a signal of a constraint to participation is not manifested in practice. The fact that 29 per cent of respondents found the new price 'too high' may indicate that the price of this facility is near a threshold beyond which price elasticity may increase. On the other hand, the strong growth in demand for the facility, despite a relatively high and increasing price, suggests either the influence of non-price reasons not tested in the research, e.g. a rising fashion for fitness, or, as suggested earlier, the attraction of new, previously untapped markets.

The evidence in Table 5.16 shows that despite the significant minorities of respondents expressing concern with the increases and levels of prices, the value for money is still felt to be generally good. This is a primary reason for the price inelasticity of demand. It is an indication that the previous levels of prices were unnecessarily low.

Such a judgement is endorsed by the evidence of Table 5.17, which defines the boundaries to customers' reference prices, i.e. the prices that they find acceptable. Table 5.17 demonstrates that the concept of reference price does not mean a single price, but rather a tolerance zone of acceptable prices. For instance, in centre 3 before the price increase, the average tolerance zone for users ranged from 13 per cent below the current price to 42 per cent above it. After the price rise the tolerance zone stretched from 30 per cent below the new price to 60 per cent above it. As the price changed, so the tolerance zone shifted.

In Table 5.17, with the exception of the one facility aiming to make a profit (the newer fitness facility in centre 1), the highest acceptable prices lie substantially above the actual price paid, even after significant price increases. The most telling indictment of the level of prices before these increases, however, is for centres 2 and 4, where the *lowest* acceptable prices lay *above* the actual prices: 27 per cent above in the case of centre 2 and 8 per cent above in the case of centre 4. In other words, the customers themselves judged the prices in centres 2 and 4, before the price increases, to be too low.

The evidence in Table 5.17 demonstrates that reference prices change with experience, as McCarville and Crompton (1987) and McCarville *et al.* (1993) have suggested. After a 15 per cent price increase in the newer fitness facility of centre 1, for example, the highest acceptable price shifted to stay 6 per cent higher than the new, higher price level. Similarly, in the case of centres 2, 3 and 4 the upper boundary of reference prices shifted as prices rose. Arguably the most important determinant of reference prices for customers is the actual price paid, and they quickly adjust their reference price to a new price.

The behavioural evidence reviewed above provides important qualitative support for the finding of price inelastic demand. It demonstrates that shifting reference prices and perceptions of value for money can compensate for any unease over large increases in prices, or relatively high levels of prices; although in the case of the highly subsidised public sector facilities monitored for this empirical investigation, this customer unease is typically small-scale.

It must be added, however, that in the catchment areas' household surveys conducted as part of the Scottish study, the reaction to the price increases was a lot stronger than that of the centres' user survey respondents. This is to be expected because the household survey will catch some of the most extreme reactions, i.e. those who have stopped or significantly cut their use of the centres. Nevertheless, the evidence of Table 5.13 would suggest that faced with increasingly stringent financial objectives, and despite the inevitable negative reaction of some customers, price increases of substantial magnitude can be implemented with the desired financial outcome and with little negative impact on total visits.

Attitudes to price levels and changes, value for money and reference prices may all be capable of being managed by the same decision-makers that change prices, as the experiments in McCarville and Crompton (1987) and McCarville *et al.* (1993) demonstrate with respect to reference prices. No evidence was taken in the Scottish study, however, to identify what measures centre management took to counteract negative reactions to the increases in prices. It may be that such marketing tactics were not necessary, given the low levels of awareness among users of the previous prices and also of the price changes. Nevertheless, as subsidy levels fall, or in lower subsidy local authorities, it might be expected that these levels of awareness will rise. As they do, so it becomes necessary to employ information and promotion tactics to alter consumers' reference prices in anticipation of, or coincidental with, increases in prices.

Because of the detailed specification of demand afforded by the market research in the Scottish study, it is possible to vindicate significantly increased entrance prices for heavily subsidised facilities, if financial imperatives are paramount. However, such a recommendation should be qualified by the knowledge that any such increase needs to be marketed effectively, to manage the behavioural determinants of elasticity of demand. These compensatory management measures may include perceptible improvements in service quality; positive promotion of service attributes and cost, to alter customers' reference prices; and protective discounts for recreationally or socially disadvantaged groups.

An important caveat to the findings of the Scottish study is that the price inelastic demand finding is strictly valid only for the sample of facilities and users tested, and for the prices investigated. Market research needs to be undertaken at other facilities before appropriate conclusions can be drawn for them.

Conclusions

The evidence on the demand for sport is at the moment patchy. However, we have been able to show in this chapter that empirical studies are yielding fruitful results both in the descriptive statistical analysis of patterns and trends in sports participation and in international comparisons in patterns of participation. Analytical models have also started to give us an insight into the factors that are most critical in determining levels of sports participation, and the demand for facilities. In particular, the factors that are important in determining whether an individual is a participant or not are the same as those that determine the intensity of participation for those that participate. Intensity of participation seems to be crucially dependent on the availability of time. The Scottish pricing experiment study tends also to support the hypothesis that time rather than money may be the major constraint on sports participation, with increases in prices of sports facilities having little effect on demand. Evidence in all these areas has increased tremendously over the past decade and no doubt will continue to accelerate.

However, the biggest constraint on further in-depth analysis of the demand for sport is the inadequacy of the coverage of the current data available, in particular the General Household Survey sports participation data with which we began this chapter. The major inadequacies relate to:

1   inability to relate sports participation to other areas of leisure lifestyle, in particular tourism and the arts – the GHS has increasingly focused on sports participation so that it now does not provide a comprehensive database for research into leisure lifestyles;

2   lack of variables to facilitate the creation of a leisure typology – despite developments in the tourism literature in terms of psychographic segmentation of leisure consumers, the GHS continues to adopt a socio-economic/ demographic approach which restricts the level of analysis possible;

3   lack of expenditure data (on sports equipment, clothing, shoes, etc.) – it is possible to obtain only a limited picture of consumer behaviour because participation rates cannot be related to other indicators of demand such as consumer expenditure;

4   lack of time expenditure – although frequency of participation is one measure of the intensity of participation, it is also important to know how long participants spend on average on each occasion of participation, which was available in the HALS but is not available in the GHS data;

5   lack of data on supply of facilities facing respondents (e.g. distance to nearest sports centre) this is probably the biggest single problem with the GHS data. Participation rates for individual sports are not an indicator of demand for sport; they are indicators of the outcome of the interaction between demand and supply. Without information on the supply of facilities faced by the consumers it is not possible to separate out the different influences of demand and supply. This prevents any serious estimation of demand models using these data.

These problems relate specifically to the GHS and its use for research into participation and lifestyle. In fact no data-set currently exists in Britain which is adequate for the testing of the theories of lifestyle and participation that have been developed over the past 20 years. In the 1960s, two surveys were carried out that were specifically targeted at research into participation and lifestyle, the Pilot National Recreational Survey (British Travel Association/University of Keele, 1967) and *Planning for Leisure* (Sillitoe, 1969). At that time little information was available and few attempts had been made at developing theories. In the 1990s the GHS is still collecting very similar types of information to those earlier surveys, even though leisure researchers have moved on considerably in theory formulation.

Despite this data constraint, we have tried to show in this chapter that it is possible to carry out empirical research into the demand for sport, although in the two detailed analyses used here the data for such work are not available on a regular basis.

Part III
Supply

6   Government and sport

Introduction

Government has considerable involvement in sport in a variety of ways, particularly through the national Sports Councils, through the Sports Lottery Fund, and through local authorities. The purpose of this chapter is to explore the scale and scope of this involvement; explain the economic rationale for it; examine possible problems with such interventions; and, finally, analyse some key issues in public sector supply of sport.

The scale of government expenditure in sport

In Chapter 2 we identified the economic importance of sport. Two of the sectoral accounts identified are central government and local government, and together they accounted for just under 10 per cent of the value added in sport in 1994 (see Table 2.3) and over 13 per cent of sports employment in the UK in 1995 (see Table 2.4). Central government in 1995 was estimated to spend £885 million on sport, but at the same time it was estimated to have taken over £4 billion in tax revenue from sport. In contrast, local government in 1995 was estimated to have spent £1,769 million on sport – more than the £1,351 million it raised in income from sport (LIRC, 1997a).

Tables 6.1 and 6.2 provide the details of these government expenditures on sport and incomes from sport. Central government clearly earns a substantial tax revenue from sport, both indirectly, on expenditure, and directly, on incomes. Central government's principal expenditure on sport is through its grant to local government, both for sports services and for that part of education which is devoted to sport and physical education. It also funds major agencies such as the Sports Councils for the four home countries and the UK.

Both central and local government benefit from lottery awards and partnership contributions – £38 million for central government and £86 million for local government – although the full scale of lottery awards was not reached in 1995. Under central government income the lottery awards were obtained by schools, colleges and universities directly funded by central government; under local government income the awards were largely for sports services and schools funded by local authorities.

Table 6.1 Central government income from and expenditure on sport, 1995 (£ million)

Income	
Taxes	
on expenditure	1,743
on incomes generated in	
commercial sport	547
voluntary sector	240
commercial non-sport	1,313
local government	260
Factor income	
rail receipts	54
Total income	*4,157*
Lottery awards	23
Lottery partnerships	15
Expenditure	
Transfer payments	
Grants via Sports Councils	64
Grant support for local authority expenditure on	
sport (net spending)	362
education	266
Foundation for Sport and Arts	54
Football Trust	12
subsidy to central government employees	45
Factor expenditure	
Sports Councils	22
rail	42
prison service, MOD, Royal Parks	18
Total expenditure	*885*

From Tables 6.1 and 6.2 it can be seen that local authority expenditure on sport is twice the level of central government expenditure on sport. This impression of the imbalance between central and local government support is something of an illusion, however, since local authorities receive nearly half their revenue from central government grants (see Table 6.2). Nevertheless, the balance between central and local government subsidy for sport changed markedly in the late 1980s and early 1990s. In the mid-1980s local authorities' subsidies to sport were more than twice the amount given by central government. Since then there has been a continued increase in central government subsidies but local authorities' subsidies have declined in real terms for the first time in two decades and for one or two years they have declined in money terms too.

Central government intervention in sports markets not only takes the form of direct funding, it also imposes significant 'regulation' of the sports market as it does of all other markets. Arguably the two most significant regulations by central government on the operation of the UK sports market are: first, the long-standing regulations governing gambling in sport, particularly the regulations on the operations of betting shops; and second, and more recently, the National Minimum

Table 6.2 Local government income from and expenditure on sport, 1995 (£ million)

Income	
Local authority sports facilities	
fees and charges	202
sales of equipment	48
ground hire	28
Grants from central government	
to fund net expenditure on sport	362
sport education	266
via Sports Council	10
via Foundation for Sport and Arts	13
Rates	
voluntary sector	53
commercial sport	61
commercial non-sport	159
Local transport	54
Payments for policing	9
Lottery awards	52
Lottery partnerships	34
Total income	*1,351*
Expenditure	
Current expenditure	
Direct gross expenditure	
wages	466
other current expenditure	397
Education	
wages	327
research	15
Local transport and policing	
wages and other inputs	93
Grants to voluntary clubs	25
Capital expenditure	
Investment	446
Total expenditure	*1,769*

Wage. As with the leisure sector as a whole, many jobs in sport, particularly in the commercial sector, are traditionally low-paid, and the impact of the National Minimum Wage is to have increased labour costs at the bottom end of the sports labour market, with consequences on labour costs for those already paid more than the minimum wage of £3.60 an hour to the extent that wage differentials have been protected.

Since 1995 the National Lottery has made a large impact on funding of sport, and it is arguable whether or not this is part of government funding. In one sense it is no different to tax revenue – the government collects the money and spends it through appointed authorities, the Lottery Panels. However, in other ways it is very different to tax revenue – people choose to pay; the payment can be seen as more akin to a charitable donation than to a tax payment – and on this

Table 6.3 Local authorities' net expenditure on sport and leisure, 1995–1996 (£ million)

Swimming pools	98
Sports halls with pools	210
Sports halls without pools	65
Community centres, public halls	68
Outdoor pitches	53
Golf courses	(11)*
Urban parks, open spaces	480
Total sport	*963*
Total arts	*277*
Total other	*296*
Total leisure	*1537*

Source: *Leisure and Recreation Statistics Estimates CIPFA* (1995–1996).

* Golf courses are in surplus.

Table 6.4 Percentage cost recovery of different local authority sports and leisure facilities

	1979–1980	*1985–1986*	*1990–1991*	*1995–1996*
Swimming pools	12	33	36	24
Sports centres	27	47	44	36
Community centres and public halls	16	30	25	26
Outdoor pitches	19	27	22	23
Golf courses	68	93	109	142
Urban parks and open spaces	4	14	12	12
Theatres and art centres	34	41	40	50
Art galleries and museums	6	15	16	21

Source: *Leisure and Recreation Statistics Estimates CIPFA.*

interpretation it is not really accurate to include it as part of government funding of sport. However, for convenience as much as any sound principle, National Lottery expenditure on sport is conventionally identified as part of government spending.

Table 6.3 shows net expenditure (i.e. subsidy) for different kinds of sport and leisure facilities operated by local authorities. The largest element, nearly half of local authorities' so-called 'sports' expenditure, is on urban parks and open spaces, much of which is not really utilised for sport and probably not for very physical recreation – only selected parts are for sport, such as tennis courts and bowls greens.

Table 6.4 shows that the cost recovery of various local authority sport facilities improved over the first half of the 1980s, but in many cases it deteriorated slightly in the second half of the 1980s and fell further in the first half of the 1990s. This deterioration in cost recovery is particularly apparent in built sports facilities subject to compulsory competitive tendering (CCT), i.e. swimming pools and sports centres, which is contrary to expectations given the incentive for more commercial objectives under CCT and the tighter financial environment of local government generally.

One major reason for the lower cost recovery in swimming pools and sports centres in the early 1990s is that the estimates by local authorities of their direct income from fees and charges were declining. There are two additional 'statistical' explanations. First, different accounting procedures within local authorities increased the costs attributed to facilities. In the increasingly stringent local authority financial climate, together with client–contractor relationships under CCT, more realistic (i.e. higher) central administration charges, 'client costs', were allocated to individual services such as sport. Second, the response rate for the CIPFA Leisure and Recreation Statistics Estimates, from which the data in Table 6.4 is drawn, has been lower in recent years (77 per cent in 1995–1996), presumably because of CCT. With a lower response rate there is the possibility of sample error, particularly that authorities with facilities under private contractor operations, with higher cost recovery, are not responding to the CIPFA survey.

Some types of facilities in Table 6.4 – particularly golf courses – continued to improve cost recovery throughout the 1980s and early 1990s. It has always been acknowledged that golf courses have the potential to be profitable, mainly because of the strength of demand and willingness to pay by participants.

Economic rationale for government intervention: market failure

Why does the government spend money on sport and recreation and regulate the markets in which they operate? This is an important question if only because of the importance placed on intervention in sports markets by central and local government. Consumers' expenditure on sport and recreation accounts for a relatively small share of total consumers' expenditure on leisure, and yet government expenditure on sport and recreation is one of the largest components of total government expenditure on leisure. In addition, expenditure on sport and recreation has been the fastest growing component of public expenditure on leisure over the past 20 years.

Economic welfare principles provide us with reasons for this government interest in sport. When a private market operates successfully, but still fails to cater adequately for the full effects of the market on the welfare of society, economists call this a situation of 'market failure'. Several causes of market failure are relevant to the market for sport. In each case the existence of a market failure is in principle a reason for government intervention, since intervention has the potential to prevent or compensate for the market failure.

Two broad categories of sports market failure can be distinguished: efficiency-related and equity-related. If sport generates social (collective) benefits over and above the private benefits for the participants, then the market may be efficient for the participants but it is not necessarily efficient for society. An efficient market solution takes account of the value to the participating individuals and the cost of supply, but it fails to take account of any additional social benefits. Thus the socially desirable output will not be produced by the market, which will under-provide resources to the sport and recreation market.

Individual consumers, through their purchasing behaviour, will not encourage the socially optimal level of production (i.e. a level that generates not only sufficient private benefits but also optimal social benefits). This is because they can get any social benefits going for nothing, i.e. they can be 'free riders'. One way to generate the socially optimal level of consumption is to reduce prices, but this is unlikely to be done by private market suppliers in the interests of public welfare! Government, accepting responsibility for social welfare, has a reason to encourage higher production and consumption of sport – by subsidising consumers, subsidising suppliers in the commercial and voluntary sectors, or directly supplying the product at a lower price than the private producer would offer.

Regarding equity, a distribution of resources and products according to the private market may not be consistent with what government deems to be a fair distribution – the market in this case is inequitable. Again, government may use this as a reason for subsidising certain consumers, or suppliers, in order to achieve a more equitable distribution of products, resources and sporting opportunities.

Market failures relevant to sport include health, crime, public goods and equity considerations. We now review both the theory and evidence of such market failures and the implications for government intervention in sports markets.

Sports participation and health

The 1975 White Paper *Sport and Recreation* indicated that the relationship between sports participation and health was one of the reasons for increasing government interest in promoting sports participation. It pointed to the physical and mental health benefits of exercise:

> For many people physical activity makes an important contribution to physical and mental well-being. There is some evidence to suggest that vigorous physical exercise can reduce the incidence of coronary heart disease which in 1972 accounted for about 27 per cent of the deaths of those over 40.

The evidence on the sports participation/health relationship has been building up consistently over the post-war period. It is in the prevention of coronary heart disease that exercise has been established to have its most significant positive effect on health. Over 45 years ago, Morris *et al.* (1953) found that bus conductors (spending most of the day walking up and down stairs and rarely sitting down) were at less risk of having heart attacks than sedentary bus drivers. The obvious question raised is whether it is possible for sedentary workers to obtain health benefits by physical activity in leisure time.

Epidemiological studies seem to indicate that it is. Morris *et al.* (1973, 1980) investigated the leisure-time activities of 17,944 middle-aged British civil servants. They found that those who reported regular vigorous physical exercise (mainly through involvement in sport) had less than half the risk of coronary heart disease over the 8-year follow-up period than those who did no vigorous exercise. Other studies have shown that the reduction of risk of heart attack is not the only health benefit of exercise. Thomas *et al.* (1981) indicate that physical exercise can have a beneficial effect in the prevention and treatment of hypertension, obesity, diabetes mellitus, anxiety, depression, and asthma. In a position paper on health for the Council of Europe, Vuori and Fentem (1995) conclude that 'There is firm scientific evidence to indicate that regular, moderate leisure time physical activity has numerous and substantial effects on health, functional capacity and well-being'. They cite the President's Council on Physical Fitness and Sports in the USA as an example of translating the known evidence into public health policy: 'Every American adult should accumulate 30 minutes or more of moderate-intensity physical activity over the course of most days of the week.'

In addition to this epidemiological evidence, Gratton and Tice (1989) produced evidence on the beneficial effects of sports participation and health using data from several General Household Surveys and the Health and Lifestyle Survey. Their evidence suggests that sports participants are healthier and lead healthier lifestyles than non-participants. It also suggests that participation in sport is associated with an enriched quality of life, since sports participants also take part in a much wider range of non-sport leisure activities than non-participants – this is the non-pecuniary investment benefit identified in Chapter 1.

The question arises of whether such health benefits are purely private or social. If the main beneficiary of such benefits is the participant, then we do not have a strong case for government intervention on health grounds. There are, however, several aspects to the sports participation and health relationship where government intervention may lead to an increase in social welfare.

One argument relates to the possible difference between the benefits of exercise as perceived by the consumer and the real private benefits. Grossman's model (1972), reviewed in Chapter 4, assumes that the individual has perfect knowledge of both the health production function and the rate of return on health capital. In reality, people are uncertain of the impact of exercise on their health capital, but even more uncertain as to the rate of return on health capital. This uncertainty is likely to cause inefficiency in consumer decision-making in the form of under-consumption of 'exercise for health reasons'. This is a specific form of market failure, since the market left to its own devices does not give sufficient knowledge. In the terms of Scitovsky's analysis examined in Chapter 4, there is a lack of consumption skill.

Testimony to this consumer ignorance is provided by the Allied Dunbar National Fitness Survey (1992), which measured the physical activity and fitness levels of over 4,000 English adults. This survey revealed extremely low levels of cardio-respiratory fitness in the population: seven out of ten men and eight out of ten women do not do enough exercise in an average week to keep themselves healthy. It also revealed a major misperception by both men and women of all ages – although 80 per cent correctly believed that regular exercise is important for health, the majority incorrectly believed that they did enough exercise to keep fit.

In order to overcome inefficiency due to consumer ignorance, therefore, there is a justification for government intervention to educate consumers on the nature of the benefits from exercise. In Britain this is one of the roles of the Health Education Authority, which has been responsible for several exercise-related promotional campaigns such as the 'Look After Yourself' campaign. The Sports Council emphasised the health benefits of exercise in its sports promotions campaigns. The effects of ignorance can also be counteracted by offering subsidised exercise opportunities for health reasons. This is a 'merit good' approach – enticing the 'ignorant' consumer to consume greater quantities than they otherwise would have done.

A second argument for government intervention concerns the benefits of releasing healthcare resources for others. Fentem and Bassey (1978, 1981) identified the main health beneficiaries from sports participation to be those most dependent on healthcare services. Such services, provided mainly by the government-funded National Health Service in Britain, are expensive. If, because of the health benefits of sports participation, health services are released to concentrate on less preventable health problems, there may be efficiency gains. This depends on the relative values of, on the one hand, the cost of prevention via subsidies to sports participation and, on the other hand, the consequent health gains in less preventable problem areas.

Gratton and Tice (1987) have provided further evidence on the importance of this social benefit. Using data from the General Household Survey for 1977 they found that among the chronically ill, those that take part in sport use health services less than non-participants. Further cross-tabulations allowing for both age and income show that the sharpest differences between non-participants and participants occur for the older age groups and the lower income groups, that is, those groups most prone to illness and those making the heaviest demand on health services. This evidence indicates that the importance of this benefit has probably been seriously underestimated up to now.

The implication of this argument is that there is a role for government over and above the educational one. A more efficient means of achieving health policy objectives may be to redistribute resources from health services to direct expenditure on the provision or subsidisation of active recreation facilities, i.e. prevention rather than cure. There is a temporal problem here in that benefits from any increased participation are likely to take many years to show through in a reduced demand for health services. In the short term, it is unlikely that any increase in public expenditure in sport would lead to an immediate reduction in expenditure on health.

A third argument in favour of government intervention is that since exercise contributes to health (and a healthier workforce means an increase in productivity and fewer days lost in industry due to illness), this is a social benefit as the whole nation benefits from a stronger economy. Shepherd (1990) summarises these benefits:

The gains realized by companies which have implemented work-site fitness programmes include an improvement of corporate image, a selective recruitment of premium workers, an increase in the quality and the quantity of production, a decrease of employee absenteeism and turnover, and a reduction of industrial injuries. In situations where full or supplementary medical insurance is offered to employees, it may also be possible to negotiate lower premiums with the insuring company.

Gratton and Tice (1989) use General Household Survey data to show that sports participants in Britain not only take part in a broader range of recreational activities than non-participants, but they also work longer hours. Gratton and Taylor (1987) show that there is evidence that absenteeism is a major problem in British industry, and that over the post-war period it has been on the increase. Between 1962 and 1982 the number of days of 'certified incapacity for sickness and invalidity' rose by 28 per cent for men and 17 per cent for women. 'Certified incapacity' refers only to those whose illness lasted for three days or more and thus required a doctor's certificate. (Unfortunately this absenteeism data is not available from 1983 onwards because of the introduction of self-certification of illness.) This rise in the number of days lost because of illness cannot be explained by changes in employment since, over the same period, male employment fell by 18.4 per cent and female employment rose by 8.8 per cent. Thus the number of days lost for men increased considerably over a period when employment decreased considerably.

Figure 6.1 shows that sports participants are less likely to be 'away from work last week' than non-participants. This is true for every age category and every income category. It seems, then, that participation in sport is associated with reduced absenteeism. Such reduced absenteeism is a social benefit in that it reduces public expenditure through the statutory sick-pay scheme.

However, employers are probably the main beneficiaries of any reduction in absenteeism. Not only do they bear a considerable cost burden in terms of occupational sick-pay schemes (particularly for senior staff), but under the self-certification of illness arrangements they also carry the main administrative costs of the statutory sick-pay scheme. They pay out the money initially and then recover it from their national insurance remittances to the Department of Health and Social Security. We should expect, therefore, to see employers providing exercise programmes and facilities for their staff. At the moment, in Britain, there is little evidence that this is happening, with firms offering membership of private health insurance schemes in preference to direct provision of exercise facilities. In taking this 'treatment rather than prevention' approach, firms, like health policy, may be making an expensive mistake.

The arguments discussed so far in this section provide a considerable case for government intervention in the sport and recreation market on health grounds. However, up to now we have only considered the positive side of the relationship between sports participation and health. There is also a negative side – sports injuries. It is such injuries that make up the cost side of the balance sheet of the sports participation and health relationship.

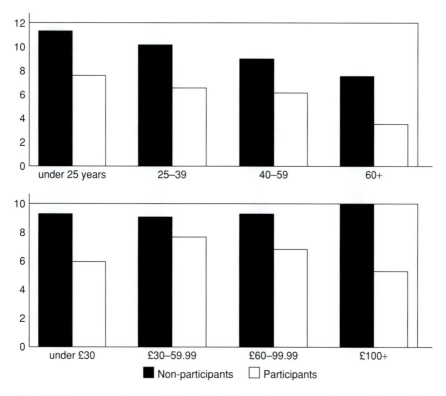

Figure 6.1 Percentage of non-participants/participants in sport away from work in previous
        week, according to age and income.
Source: Gratton and Tice (1987)

The most authoritative evidence on sports injuries is provided by a national
survey conducted by Nicholl *et al.* (1991) for the Sports Council. Out of 17,564
respondents, 45 per cent had taken part in vigorous exercise or sports in the
previous four weeks, and 18 per cent of these had been injured in doing so.
Three-quarters of the injuries were to men, and half occurred in the ages group
16–25 years. The most risky sports were rugby, martial arts, soccer, cricket, and
hockey. This study estimates a cost to public and private health services from
sports injuries of at least £250 million each year, with an estimated value of lost
production due to time off work of £405 million per year.

In a subsequent paper, Nicholl *et al.* (1994) estimated the value of health
benefits from exercise and set this against the estimates of health costs through
injury. Their conclusion was that in younger adults (15–44 years) the average
annual medical care costs resulting from injury as a result of regular participation
in sport would exceed the costs that might be avoided by the disease-prevention
effects of exercise. For older adults (45 years and over), however, the value of the
benefits greatly outweighed the injury costs. However, these results do not take

account of the fact that there is a strong inter-temporal linkage in sports participation, with those who participate when young far more likely to reap the benefits by participating when older.

The policy implications of this review of the health justification for public subsidy of sport are complex. On the one hand, some of the evidence suggests very selective subsidisation, targeting those at greatest risk, those with the lowest injury risk, and with the largest benefits to be gained, such as the poor, the elderly and the ill. On the other hand, there is sufficient general evidence of the health benefits from sports participation to suggest that a more universal policy of subsidy for sport on health grounds is justified. Even this policy inference needs to be qualified, however, with obvious exceptions such as sports with very high injury risk or very low physical activity content.

Sport and crime

It has been claimed that participation in sport will 'improve life for many who would otherwise be attracted to delinquency and vandalism' (Department of the Environment, 1977). One of the target groups often chosen by sports providers is young people, particularly young males, and both implicitly and explicitly it is often recognised that provision of sporting opportunities for this group will help promote constructive leisure pursuits, at the expense of more negative activities such as crime and vandalism.

If the channelling of energies and effort into constructive leisure pursuits such as sport helps to reduce the likelihood of criminal activity by the individuals concerned, then obviously it is not just these individuals that benefit. Their potential 'victims' also benefit – an 'external' or social benefit which individuals would not pay for, not even the actual 'victims' since they do not realise their parlous state until the crime actually happens. In such circumstances the government may be justified in subsidising and/or supplying sports opportunities, for much the same reason as one of those used above in the context of health and sport – prevention is less costly than cure.

Despite the frequency with which policy-makers refer to this relationship between involvement in sport and reduction in anti-social behaviour by, in particular, young adolescents, analysts such as Robins (1990) and Coalter (1990) have suggested that there is neither much evidence of the effects of sport on crime nor clear programme rationales and objectives. The theory of stimulation-seeking leisure behaviour offered in Chapter 4 may help here. As Scitovsky (1981) suggests:

> an underlying assumption . . . is that different sources of excitement are good substitutes for each other. If true, that points the way to reducing violence and crime by providing socially more acceptable sources of risk, danger and excitement. . . . City officials in the United States are very slowly beginning to recognize man's need to face danger and take risks for excitement's sake, and the absurdity of 'honey and milk toast' activities in urban recreation

programs. To quote one official, 'What an indictment against our programs that almost everything children do that is risky and fun is done off the playground'.

As well as blaming inadequate provision, the market failure demonstrated by anti-social behaviour is a lack of information about constructive alternatives, and a lack of consumption skills with which to enjoy them.

A major complication in defining a clear rationale for sports programmes aimed at reducing crime is that a range of intermediate objectives act either individually or collectively to reduce crime. These include the constructive relief of boredom, increased self-esteem brought about by sporting achievement or increased physical fitness; the influence of sports leaders as positive role models; and enhanced employment prospects. The exact relationship between these objectives and reducing crime will depend on the specification of the programme and on the individual participant.

In order to justify the subsidy provided for such programmes, it is necessary to estimate the value of the benefits of the programmes, in comparison with the costs of providing them. Unfortunately, there is little evidence for the effectiveness of physical activity programmes in reducing crime. For example, Robins (1990) reviewed eleven schemes designed specifically to use sport as a means of diverting young people from criminal behaviour, and concluded that 'information about outcomes was hard to come by'. This impression is confirmed by Utting (1996) in a review of programmes in the UK, including several using sport. Recently evidence has improved with research into Probation Service programmes using demanding physical activities. First, Nichols and Taylor (1996) examined the effects of the West Yorkshire Sports Counselling Scheme and provided substantial and positive evidence of the effect of the programme on crime, with a significant reduction in reconviction for young offenders participating in the programme for 8 weeks or more. Unfortunately, the sample size of young offenders was insufficient to provide a statistically reliable estimate of the value of the benefits gained, to set against the cost of the programme. This research built on earlier positive findings from a similar programme, the Solent Sports Counselling Project (Sports Council Research Unit, North West, 1990).

The Probation Service research was extended to a national survey by Taylor *et al.* (1999), which identified fifty-four programmes operating in thirty-four of the fifty-four Probation Service areas. A major characteristic of the research was the variety of programmes on offer, particularly in terms of their duration, scale and intensity (from 1-day taster sessions to 2-week residentials), the activities offered, and the programme rationales. This diversity of programmes can be interpreted in one of two ways: either as a reflection of uncertainty about both why the programmes are provided and what is effective; or as an indication that with such a complex set of intermediate outcomes there are many possible ways to achieve one or more of them. From the economist's perspective, the most disappointing finding was that few programmes monitored their effectiveness of achieving objectives in a way which facilitated the valuation of the outcomes, so that the efficiency of the programmes could not be identified. Evaluation was identified as the most significant weakness of the programmes.

One interesting feature of the Probation Service research is that the activities used in the programmes divide between those which are local and accessible, with potential for continued, independent participation by young offenders; and one-off, potentially life-changing experiences, away from the home locality. Outdoor adventure activities are the most commonly provided, but there are no clear-cut theories or evidence that they are better than other activities for changing offending behaviour. Other researchers have focused on the impact of outdoor activities. Barrett and Greenaway (1995) have reviewed evidence of the impact of outdoor activity programmes aimed at both young people at risk and offenders. Their review concludes that there is evidence to show that outcomes of programmes include: enhancing positive self-concept, improving self-efficacy, improving social development, encouraging responsibility, improving internalisation of locus of control, improving constructive use of leisure and enhancing participant–staff relationships. Once again, however, valuing these benefits in monetary terms was not possible.

Another national survey (Nichols and Booth, 1999) has been conducted of local authority sports schemes in Britain which have the objective of reducing crime. Out of 109 responses, forty-nine authorities did not have such a programme, but sixty authorities supported a total of 116 programmes. Only a small minority of programmes monitored their impact on crime reduction, but that is partly because many programmes were more concerned with crime prevention and reducing social exclusion, rather than crime reduction. This illustrates an even more difficult evaluation problem than those facing Probation Service programmes for young offenders – how to identify the extent to which crime is prevented by a programme.

There is some evidence, therefore, that crime and vandalism may be reduced by greater participation in sport. The evidence does not extend, however, to proving that the value of the crime reduction is greater than either the costs of providing the programmes or the costs of dealing with crime after it has taken place, and more work is needed on these cost–benefit questions. In the meantime, government subsidies for sports programmes with crime reduction or prevention as a major objective are in a fragile position, because the necessary evidence of effectiveness or efficiency is so hard to assemble (Nichols and Booth, 1999; Taylor *et al.*, 1999). Such programmes continue to rely, therefore, on political will and the commitment of those with expertise in operating them. Nevertheless, there is a substantial and growing body of qualitative evidence demonstrating the worth of government subsidised sports programmes for young people 'at risk' of offending. Of necessity, such programmes have been and will continue to be targeted at young people and urban areas.

Of course, it is important to recognise that as well as having the potential to generate external benefits associated with crime reduction and prevention, sport has also achieved notoriety for being associated directly with crime costs, particularly in the form of football hooliganism. However, this association is a spurious one for the purposes of this chapter. The efficiency arguments used to justify government intervention in sports markets are applicable to participation, not to spectating.

Public goods

Some sport and recreation products demonstrate characteristics which qualify them for recognition as 'public goods' (also referred to as 'collective goods'). The principal characteristics attached to such goods are that they are non-rival and non-excludable in consumption. Non-rival means that one person's consumption does not prevent another person from enjoying exactly the same product at the same time. Non-excludable means that no consumer can be prevented from enjoying the product. Under these two conditions private market provision is not worthwhile, so public goods will be under-provided by the private market.

It has been argued that large, natural, resource-based recreation resources, such as forests, lakes and reservoirs, mountains, rivers and coastlines, are public goods. The benefits provided to users of such recreation resources are non-rival (until the exceptional case where congestion becomes a problem). Also, such areas are often difficult or expensive to exclude non-payers from. Such areas are not pure public goods, but there are certainly elements of collectiveness to the benefits they generate.

Public sector involvement in natural recreation resources of this type can be split into three groups: National Parks; water-based recreation resources; and local and countryside parks. Unlike the USA, where provision of National Parks is a major area of government expenditure in recreation, in the UK public expenditure on National Parks is a small area of total government expenditure on leisure. Similarly, although many water-based recreational areas have been publicly owned for many years, recreation is often a minor objective of the water authorities and the British Waterways Board. It is only in the area of local and countryside parks that we see substantial public expenditure and yet, in this area, benefits are often excludable and rival.

International sporting success is a more pure form of public good. A quote from the White Paper *Sport and Recreation* (1975) makes the point:

> Success in international sport has great value for the community not only in terms of raising morale but also by inspiring young people to take an active part in sport.

Because many of the benefits of international sporting success (e.g. improved national morale, increased interest in sport) are such that nobody can be prevented from feeling them, they are non-excludable. Because everyone can enjoy these benefits together with no congestion in consumption, they are non-rival. A free market would under-provide such public goods, because there is always the temptation for consumers to become 'free riders', benefiting from the products without paying for them. Government can ensure that adequate provision is made for excellence in sport to be produced, and can also ensure that those who benefit from this public good pay, through taxes.

The public good effect of sporting excellence has several variants, illustrated as follows in the Coe (1985) report on British sport's preparation for the Olympics.

1   Sporting success for Britain makes people proud to be British. Sporting failure or decline has the reverse effect; we blame each other and ourselves and we feel less committed to the national cause.
2   The link with prestige abroad is important. . . . If our teams and individuals are successful, they help the country's image abroad; thus, directly and indirectly, they can help to sell our products and services and earn foreign currency.
3   Sporting achievement in the Olympics is also a vital contributor to the Government's and the Sports Council's strategy to boost participation in sport and recreation. The Olympic Games create heroes and heroines. These encourage and inspire youngsters – and indeed people of all ages – to participate in sport, to develop and to enjoy themselves.

First, there is the simple utility boost to anyone who enjoys success by national sportspeople. Second, an indiscriminate (non-rival) and universal (non-excludable) economic impact results from excellence in sport; various organisations, such as the Confederation of British Industry, the Trades Union Congress, and the British Council were cited by the Coe Commission as supportive of this view.

Third, there is a 'demonstration effect' which will almost certainly beneficially affect the number of people participating in sport, their frequency of participation and/or possibly the number of years they participate. However, what is not clear is the extent to which such demonstration effects are internationally as opposed to domestically generated: in other words, is it just exposure of any major event that promotes participation, regardless of who is winning, or does success by domestic teams and individuals generate a stronger demonstration effect?

Public good benefits apply at the local level too – regional, national and international sporting successes bring about local public good effects, especially to the home area of the successful sportsperson.

However, whereas it is easy to define likely public good benefits arising from sporting success, unfortunately they are very difficult to measure and so their importance is difficult to assess. Nevertheless, the *ad hoc* evidence and 'expert opinion' suggests that the public good effects of excellence in sport are significant. The Coe Commission produced its report as an appeal for funding for British sport's preparation for the 1990 Olympics – especially support from the Government. The Commission was aware that left to 'the market' there would be insufficient funding, inadequate preparation and therefore underproduction of British successes in the Olympics. In similar fashion, the recent initiative by both the Conservative and Labour governments in the UK in the mid to late 1990s to develop the National Institute of Sport can be seen as a reaction to perceived sporting failures on the international stage (cricket, football, athletics) which can be directly related to market failures. The policy reaction is to offer more government support for the production of excellence, albeit from the National Lottery.

On the basis of the public good arguments alone we would expect to see government involved in the promotion of excellence of sporting achievement and the financial support of élite sportsmen and sportswomen. In 1985–1986, for example, of the £164 million estimated total expenditure on excellence, 10 per cent came from the public sector (Taylor, 1993). One part of this expenditure, the subsidisation of National Sports Centres, may be justified on the grounds that such facilities are vital to the production of a public good, excellence. National Centres, and the new UK Sports Institute, can charge élite sportspeople and their clubs for the use of their facilities, but they cannot extract the true value of the resulting excellence from the wider public, who receive the public good benefits. Only the government can 'internalise' these collective benefits by subsidising National Centres and/or the excellent users of National Centres, through general taxation.

Another example of the failure of the market to produce efficiently the public good of excellence in sport is sponsorship: 'many of the characteristics of sponsorship are not conducive to effective or efficient production of excellence in sport' (Taylor, 1993). The volatility/uncertainty of sponsorship prejudices a continuous production flow of excellence. Furthermore, sponsorship is usually directed towards financing events. Hardly any goes to other inputs at least as important as events in the production process, such as training, coaching, facilities and support services.

Another form of public good which merits government subsidisation is given the term 'preservation values'. This reason for government expenditure relates, rather unusually, to benefits to non-users from the provision of sporting opportunities and facilities. Preservation values include option, existence, and bequest demands. In the context of sport, option value is the willingness to pay for the opportunity to participate in sport on some future occasion; existence value is the willingness to pay for the knowledge that a sporting opportunity is protected *per se*; while bequest value is the willingness to pay for the endowment of sporting opportunities to future generations.

The term 'willingness to pay' expresses real values to individuals but not ones which can be fully realised through market exchange. Furthermore, as Loomis and Walsh (1997) identify, 'These preservation values are nonmarket and public goods, which means their consumption is both nonrival and nonexcludable'. As in the case of external benefits such as healthcare savings or crime reduction, the presence of option, existence and bequest values requires sport and recreation provision above the level which the private market supplies. The government has a social welfare reason for ensuring greater production through its own supply or through subsidisation of sports facilities and/or consumers.

Even though preservation values are non-market, they can be empirically identified through appropriate market research. Many of the studies attempting such empirical estimation have been conducted in North America, estimating the preservation values of outdoor recreation activities and amenities (Mitchell and Carson, 1989; Loomis and Walsh, 1997). There is some evidence that the main benefits (in terms of willingness to pay) accrue to those who participate in recreation activities, i.e. direct users are the ones who are also the major indirect consumers, in which case it may be possible to internalise such benefits by some sort of extensive membership scheme, such as the National Trust operates in Britain.

A UK example of preservation value estimation was conducted for the Sports Council as part of an estimation of the value of output of Plas y Brenin National Mountain Centre (Nichols and Taylor, 1995). The centre runs courses in mountaineering, canoeing, orienteering and skiing and therefore provides direct, priced services to individuals: in this sense it is a private traded product. A large proportion of the centre's work is involved with the training of outdoor leaders through the award schemes of the relevant governing bodies. As the primary provider of many of these training and assessment courses, and the only provider of assessment courses at the highest level, it has a significant role in setting training standards and developing leadership training in the sports concerned. In this sense it is placed at the pinnacle of a structure of mountain leadership which stretches down through highly skilled participation to an expanding base of recreational participation in mountain activities.

There has been increasing concern with standards of leadership and participant behaviour in outdoor activities in Britain, stimulated by an alarming number of fatalities in the Scottish highlands, and conspicuous incidents such as the Lyme Bay canoeing tragedy, in which several teenagers died. As the officially designated National Mountain Centre, Plas y Brenin shoulders some of the responsibility for responding to such concerns. It also gives the sports it represents a degree of credibility and it is able to act as a focal point for information and advice concerning these sports.

Many of these aspects of the centre's work might be seen as public good benefits, extending beyond the benefits gained by individuals attending courses at the centre, and not reflected in the prices paid by these individuals for courses there. Public good benefits from the National Mountain Centre's activities, such as safer standards of leadership and behaviour in mountain activities, are received by more than just the users of the centre – they reach a broader public, many of whom will be unaware of them but may be prepared to put a positive value on them as being desirable for society.

The research used a contingent valuation method (Mitchell and Carson, 1989) to find out what value, if any, users and non-users placed on the centre's preservation (for users this value was over and above whatever they paid to use the centre). The method involved asking what users and non-users would pay to keep the centre open if it were threatened with closure. The results are given in Table 6.5. The mid-range estimate of £476,968 non-user preservation values is 22 per cent higher than the annual subsidy given by the government (via the Sports Council) to the centre at the time.

In an era of tightening public expenditure budgets, it is tempting to think that those services which are already traded as partially private products are most

Table 6.5 Annual total preservation values for the National Mountain Centre, 1993

	Population	Total preservation values (£)	95 per cent confidence interval for total preservation values (£)
Users			
All users*	2,260	16,475	14,848–18,103
Non-users			
Mountaineering	60,000	374,700	301,800–447,600
Canoeing	16,500	78,870	54,780–102,795
Orienteering	7,300	22,345	15,403–29,273
Skiing†	200	1,052	894–1,210
All non-users	84,000	476,968	372,877–580,878

* The attendance records of the National Mountain Centre do not enable an accurate breakdown to be made of users by type of sport.
† The population of skiing non-users is confined to the membership of two major clubs in North Wales, the region where the National Mountain Centre is located.

suitable for budget cuts, because they are already practised at functioning in the marketplace. The National Mountain Centre is just such an amenity. However, even though the centre is part-traded, it has substantial public good benefits which the application of the contingent valuation method helped to make explicit. When monetary values were put on the public good benefits arising from the National Mountain Centre, it was in a better position to justify its subsidy from national government.

Sport and economic development

The final argument for government intervention on efficiency grounds is a relatively new argument. In the 1980s and 1990s the public sector has been increasingly involved in sport (and in the arts) for economic development reasons, particularly in urban areas. The catalyst for this development has often been a substantial collapse in manufacturing employment, particularly in the 1970s and 1980s. Examples include 191,000 jobs lost in Birmingham between 1971 and 1987; 60,000 jobs lost in Sheffield between 1978 and 1988; 50,000 jobs lost in Manchester between 1971 and 1981 (Loftman and Spirou, 1996). In each case the majority of jobs were lost in the manufacturing sector, with associated losses in services for these manufacturing firms.

The market failure here is that the adjustment process can take far too long – decades and more – if left to normal commercial mechanisms. Spatial imbalances are inefficient and yet, without a specific catalyst for change, severely depressed areas have little to attract new businesses, while there are considerable constraints (especially housing) to the movement of labour to growth areas. Attracting manufacturing industry into inner cities is not a feasible solution. Rather, cities needed to be revitalised through investment in infrastructure and facilities that would attract the growing service industries.

Sport has been used as a lead sector/catalyst in regeneration by a number of cities in the UK and the USA. Conspicuous UK examples include the bids of Birmingham and Manchester to host the Olympic Games, Manchester's hosting of the Commonwealth Games and Sheffield's development of facilities to host the 1991 World Student Games. In the USA the most common examples involve building stadia or arenas to host major league, professional team sport franchises, e.g. Coors Field in Denver; Jacobs Field in Cleveland, Ohio; and Camden Yards in Baltimore (Loftman and Spirou, 1996).

The catalyst for such urban regeneration initiatives has traditionally been public sector investment. Much of the necessary public funding in two of the UK examples cited was generated from the cities' own resources. In the case of Sheffield's three major sports facilities (Ponds Forge International Sports Centre, Don Valley Stadium and the Sheffield Arena) and Birmingham's National Indoor Arena, loans were the principal source of capital finance. In the case of Manchester, central government has provided a substantial input to the capital funding of the indoor arena, a new stadium and the velodrome. These sources lie outside other standard funds for urban regeneration, such as central government's Single Regeneration Budget and the European Union's European Regional Development Fund and European Social Fund.

A city or region develops new sporting facilities for a number of possible economic reasons, including to change the image of the city and attract tourists; to create direct employment in the local sports economy; and to attract inward investment to previously derelict parts of the city. In addition, it is often claimed that the economic regeneration is paralleled by social regeneration, the improved image helping citizens to feel better about their city, and providing the local population with excellent facilities within which to participate in sport.

However, although the objectives of using sport for urban regeneration are well rehearsed, and hundreds of millions of pounds of government funding has been used to support such objectives in the UK, the evidence of regeneration outcomes is far less apparent. Consultants' estimates include 1,900 full-time equivalent jobs created by the National Indoor Arena for the West Midlands, over 3,000 jobs created by the new facilities in Sheffield, and 2,400 jobs in the construction alone of the Manchester facilities (Loftman and Spirou, 1996). However, the first two of these estimates have been subject to criticism (Foley, 1991; Hughes, 1993), principally for being exaggerated and too short-term, and it remains the case that no reliable estimates exist of the economic outcomes of the sports initiatives in these three major UK cities.

Similarly, despite many economic impact assessments of sports stadia in the USA, there is considerable scepticism about their accuracy (Baade and Dye, 1988; Crompton, 1998b), with the distinct impression that many assessments are conducted to convince a doubting local population of the legitimacy of the public investment, rather than to provide an objective assessment of economic impact. According to Loftman and Spirou (1996):

Though incentives provided by cities are often expected to generate local economic development, it has been shown that, in the majority of the situations, this is not the case. . . . The economic impact studies in sports most often tend to exaggerate the benefits making these reports misleading and unnecessary.

The use of sport to help or lead urban regeneration is often centred on conspicuous facilities designed to host major events. The economic impact of major sports events is explored further in Chapter 10.

Equity in sport

The efficiency arguments reviewed above all suggest that government intervenes in the market for sport and recreation because a market allocation would underprovide resources to this market, since the market ignores the collective nature of the consumption benefits of sport. All the efficiency arguments are based on the same premise: it is possible to increase social welfare by altering the market allocation. Equity is concerned not so much with the total level of social welfare attained as with how that total is distributed over members of society.

Equity considerations are essentially to do with the distribution of income. A primary policy argument based on equity is that willingness to pay is not an acceptable criterion for certain goods and services, since many groups in society do not have the ability to pay due to the existing distribution of income. The policy solution does not necessarily rely on altering the distribution of income, however. The equity argument for government intervention in the sport and recreation market is an argument for a more equal distribution of the benefits generated through sports participation (both private and social), to compensate in some measure for the distribution of income which the market produces.

Perhaps the most obvious manifestation of the equity objective is the 'Sport for All' slogan used initially by the Sports Council, but subsequently adopted by many local authorities as a reason for the provision of subsidised sports facilities. More recently the current government's initiative to pursue 'social inclusion' has been a direct expression of intervention on the grounds of equity.

The equity argument has always been a problem for economists because it involves essentially normative arguments and value judgements, which are difficult to support or verify by appeal to the facts. 'Sport for All', for example, may be interpreted in a variety of ways, from literally 'sport for all people' to sport for a few 'recreationally disadvantaged' groups, depending on the equity value judgement of the policy-maker. The concept causing problems here is that of 'vertical equity', which concerns the choice of different policies for consumers of different types and circumstances. In order that equity is achieved in matters such as access and opportunity in sports participation, value judgements are needed to specify what equity means.

Vertical equity can be interpreted to mean any one of a number of policies, depending on the values adopted. Utilitarian equity aims to achieve the greatest utility for the greatest number. Rawlsian equity seeks to maximise the benefits to the most disadvantaged (Rawls, 1971). A natural endowment approach to equity would direct policy towards the gifted, who are better able to benefit from the policy. A needs approach would direct policy towards those with greatest need, as identified either relative to others or in relation to a specified social minimum. Equity has been interpreted literally as equality: equal provision for all, regardless of factors such as income and access. Finally, equity according to deserving would attempt to distribute benefits according to whatever criteria of deserving are adopted, which could vary from one extreme (e.g. inability to pay) to another (the amount actually paid indirectly through taxes for public services).

Needless to say, not all these interpretations of equity and their associated policies are compatible with each other, since they are based on different value judgements. It is Rawlsian equity – seeking to improve opportunities for the poorest in society – that is dominating current policy in the form of 'social inclusion'.

There is an important link between the equity objective and the concept of need. Culyer (1980) points out the difference between need and demand:

> Whichever view one takes of need, we should note that they each involve a judgement being made independently of the receiving individual's preferences. It is this that makes a need based on caring preferences different from demand, for a demand is a want for some good or service backed by a willingness to sacrifice resources for it. Where demand and need come together is when one individual wants something for someone else and is prepared to sacrifice resources for it. Need is thus an external demand. It represents one party's view of what another should have.

Thus need is directly related to the concept of equity. However, whereas there is a broad consensus on the existence of housing, education and health needs, the concept of recreational need is relatively new. Dower *et al.* (1981) examined the nature of leisure and recreational needs and argued that leisure provision in general catered to expressed demand rather than need, and as a result many groups were recreationally deprived.

A rationale for government intervention, therefore, is that certain individuals in society, who may or may not participate themselves, receive an increase in welfare from the participation of specific target groups whom they identify as having need because of an equity problem. The target groups on this basis would specifically be those on low incomes, but a similar argument could be made for ethnic minorities, the elderly and the unemployed, where low income is often compounded by other barriers to participation. They might also include excellent sportspeople to the extent that they are felt to have special needs and the market fails to reward many of them adequately for the sacrifices they make.

Concern over equity considerations across public policy have heightened in the UK because of clear signs of an increasingly divided society. In 1994 the Commission for Social Justice provided a damning picture of modern Britain as a divided society. This was endorsed by a Joseph Rowntree Foundation Inquiry into the Distribution of Income and Wealth in the UK, in 1995. Some of the main findings of these reports show the magnitude of the Rawlsian problem. Between 1979 and 1992 the poorest tenth of society suffered a real decline in their incomes of 17 per cent, while the top 20 per cent enjoyed an increase in their real income of around 50 per cent. Income inequality in the UK reached a higher level than recorded since the Second World War. A quarter of the population and a third of children live in poverty according to official Government Income Support criteria. One million pensioners live on Income Support or less, while many pensioners are comparatively wealthy because of occupational pensions. One in four men between the ages of 16 and 64 are economically inactive; 40 per cent of the unemployed are long-term (over 1 year).

In the face of this evidence of increasing social and economic divisions, an interventionist sports policy might hope to improve sporting opportunities for the socially excluded. In principle this has been a strong tradition in local authority sports provision, with 'sport for all' policies tending to be interpreted as increasing opportunities for socially and recreationally disadvantaged groups such as people on low incomes, the unemployed, women with young children, the disabled, the elderly, and ethnic minorities.

The policy instruments which have been used to try to achieve this equitable goal have evolved slowly. Twenty years ago the norm was 'blanket subsidies', i.e. generally low prices (with standard discounts for children) which necessitated large and persistent subsidies provided for local authority facilities. Such subsidies were heavily criticised by the Audit Commission (1989) for lacking a clear rationale and being ineffective:

> authorities assume that low prices and blanket subsidies encourage use and help ensure social objectives are met. But, sports participation is biased towards people with a professional and managerial background who benefit disproportionately from low prices. Across the board subsidies may therefore have a reverse effect from a redistributional perspective. Many poorer people are, through their rates, paying to subsidise the pastimes of the rich.

This picture suggested that nothing had changed since the 1970s. The most authoritative evidence from that era comes from an unpublished report for the Sports Council by Veal (1981), which demonstrates that in the use of public leisure facilities the professional and managerial classes were over-represented, making up an average of 24 per cent of users yet representing only 14 per cent of the population. Semi-skilled and unskilled groups, on the other hand, made up 13 per cent of users but were 27 per cent of the population.

In 1997 Sport England commissioned user surveys in 155 local authority sports centres and swimming pools, with a total of 41,000 respondents (Sport England, 1999). The results provide the most authoritative and conclusive evidence to date of some enduring inequities in participation in such facilities. Seventy-two per cent of users of both sports halls and swimming pools came

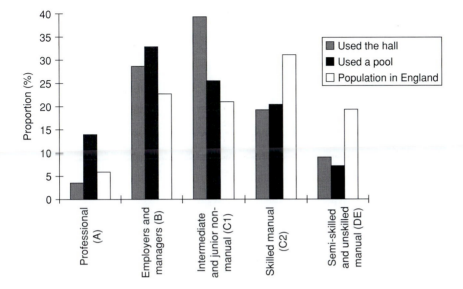

Figure 6.2 Socio-economic group (SEG) of users (relates to SEG of household's chief
income earner).
Base: all visitors aged 16 and over, i.e. excludes 'not stated' and those aged 15
and younger.
'Population in England' from Office for National Statistics (General Household
Survey, 1996): data for head of household.
Source: Sport England, 1999

from a household where the chief income earner was classified in social groups
ABC1; this compares with just 50 per cent of the population of England in these
groups. In addition, those over 45 years, the disabled, and the unemployed were
all significantly under-represented in the usage of the facilities. The detailed
evidence is contained in Figures 6.2 to 6.4 and Table 6.6.

It is not necessarily realistic to expect socially disadvantaged people to be well
represented in the usage profiles of local authority sports facilities. Many constraints other than price prevent them from participating, some of which may be
beyond the reach of public policy. Nevertheless, the enduring nature of their
under-representation is of concern if the subsidy has been used for equity reasons,
to sustain a 'sport for all'/social inclusion policy.

Recently, price discrimination has become more sophisticated than blanket
subsidies in many authorities, with nearly half the authorities responding to a
survey by Taylor and Foote (1996) having adopted the use of 'passport to leisure'
schemes. Passport schemes are a price discrimination device which allows subsidies to be directed towards target groups. However, as Taylor and Foote report,
the stated objectives of the passport schemes in use by local authorities are more
likely to reflect general usage (e.g. encourage use of facilities, equal opportunity
for all) than a more targeted approach to the socially excluded.

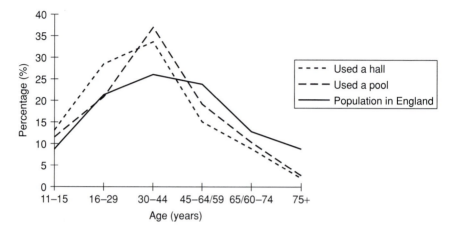

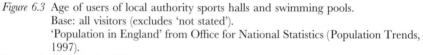

Figure 6.3 Age of users of local authority sports halls and swimming pools.
  Base: all visitors (excludes 'not stated').
  'Population in England' from Office for National Statistics (Population Trends, 1997).
Source: Sport England, 1999

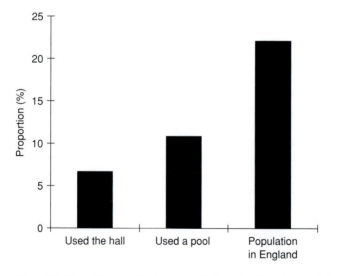

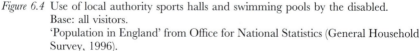

Figure 6.4 Use of local authority sports halls and swimming pools by the disabled.
  Base: all visitors.
  'Population in England' from Office for National Statistics (General Household Survey, 1996).
Source: Sport England, 1999

Table 6.6 Employment status of users (base: all visitors aged 16 and over; i.e. excludes not stated and those aged 15 and under)

	Hall users (%)	Pool users (%)	Population in England* (%)
Working full-time (30+ hours)	56.5	49.1	39.2
Retired	12.6	14.8	23.8
Working part-time (less than 30 hours)	12.5	16.2	15.9
Housewife/husband/full-time in the home	6.1	8.3	8.6
In full-time education (school/college/university)	9.8	6.9	2.2
Unemployed	1.8	2.5	4.4
Permanently unable to work (due to illness/disability)	0.6	2.0	3.9
On government work training programme	0.1	0.3	0.5
Weighted base (*n*)	419,548	686,649	13,352

Source: Sport England, 1999.

* *Office for National Statistics (General Household Survey, 1996).*

Government failure

The arguments examined so far in this chapter follow a conventional welfare economics approach, with examination of the rationale for government intervention followed by a critical evaluation of the extent to which the effects of actual intervention match its purpose. It is clear, however, particularly in the case of the equity justification for intervention, that there is not a great deal of evidence that government intervention is achieving its economic justifications.

One of the problems with the welfare approach to government intervention taken above is that it makes ambitious assumptions about the way in which government behaves (Gratton and Taylor, 1991). First, government's motives are assumed to be impartial, objective and geared towards the 'public purpose', i.e. no vested interests. Moreover, the most demanding objective – maximising social welfare – is held to be relevant; nothing less will do. Second, government is assumed to have all the information necessary to intervene effectively, or at least better market information than individual market participants (consumers and suppliers). Third, government is supposed to be representative of society's group preferences – i.e. majority opinion. Fourth, intervention by government is assumed to be cost-effective, meaning that objectives are achieved at minimum cost to the taxpayer.

These assumptions, and hence the welfare approach, have been criticised by 'liberalist' and 'new right' economists as being unrealistic. Their alternative model is one of government failure, attempting to disprove the theory that government can intervene in markets effectively (achieving clear objectives) or efficiently (doing so at minimum cost). It is not surprising that the major policy implications of this theory are to reduce the direct supply of government services and substitute, where the market is not appropriate, alternative mechanisms. However, the objective is not necessarily to abolish government intervention altogether in markets such as sport, although this is one policy option. The behavioural model does not deny that there may be market failures, nor does it imply that equity is necessarily well served by the market mechanism. Rather it suggests that the outcomes of the welfare approach are so flawed that a preferable outcome is obtainable from an approach which instils more market discipline into government organisations.

In the liberalist package to achieve effective and efficient government intervention are many measures that are becoming more common in public services. These include performance-related pay; contracting of government services; partnerships with private, not-for-profit suppliers; and vouchers for potential users rather than subsidies direct to facilities. Of these measures, only vouchers have remained largely untested in the supply of public sector sports services. Vouchers have clearly-identified problems (particularly administrative cost), and the targeting of subsidies that they have the potential to achieve is also possible with other, more practical methods, such as passport to leisure schemes.

The government failure model has done much to modify the supply of public services in the UK, including provision of sport. However, rather than replacing the welfare approach described above, the 'new right' measures have been used as a supplement to it in a concerted attempt to ensure that government intervention is cost-effective.

Conclusions

Economics provides a very clear basis for government intervention in sports markets, at least in principle. However, evidence of the outcomes from such government intervention is in many cases patchy, weak or simply contradictory to the expected outcome. This means that not only is there scope for substantial improvements in the quantity and quality of research to test the achievements of government intervention, but there is also considerable licence to consider models of government failure, which leads in the direction of either less, or substantially modified forms of, government intervention.

Efficiency arguments for government intervention lead to similar conclusions to the equity arguments, i.e. in order to produce a socially optimum level of collective benefits from sport, public expenditure should be targeted at specific groups. If sports participation by adolescents reduces crime and vandalism, then such social benefits are only generated if public provision encourages adolescents to take part in sport. Health status declines with age and is lower for low-income groups than for high-income groups, such that a policy of sports promotion for health externality reasons might concentrate on these as priority targets. Caring for the socially excluded requires targeting of groups such as the elderly, those on low incomes, and the unemployed.

7   The voluntary sector and sport

Introduction

In the UK and in many other countries a large proportion of sporting opportunities, from the recreational to the competitive élite, is provided outside the
government and commercial sectors. This third major provider of sport, the
private not-for-profit sector, is made up of a number of different types, but all
characterised by private ownership and the lack of a profit motive. The first
and most significant part of it is the voluntary sector, which has one essential
characteristic, voluntary labour, that makes it difficult to measure and analyse by
conventional means. Voluntary labour in sport is not recorded systematically on
a national basis and the actions and consequences of voluntary organisations
are not monitored by official statistics. However, as a result of a recent study
(LIRC, 1996), both the size and the value of the voluntary sector in UK sport
have been identified and will be reported in this chapter.

Second, and of increasing importance in the UK, is the charitable sector, to
which belongs a growing number of charitable trusts specifically formed to take
ownership of leisure facilities, many of which were previously owned by, and are
still subsidised by, local authorities. Third is the industrial sector, through which
sports facilities and clubs are organised at industrial premises, often with explicit
subsidies from commercial firms and with organisation largely on a voluntary
basis. Little is known about the national scale of provision for sport through the
charitable and industrial sectors, but there is some evidence in the UK that while
the former is growing, the latter is in substantial decline.

Most sports in the UK are organised around voluntary clubs. These and their
parent organisations, the national governing bodies of sport – many of which are
also organised voluntarily – provide the backbone to the whole structure of
sports development in many sports, from foundation through participation and
improvement, to excellence. The chapter begins, therefore, with a description of
the size, structure and value of the voluntary sector. It then explores the economic
rationale for the voluntary sector. A number of organisational considerations are
examined, which help to assess the economy and efficiency of voluntary sports
organisations, including the costs and benefits of volunteer labour. Finally we
explore some policy considerations, not least of which is the extent to which the
voluntary sector needs government support.

The structure and scale of voluntary sport

Many sports are organised through voluntary clubs, with typically a structure of organisation above club level represented by national governing bodies of sport (NGBs). It is not unusual within the UK to have a multiplicity of NGBs for one sport; the single governing body in sport is very much the exception. Often, as well as a Great Britain governing body, there will be separate bodies for Scotland, Wales, England, and Northern Ireland. For many sports, the main purpose of these separate bodies will be team selection and organisation for the Commonwealth Games, one of few major international competitions remaining where England, Scotland, Wales, and Northern Ireland send separate teams. Many sports have separate schools associations; several have separate disabled/wheelchair associations – indeed, disabled sport has a whole structure of its own governing bodies. There are at least fourteen NGBs in the martial arts, including four for karate, and others representing kung fu, ju-jitsu, aikido, kendo, shorinji kempo, and Thai and Korean martial arts.

In some sports many participants join neither club nor national governing body. Facilities may be provided by the commercial, public, or voluntary sector and the participant simply pays a charge for each occasion of participation. In the General Household Survey three of the largest sporting activities are walking (over two miles, for recreational purposes), indoor swimming, and keep fit. All three of these sports are organised principally outside the club and governing body structure, informally in the case of recreational walking and swimming, and via commercial provision in the case of keep fit.

Whereas some voluntary organisations are entirely devoted to supplying sport on a continual basis, such as governing bodies of sport and sports clubs, others are temporary, e.g. to organise specific major sports events. Furthermore, sport may be offered as only part of the remit of more general purpose organisations which use volunteers, such as in schools, youth organisations and organisations for the disabled, so volunteering for sport in these may be by sports specialists or part of the functions of multi-purpose volunteers.

These examples serve to indicate that the voluntary sector in sport is very diverse. The current organisational structure for any sport is a result of a range of influences: historical factors, different disciplines and abilities within the sport, different interests and policies in different regions and countries, demands of international bodies, and organisational developments related to interactions with national Sports Councils, upon which many depend for funding. It is perhaps not surprising that the interaction of such factors leads to very different organisational structures in different sports.

Until recently it was not known even approximately how big the voluntary sector in UK sport was. However, a recent study conducted for the Sports Council has disclosed for the first time an accurate picture of the scale and extent of this sector (LIRC, 1996). For this study the measurement of size was in terms of the numbers of volunteers working in sport, and the time they put into sport in a year. The data was assembled from primary research to establish how many

Table 7.1 The extent of volunteering in UK sport

Type of sports volunteer	Number of volunteers	Number of hours per year	Number of hours per week
Governing bodies and sports clubs in 94 sports	1,166,688	165,528,565	142
International events hosted in UK	5,047	277,680	n.a.
Disabled sport	25,217	3,162,744	125
Schools	37,897	2,576,972	68
Youth organisations	233,389	11,617,709	50
Total	1,468,238	183,163,670	125

Source: LIRC (1996).

volunteers existed on average per club/organisation and how much time they devoted to sport. From this information it is possible to put an economic value on this important sector.

Table 7.1 presents the overall size of the volunteer labour market in UK sport. These results signify nearly 1.5 million volunteers in UK sport, putting in an average of 125 voluntary hours per year, or just over 2.5 hours per week for 48 weeks per year. To put these data into perspective, the number of volunteers involved in sport is more than three times the number of people working in paid employment in sports-related activity. For 1995 the Leisure Industries Research Centre (LIRC, 1997) estimated the total paid employment in sport-related activity in the UK as 414,950 people. Assuming a standard working week and year, the hours worked by the estimated volunteer workforce in Table 7.1 are equivalent to over 106,000 full-time-equivalent workers added to the sports labour market.

As well as the categories of volunteering in sport identified in Table 7.1, one other category was explored in the LIRC (1996) research – volunteering in clubs not affiliated to recognised governing bodies of sport. This part of the voluntary sector was not picked up in the main primary research because this was conducted through governing bodies of sport recognised by the Sports Council. For the few sports identified by Sports Council liaison officers and governing bodies' representatives as possibly having high levels of unaffiliated activity, insufficient information was available on the extent of such activity. Therefore, this remains the one area of volunteer activity in sport still to be estimated.

It must be emphasised that the estimates provided by the LIRC study are conservative in one important respect. They only include volunteers working within organisations such as clubs and governing bodies – these are termed 'formal' volunteers. They do not include volunteers who help in the delivery of sport in a more 'informal' capacity, such as parents driving their children and friends to sports facilities and events, friends who coach or train sports participants outside the formal organisation of a club. The National Survey of Voluntary Activity (NSVA) measures both formal and informal volunteering (Lynn and Davis-Smith, 1991) and its evidence leads to estimates for sports volunteers which are a lot higher than those of LIRC as a consequence. Using NSVA data provides an estimate of 5.75 million 'current' sports volunteers, i.e. who had volunteered at least once in the previous year. This figure included 2.18 million weekly volunteers (who had volunteered in the week before the interview); another 1.06 million volunteers who volunteered at least once a month and 2.51 million volunteers who volunteer less frequently than once a month.

Individual sports

Three sports feature significantly in the 26 selected for primary research in the LIRC study – bowls, association football, and cricket. These three sports account for 37 per cent of the total numbers of formal volunteers in organised UK sport. They are important to volunteering for different reasons: football because a moderate amount of volunteering per club will still aggregate to a large number because of the sheer size of the game in the UK; bowls because a high proportion of club members tend to volunteer, possibly for social reasons; and cricket because a high proportion of club members tend to volunteer for a variety of reasons.

The total numbers of volunteers and volunteer hours are dominated by club-level activity – clubs account for most of the 79 per cent of volunteers and 90 per cent of volunteer hours attributed to NGBs and clubs in Table 7.1. In terms of volunteer hours worked per week however, there is a clear relationship between level and number of hours – the higher the level, the larger the number of hours worked. On average each volunteer at the national level works 13.8 hours per week, compared with 5.8 hours per volunteer per week at middle levels and 2.7 hours per volunteer per week at club level. These estimates take account of seasonal variations and assume a 48-week year for the purposes of voluntary work. It is the norm that volunteering in sport does not stop out of season. It may reduce in hours and often the tasks to be done change, but it continues in the off-season. There is considerable variation between sports around the overall averages reported above. For example, at the national level the average hours worked per volunteer per week range from less than 1 in hockey to 36 in table tennis.

There is not a strong relationship between the size of volunteering and the size of participation in a sport. Some of the most popular sports are not among the most significant for volunteering, e.g. cycling, walking and swimming, because a lot of participation in these sports is informal, casual, uncompetitive and there-fore not in need of volunteer support. However, because they are such large participation sports, even a proportionately small volunteer support is significant in terms of total numbers of volunteers. Other relatively minority sports have a very high percentage of participants in organisations which rely on volunteers, such as cricket, rugby and hockey; they are high in the ranking of sports accord-ing to voluntary activity because they are largely played in a formal club environ-ment and need a full range of volunteer support, including administration of competitions, coaching and grounds maintenance. Yet another type of sport has a high percentage of participants in clubs but does not need as much volunteer support because it has significant commercial provision, e.g. sailing.

There are some extreme figures for average voluntary hours worked, but the normal range of average hours worked across the sports investigated is in the range of 2 to 5 hours per week. These averages are dictated largely by the very high proportion of volunteers that operate at club level.

The number of club members per volunteer is an indicator of the intensity of volunteer support, with low numbers implying high intensity and high numbers implying low intensity of volunteer support. A lot of the sports have very low numbers/high intensity, possibly because of the large range of voluntary functions required to be done. Sports with high numbers/low intensity can be categorised as those with no competitive structure and few technical coaching/leadership demands, such as walking, angling and recreational cycling, and those where significant commercial provision means that fewer volunteers are required, such as golf, sailing and keep fit.

Major international events

Volunteering in individual sports includes regularly held events within the domestic calendar of each sport. Additional to these regular commitments, however, are occasional major international events which are hosted in the UK. These range from multi-sport events such as the World Student Games in Sheffield in 1991 and the Commonwealth Games to be held in Manchester in 2000, to the single-sport World and European Championships. Whereas each event of this type is held in the UK only periodically, in any one year a number of such events are likely to be hosted. At the time of the research into the voluntary sector in UK sport, the most recent year, 1995, had seen the UK host World or European Championships in eleven sports.

The amount of volunteering required for major international events can be very significant. For example, the European Swimming Championships held in Sheffield in 1993 involved 700 volunteers working an average of 8 hours a day for up to 17 days, giving a total of about 95,000 hours – equivalent to another 3.6 per cent on the estimated annual swimming volunteer total for the UK. The volunteering for the World Netball Championships hosted in Birmingham in 1995 was equivalent to an extra 2 per cent on the annual amount of volunteering in netball.

The level of volunteering required for major international events varies enormously between different types of events, and is not simply a function of the number of participants. Some events require functions such as drivers, attachés, and technical officials in much greater numbers than others. Some events use a lot of paid staff rather than volunteers.

Major events, not surprisingly, have very intensive volunteer efforts. It is not unusual to find the number of competitors outweighed by the number of volunteers. The average hours per volunteer varied from 11 in cross-country to 120 in the netball event, although some volunteers worked for a considerable time before the event – e.g. 2 years' effort by one volunteer before a canoe slalom event.

Disabled sport

Disabled sport comprises a number of organisations, many of which are sport-specific but some of which are more general and have sport as only one part of their programmes, e.g. Gateway Clubs. The estimate in Table 7.1 is based on evidence from nine major organisations: British Amputees Sports Association, British Blind Sport, British Deaf Sports Council, British Les Autres Sports Association, British Paralympic Association, British Wheelchair Sports Foundation, National Federation of Gateway Clubs, Riding for the Disabled Association, and Special Olympics GB. There are an unknown number of minor organisations for the disabled which will help in the provision of sports opportunities, so the estimate for disabled sport in Table 7.1 is cautious, but there is insufficient information to be able to judge by how much it underestimates the real position.

The number of volunteers in disabled sport is dominated by the Riding for the Disabled Association, which not only has a lot of members but has on average one volunteer helper for less than two riders. Not surprisingly, there is generally a low ratio of members per volunteer – typically less than 5:1.

Schools

The Department for Education and Employment (DfEE) conducted, in 1996, a national survey of PE and sport in schools. This survey included questions on the number of volunteers who helped with extracurricular sport and the time that they put into such volunteering per week. This evidence was collected for primary, secondary and special schools. From the evidence provided by the DfEE on the findings of these questions, it is possible to construct national level estimates of volunteering in school sport, which are summarised in Table 7.2.

Assessing volunteer activity for sport in schools is complicated by the fact that a lot of teachers work extra time for no extra pay in order to supervise extra-curricular sport in schools. However, this could be seen as part of their contract of employment and the definition of volunteering used in the LIRC project does not include unpaid overtime, so such time is excluded from the estimates of volunteering reported.

Table 7.2 Volunteering in school sport

Type of school	% of schools with volunteers for sport	Number of volunteers	Number of annual volunteer hours	Annual hours per volunteer*
Primary	57%	33,098	2,323,480	70
Secondary	36%	3,705	202,293	55
Special	19%	1,094	51,199	47
Total		37,897	2,576,972	

Source: LIRC (1996). Estimated from findings from DfEE Survey of PE and Sports in Schools, 1996.

* Annual hours are based on an assumed 39-week year.

Clearly there is a significant difference between volunteering at the three different types of school, with a substantially higher percentage of primary schools using volunteers for sport, as well as higher total numbers of volunteers and greater average time input in primary schools compared with secondary schools. Sports sessions for primary schoolchildren are more demanding in terms of child management, since they are less able to adhere to codes of behaviour, so a higher ratio of leaders to children is necessary.

In special schools the scale of volunteering is clearly the lowest, with less than a fifth reporting use of volunteers for sports activity. However, some voluntary activity concerning special schoolchildren will occur in the specialist disabled sports organisations reviewed above, such as Riding for the Disabled. It is apparent from the DfEE survey that sport is practised as a much broader concept in special schools than in other schools, embracing such forms as physiotherapy and stretching, for which volunteering is less necessary than in traditional sports. Also, extracurricular activity is heavily constrained in special schools by transport arrangements and the longer travelling distance for pupils compared with primary and secondary schools.

Youth organisations

As with the estimates for volunteering for disabled sport, the findings for youth organisations are confined to major national organisations: the Air Training Corps, Army Cadets, Boys Brigade, Boys Cubs, Combined Cadets, Girls Brigade, Guides, Methodist Youth Clubs, Scouts, Sea Cadets, YMCA, Young Farmers, Youth Clubs UK (the Duke of Edinburgh's Award Scheme is conducted largely through other organisations, so few volunteers are specific to it). There are an unknown number of minor organisations which will help in the provision of sports opportunities for young people, so the estimate in Table 7.1 is cautious.

Whereas the Guides and other youth organisations may have a fairly stable programme for meetings, which may almost always contain some physical games, this is not the case for all youth organisations – in some sport may feature heavily in one meeting but not in another. In some youth organisations sport is loosely defined as physical activities and games which may only last, as in the case of the Guides, a quarter of an hour as part of the programme of an organised weekly meeting. However, even a quarter of an hour per week is significant if volunteers are leading such sessions for a large proportion of the year: in the case of the Guides a quarter of an hour per week aggregates to over 900,000 hours of volunteering for sport per year.

The value of volunteering in UK sport

Whereas monetary values can be attached to the estimates above of the size of volunteering in UK sport, it is important to acknowledge from the outset that to put a monetary valuation on voluntary labour is in some senses a contradiction in terms. Voluntary labour is given explicitly for no monetary reward – indeed, many volunteers would find it hard to put a monetary value on their voluntary work, simply because it is not a concept that is relevant to their volunteering.

Nevertheless, from the point of view of the organisation rather than the individual volunteer, the value of voluntary labour is relevant because without this voluntary labour the main alternative is a paid replacement. Furthermore, voluntary labour is not worthless – it is clearly of value to the organisation for which it is being given. It is also a value that is relevant to an assessment of the economic importance of sport nationally and locally (see Chapter 2), for although voluntary labour is not paid for, and the output it produces is not paid for, both the labour and the output have values and contribute to the material standard of living of the sports participants who benefit.

In principle the value of voluntary labour can be approached in much the same way as valuing leisure time. Three methods are possible. First, direct questions as part of a contingent valuation approach could attempt to identify what value volunteers would ascribe to losing an opportunity to do voluntary work. No studies of this type have been conducted to value voluntary labour. Second, the hedonic pricing method would analyse the behaviour of economic agents whose prices reflected the value of voluntary labour. However, identification of such agents in this case is difficult, and again no such investigation has been conducted. The third method, the opportunity cost method, works on the premise that the alternative to doing voluntary work is to do paid work, and the rate at which paid work could be obtained is the opportunity cost or shadow wage of preferring voluntary labour. The opportunity cost approach is the one typically used in the valuation of voluntary labour time.

To compare paid employment with voluntary employment is not comparing like with like – the former is typically subject to more work discipline, training, and productivity expectations than the latter, for example. One might expect the standard of work to be lower in voluntary employment and therefore the value of voluntary labour to be below that of the equivalent paid employment. However, voluntary labour typically takes place in traditional overtime hours; indeed, many volunteers have full-time jobs as well as their voluntary employment. Given that overtime is typically paid at premium rates, it could be argued that voluntary labour should be valued at more than the normal rates of pay. There is no satisfactory resolution of this problem, either conceptually or empirically. Therefore, for the purposes of valuing voluntary labour a pragmatic line has to be taken.

A major problem in valuing the volunteer market in sport is that no accepted shadow wage rate is used. The most accurate method, adopted by research in the occupational health volunteering context (Centre for Research in Social Policy, Loughborough University) is to identify the job tasks and occupational structures in the voluntary labour force, match them to paid employment occupations and apply appropriate shadow wages for the different occupational roles. This is a very complex research task and was not undertaken in the LIRC research into the voluntary sector in UK sport.

Both the Heritage and Sports Lottery Funds provide another basis for a shadow wage for voluntary labour, because of their acceptance of voluntary inputs as

Table 7.3 The value of volunteers in UK sport

Type of sports volunteer	Number of volunteer hours per year	Value of volunteer hours at £8.31 per hour (£ million)
Governing bodies and sports clubs in 94 sports	165,528,565	1,375.5
11 international events hosted in UK	277,680	2.3
Disabled sport	3,162,744	26.3
Schools	2,576,972	21.4
Youth organisations	11,617,709	96.5
Total	183,163,670	1,522

Source: LIRC (1996).

part of the required self-funding element to set against the grant applied for from the Lottery. The Heritage Lottery Fund advises two shadow wages for voluntary contributions to Heritage Lottery projects. For manual labour its shadow wage is £5.75 an hour and for professional labour the rate is £120 a day, which, assuming an 8-hour day, is £15 per hour. Assuming voluntary labour in sport to consist of half manual and half professional work gives an average value per hour of £10.38. The Sport Lottery Fund does not offer similar advice to the Heritage Lottery Fund, although it does accept the value of voluntary labour as part of the contribution in Lottery bids. Of the submissions that include such contributions, the values for manual labour are typically £5 or £10, while for professional work the values range from £5 to £15, according to information from the Sports Lottery database. On balance, therefore, the rate of £10.38 per hour from the Heritage Lottery Fund advice is one option for valuing voluntary labour in the current project. This value has two advantages: it is derived from official sources and it emanates from a very relevant context: voluntary labour for sports and heritage organisations.

However, the Lottery shadow wage is a high value – 25 per cent higher than the average hourly earnings for all industries for 1995. While it may be true that volunteering in sport involves a higher proportion of skilled and professional work than other volunteering, there is no evidence to substantiate this. Much of the administrative work typical of sports club volunteering, for example, may be more 'clerical' than 'professional' in terms of skill requirements. A less controversial option than the Lottery shadow wage is to follow the precedent of previous national research into the voluntary sector (The Volunteer Centre UK, 1995). This research used a national average wage to value voluntary labour. Using average hourly earnings as the shadow wage gives, for 1995 (the base year for the recent research), a value of £8.31 per hour.

Table 7.3 summarises the value of voluntary labour in UK sport. The total value of over £1.5 billion is over eight times greater than the previous estimate, provided by the Henley Centre (1992a) as part of its assessment of the economic impact of sport in the UK. To be fair, this comparison is not of like with like – the Henley Centre used an arbitrary half of average hourly earnings as a shadow wage. Nevertheless, adjustments for this and for inflation, to make like-for-like comparisons, still yield a figure over four times the adjusted Henley Centre estimate. The inevitable conclusion is that previous estimates of the size and value of the voluntary labour market in sport have been seriously underestimated.

The values in Table 7.3 need to be qualified with the same point made about the estimation of numbers of volunteers in Table 7.1. The values are only for formal volunteers working in sports organisations; they do not include informal volunteering, which takes place outside such organisations.

Of the different types of organisation providing volunteers for sport, it is clearly sports clubs and governing bodies that produce the largest value – they provide over 90 per cent of the total value in Table 7.3. Furthermore, in this category sports clubs provide 90 per cent of the volunteer hours, and governing bodies 10 per cent. The top twenty sports in terms of the value of their voluntary labour each have over £10 million per annum value from their volunteers' inputs, using average hourly earnings as a shadow wage for this labour.

Economic rationale for the voluntary sector

There has been little theoretical discussion of the role of the voluntary sector in sport. However, one economist, Weisbrod, has analysed a specific role for the voluntary sector and this approach has been used by Gratton and Taylor (1991) in an attempt to apply that theory to sports clubs. Weisbrod (1978, 1988) provided an economic rationale for the existence of the voluntary sector. He saw it as essentially fulfilling the same role as government, providing collective goods. There is a need for this sector since government fails to correct for all private market failures – see Chapter 6. In other words, a combination of commercial market failure and government failure leaves opportunities for a third major provider, the non-profit supplier.

Weisbrod argued that two factors are particularly relevant to the stimulation of voluntary sector activity. Government itself lacks adequate information on consumer demands, and also government officials often follow their own personal objectives rather than acting on the basis of abstract concepts of efficiency and equity. Government may be an efficient provider of collective goods if demand for such goods is homogeneous. In circumstances where there are diverse demands, the voluntary sector is likely to be the more efficient provider.

> When a collective good is collective for only some persons – in the sense that the good enters positively the utility functions of only those persons – the potential for organising collective good activity outside of government, in voluntary non-profit organisations, appears more likely.
>
> (Weisbrod, 1978)

In effect, Weisbrod suggests that there has to be a wide degree of consensus on the collective nature of a good before government enters the market. For minority interests government is likely to fail to provide collective benefits.

> the undersatisfied demand for collective type goods is a government 'failure' analogous to private market failure. That is, the combined willingness of part of the population to pay for additional collective-type goods exceeds the incremental cost of providing them and yet government, responding to majoritarian interests, does not provide them.
>
> (Weisbrod, 1988)

Government fails to obtain relevant information on consumer demand when demand is heterogeneous and fragmented, even when the nature of the good concerned is collective. There are several reasons for this.

First, there is a motivation problem. The behaviourist model indicates that politicians are likely to be more concerned with the objective of maximising their chances of re-election than with meeting an abstract social welfare objective. Where there is a majority demand for a collective good, the two objectives are likely to lead to the same action: provision of the good. However, for minority interest collective goods, the re-election objective is not necessarily fulfilled by provision.

Second, there is an information problem. For majority interests, there is less likely to be a problem in politicians perceiving the demand for the collective good. For minority interests, it is much more difficult to establish the strength of demand.

Added to this are the inefficiencies in the implementation of the decisions of the politician through the bureaucratic process. It is perhaps not surprising that a significant part of consumer demand for collective goods goes unmet by both the commercial sector and government. The voluntary sector fills the gap.

Weisbrod's argument is specifically relevant to sport because the nature of the demand for sport is such that demand is likely to be fragmented. Data on participation rates from the General Household Survey shows that demand for any particular sport is a minority demand. The fragmentation of NGBs in sport is partly a reflection of different interests within individual sports. At the same time, participation in sport is a collective good in the sense that there are pre-sumed societal benefits (see Chapter 6) over and above benefits to individual participants. The sports club, therefore, in Weisbrod's terms, arises out of the failure of both markets and government to provide for a heterogeneous demand for sport. Markets fail to provide sufficiently because of the collective nature of the good; governments fail because of the heterogeneous nature of demand.

Weisbrod discussed the wide spectrum of types of non-profit organisation. At one end are organisations almost entirely dependent on income from members, i.e. clubs. Buchanan (1965) analysed the economic formation of clubs. The benefits of such organisations accrue only to the members of the club; in fact, Buchanan saw the objective of such a club as the maximisation of the net benefit of the typical member. The good provided is collective in a sense, but it is excludable and is made exclusive to the club members.

Table 7.4 Summary of voluntary sector income, 1995 (£m)

Factor income (monetary)	
Players' subscriptions, match fees, etc.	1,327
Equipment	4
Sponsorship, advertising	73
Raffles, gaming machines, etc.	241
Bar	1,646
Total factor income	3,291
Other income (monetary)	
Grants	79
Employers' subsidies to clubs	94
Interest	42
Foundation for Sport and Arts	40
Football Trust	6
Lottery awards	37
Lottery partnerships	44
Total monetary income	342
Total income	3,633

Source: LIRC (1997).

At the other end of the spectrum, 'collective-type non-profits, such as providers of medical research and aid to the poor, produce public-type services that bring widely shared benefits' (Weisbrod, 1988). These organisations imitate government at a micro scale. Government does not provide such collective benefits because of their minority nature or because of information inadequacies. Such organisations are, however, likely to be publicly subsidised and receive a large part of their income in the form of contributions, gifts, or grants. An example in sport is NGBs, which often rely heavily on public subsidies, as shown in evidence for the mid-1980s by Taylor (1993).

Weisbrod suggests a 'collectiveness index' to measure the percentage of an organisation's income that comes from such sources. An organisation that provides mainly private goods and services to its own members (i.e. clubs) would be expected to have a 'collectiveness index' close to zero. At the opposite extreme, any non-profit organisation providing purely collective goods (i.e. all the benefits accruing to individuals who did not pay for them) would have a collectiveness index approaching 100. Thus we have a wide variety of voluntary sector organisations.

It seems that many sports clubs (e.g. amateur football clubs, athletics clubs) would be at the 'private good' end of Weisbrod's spectrum of voluntary sector organisations. Weisbrod argued that this type of non-profit is most similar to the commercial sector. Most of the income comes from membership dues and from sales. There is little or no public subsidy since few if any benefits are generated for non-members: the collectiveness index therefore should be very low.

The Leisure Industries Research Centre (1996) estimated the total income of the voluntary sector in sport (see Table 7.4), a sector which is likely to be dominated by sports clubs but also contains governing bodies of sport. The majority of sports club income comes from two sources: membership subscriptions and fees, and bar profits. The next largest source of income is from raffles and gaming. Since it is normally the members themselves that drink in the club bar and use the gaming machines, most of the income from sports clubs comes from members. It should be noted that National Lottery awards account for a comparatively small amount of income in Table 7.4 in the year for which estimates are provided, 1995. Even though this was the first year of Lottery awards and therefore not up to the level of funding subsequently reached, the lottery is not a major source of income for the voluntary sector compared with member-derived income.

If we consider the typical amateur sports club then the picture is quite clear. The benefits provided by the club are exclusive to its members. Their participation in their chosen sport is made easier and considerably cheaper by the organisation provided by mainly volunteer labour. Although there is an element of altruistic giving in the volunteer labour provided to sports clubs, most of this labour is provided by the players themselves (the main beneficiaries), former players (and hence former beneficiaries), relatives of the players (hence indirect consumers of the benefits), or volunteers who receive positive utility through their involvement in the sport. There will always be an incentive for a player to receive the benefits without making a contribution and leave the club as soon as he or she ceases to play. This is the familiar 'free-rider' problem. However, sports clubs are also social organisations and social pressure can be an important deterrent to free-rider behaviour.

This volunteer labour is a substantial resource in the voluntary sector and distinguishes this sector from the public and commercial sectors, both of which must pay market rates for their labour. Table 7.4 shows that a substantial proportion of sports club income comes from a commercial activity that is in direct competition with the commercial sector, the selling of alcohol and other drinks (i.e. income from the bar), thus the sporting activity of the club is cross-subsidised from commercial operations. One of the reasons sports clubs can successfully do this is that they can often sell their drinks at lower prices than the commercial sector due to lower costs, and a major reason for these lower costs is the supply of volunteer labour.

Thus the product provided by the typical sports club is essentially a private product. People participate in the club for reasons of self-interest rather than altruism. The motivation of club members is not to generate collective benefits of sport for society generally, but rather to maximise benefits for club members. The fact that some collective benefits are incidentally generated may mean that the club is treated favourably by government (e.g. grants, subsidised charges for facilities or ground rental), but this is not normally the case.

Problems for sports volunteers

Voluntary labour brings about its own problems which affect the effectiveness of service delivery, as identified in the LIRC (1996) research. In the quantitative

Table 7.5 Problems encountered by volunteers in sport

Problem	Yes
There are not enough other people willing to volunteer in the club.	74%
Increasingly the work is left to fewer people.	55%
Increasingly my work as a volunteer in the club requires specialist skills.	23%
There is little time left after paid work.	19%
Things could be better organised in the club, so you feel that your efforts are sometimes wasted.	16%
Conflict with your family commitments.	16%
Any other important problems?	11%
Your children are no longer involved in the club, so you are less motivated.	2%
Other organisations which the club is in contact with place greater demands on your skills.	2%
You have stopped playing the sport, so are less motivated.	1%

Source: LIRC (1996).

survey of club committees the two most frequently cited problems – not enough volunteers and work left to fewer people – were clearly linked with each other (see Table 7.5). In many clubs there were difficulties in recruiting new volunteers, particularly for jobs seen as either time-consuming or specialist such as junior development and fund-raising. As representatives of one bowls club put it:

> Generally speaking the members that want to do the work are getting less and less, and it is getting harder and harder to attract people on and it is getting more difficult to get volunteers to stop as long as (current volunteers) are doing – they don't want to do 8, 9, 10, 15 years, it's 2, 3 years and out.

Consequent problems include overloading existing volunteers and peer group pressure for them to remain in their voluntary posts for longer than they might otherwise have expected or wished. National Survey of Voluntary Activity (NSVA) evidence for 1997 suggests that the average age of volunteers is getting higher, which is consistent with this problem (Davis Smith, 1998). In general there was found to be a lack of a system in the recruitment of volunteers. It was too often a matter of personalities rather than structures. This is probably endemic to the not-for-profit sector, given the reliance on voluntary labour and the fact that many volunteers may not wish their voluntary work to emulate paid work. Ironically, one way out of this problem is to employ paid workers to fulfil some roles in a club. Table 2.3 in Chapter 2 indicates that over time the value added in the voluntary sector is increasing, which may be because of the use of more paid inputs, including paid labour.

The roots of the problem of a shortage of volunteers was felt by LIRC (1996) to be twofold. First, the time which needed to be committed:

> I don't think people are afraid of the role, they're afraid of the time.
>
> (badminton)

> I couldn't count on being able to give the time commitment because of my job. I know I'd just end up letting people down all the time.
>
> (athletics)

The regular commitment was off-putting, possibly because of absolute time constraints – pressures from home, paid work (especially if both partners were working) and other aspects of leisure lives. In terms of time, we have seen earlier (Chapters 3, 4 and 5) how important the time constraint is for participation. Exactly the same analysis applies to voluntary work, which is a direct substitute for other leisure time activities.

The second reason for the shortage suggested by respondents in the research was a change in attitude to what being a member of a voluntary club is about. The essence of voluntary club membership is being a producer as well as a consumer; where through altruistic reasons people recognise the collective benefit to be produced within the club, by collective effort. If the respondents in the research are correct, the change that they suggest is an increasing emphasis on market exchange, where payment of membership is seen as purely a consumer choice, for participation opportunities, without necessarily obligating the member to anything further. This increases the free-rider problem identified above. Symptomatic of this change in attitude was a tennis club which had experimented with a two-tier membership charge: £200 full price or £180 for those willing to volunteer for the club. The vast majority of members had opted for the full price membership. Similarly, a netball club gave its members a choice at an AGM of giving more time to the club or paying more subscriptions – the members voted for higher subscriptions.

The problem of time is an intractable one, given that time constraints are imposed by paid work and societal factors in the main, leaving little room for choice for the individual beyond radical measures such as 'downshifting'. The problem of attitude is worrying, because it is in principle up to the individual to decide. Any growth in market exchange consumer attitudes in the voluntary sector is inappropriate to the production responsibility implied by volunteer labour. The competitive advantage of voluntary clubs lies in their low labour costs, but the recent research suggests that the basis for this advantage is under threat.

Policy considerations

One of the main findings of the LIRC (1996) research on volunteers in UK sport is that voluntary clubs are very self-sufficient. The common perception in clubs is that internal networks via the club members are capable of dealing with most problems that arise – a typical response being:

> if there's something we can't sort out then there's enough intelligence within the club to work out a solution.
>
> (football club)

Nevertheless, the research also disclosed specific areas where external support is needed, not all of which are acknowledged by the clubs themselves. The areas of need identified by the clubs themselves included help with fund-raising, particularly sponsorship and the potential for making bids to the Sports Lottery Fund; and both better information and some financial assistance for coach development/ training and junior development.

Financially, the most important development in recent years in funds for voluntary sports clubs, among others, is the National Lottery. By March 1998 the Lottery Sports Fund had allocated 1,861 awards to voluntary sports organisations in England, 68 per cent of the total number of Sports Lottery awards. By May 1998 it was estimated that 2 per cent of sports clubs in England had received an award. While there are concerns over the equity of the distribution of lottery awards, there is little doubt that it represents a major financial boost to capital development in the voluntary sports sector.

A major area of potential assistance was not acknowledged by the clubs in the LIRC research but was implicit in the problems associated with a shortage of volunteers. The implication of this set of problems is that support is needed for voluntary clubs to manage the whole process of securing, maintaining and satisfying volunteers. However, clubs in the research were not only unlikely to suggest the need for such assistance, when the possibility was raised many were also hostile to the prospect, seeing the idea as unnecessary. The general weakness in recruitment planning is not helped by such a dismissive attitude to training for administrative functions by clubs. There is a clear perceptual barrier to overcome in getting clubs to acknowledge a source of inefficiency for which external assistance might be appropriate.

Where assistance from outside the club network is necessary, the LIRC research suggested that the organisations capable of 'reaching down' to the level of the individual club are either from within the voluntary sector, in the shape of the club's own governing body, or from the public sector in the form of the club's local authority. Even programmes devised at a national level, such as the Sports Council's 'Running Sport' programme, can impact on voluntary clubs effectively.

In response to the LIRC research findings, the English Sports Council devised a Volunteer Investment Programme (VIP) designed to provide more information, more training, and more recognition for sports volunteers. One important route for delivering these initiatives is through national governing bodies – thirteen had incorporated the VIP programme into their volunteer support strategies by the end of 1998. Subsequent research by the English Sports Council found that over a quarter of club secretaries were aware of the programme (considerably more than previously), nearly all governing body representatives questioned were aware of the programme, and the training programmes were well attended and well received by volunteer delegates (Nichols and Taylor, 1998).

Why should support for voluntary clubs be offered by the public sector, given that they operate largely for a self-contained set of benefits which are exclusive to members? On both national and local levels there has been an increasing concern to see the not-for-profit sector realise its potential. The main reason is that through a flourishing not-for-profit sector it may be possible not only to achieve development and growth, but at the same time to reduce government activity and expenditure. Such a strategy is consistent with the collective benefits produced at the micro scale by voluntary clubs, which when multiplied by thousands of clubs probably represents a not insignificant benefit (although it is as yet unmeasured).

Taylor and Page (1994) identified a substantial interest on the part of local authority departments responsible for sport and recreation in developing partnerships with both the commercial and not-for-profit sectors – 73 per cent of local authorities were either involved or interested in partnerships with the commercial sector; 71 per cent with the voluntary sector. Since these findings were in connection with a survey about local authorities' financing of sport and recreation, it is reasonable to suggest that the interest in partnerships was primarily driven by the desire to achieve financial savings on current operations, or to achieve growth with a minimum of expenditure commitments. Interest in partnerships with the voluntary sector may also be in acknowledgement of the advantages of empowerment – greater effectiveness and economy in producing collective benefits by placing control of the services in the hands of the community which receives these benefits.

Others (Riiskjaer, 1990) have argued that such an approach by government towards the voluntary sector destroys the essential nature of voluntary sector activity. It changes the voluntary sector from co-operative bodies with largely voluntary labour to neo-corporate bodies with paid officers, which are little more than agencies of government. Riiskjaer sees the increasing direction of the voluntary sector by government, and financial dependency on government, as a dangerous combination.

Conclusions

The voluntary sports club is typically independent and inward looking, not explicitly seeking to provide collective benefits. Yet an important part of the economic rationale for the existence of the voluntary sector is that taken as a whole it is capable of providing collective benefits from a very heterogeneous structure, which complements what government traditionally provides.

Despite its independence, the voluntary sector in sport is not without its problems, particularly with shortages of volunteers. Government may be able to help with such problems through finance, advice, training, and partnership. Government has an incentive to do this because it may be more cost-effective than defending or developing its own direct provision, and the sheer scale of voluntary sector sport is very inviting for policy purposes. An intractable problem may be the reluctance of many voluntary organisations to work in partnership or in a perceived state of dependency with government. The National Lottery may be a catalyst for a change in this attitude, and so might the problems with recruiting volunteers. However, if this is the case there remains a worry that the nature of the voluntary sector may be changing, at a cost of losing some of its autonomy.

8 The commercial sector and sport

Although the voluntary sector has been the key lead sector in sport over the past two centuries, and government has played a significant role at specific periods, as we enter the new millennium it is the commercial sector of sport that is the most dynamic sector of the supply side of the sports market. It is now realistic to talk about 'the sports industry' as an important generator of economic activity and employment, and it is the commercial sector in sport that accounts for the major share of sport-related economic activity and employment. In this chapter we define the boundaries of the sports industry and outline the key contributors to its economic importance.

Certain sections of the commercial sector in sport have become so important over the recent past that we devote separate chapters to each of them in the final part of this book. These are sports sponsorship, major sports events, professional team sports, and sports broadcasting. We indicate their place in the commercial sector in sport in this chapter, but detailed analysis is left to the last part. The core of the sports industry is the sports goods sector: sports equipment, sports clothing, and sports shoes. The major part of this chapter is devoted to this sector, and we consider a specific issue within the sector: the inherent instability and volatility of demand for sports goods.

However, there are other commercial sports service sectors in addition to the four covered in the last section of the book. The most notable of these is the commercial provision of health and fitness facilities, and one specific issue in this area is considered in this chapter: the issue of unfair competition with the subsidised government sector.

The definition and structure of the sports industry

Figure 8.1 shows a breakdown of the commercial sector in sport: the sports industry. The commercial sports sector consists of the sports goods sector and the sports services sector. The sports goods sector includes all products which are bought for use in sport: sports equipment, sports clothing and sports footwear. The sports goods market accounts for about one-third of all sport-related consumer expenditure (see Table 2.1). Sports services include expenditure on admissions to spectator sports, fees and subscriptions for participation sports,

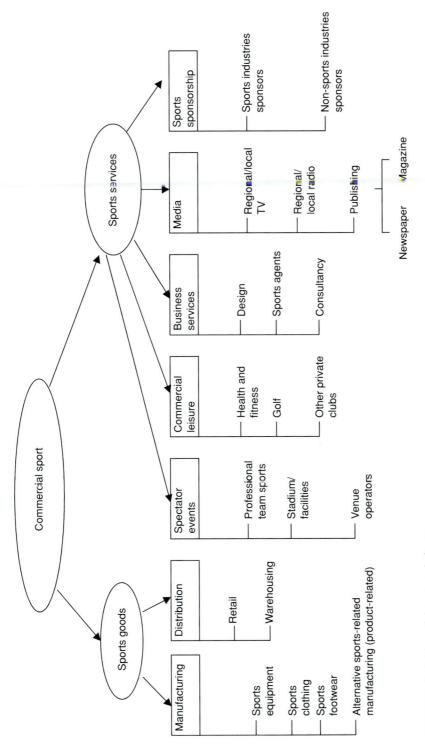

Figure 8.1 Definition of the sports industry.

Table 8.1 Commercial sports sector income in the UK, 1995

	£ million	%
Spectator clubs	633	12
Participation clubs	362	7
Retailers		
equipment	692	14
clothing and footwear	2,099	41
media	539	11
Manufacturers' sales (including exports) of		
equipment, clothing and footwear	486	10
TV and radio	249	5
Other	2	0
Total	5,062	100

Source: LIRC (1997a).

sports-related expenditure on television, and expenditure on health and fitness clubs. Expenditure on sports services accounts for 25 per cent of total consumers' expenditure on sport. Although some of this goes to the government and voluntary sectors, most of it goes to the commercial sports sector.

The other major items of sport-related consumers' expenditure are part of the non-sport commercial sector. That is, they are sport-related expenditures by consumers but the firms that supply these demands would not classify themselves within the sports industry. They include travel, gambling, and expenditure on books, magazines, and newspapers. Sport-related travel accounts for 7 per cent of total expenditure on sport, sport-related gambling for a massive 30 per cent, and sport-related expenditure on books, magazines, and newspapers for a further 7 per cent.

In the commercial sports sector, the sports product sub-sector accounts for a much higher proportion of total income than the contribution it makes to consumer expenditure on sport, since much of the latter goes to the government and voluntary sectors. Table 8.1 summarises the income earned by the commercial sports sector in 1995, with sports products representing 51 per cent of the total income earned. Clearly for the health of the commercial sports economy, sports products as defined (equipment, clothing, and footwear) are very important.

Another important indicator of the economic importance of sport, employment, is given in Table 2.4 in Chapter 2. Sports retailers and manufacturers employ 18 per cent of the total employment estimated for sport in the UK. By far the largest proportion of employment (47 per cent) in sport is in the commercial non-sport sector.

A final indicator of the economic importance of sport is the balance of international trade in sport, which shows a clear deficit. Sports clothing, footwear and equipment in 1995 had imports worth £635 million, including the import content of UK sports products, and exports worth £442 million (LIRC, 1997).

According to figures from the Department of Trade and Industry (DTI, 1999), the balance of trade for sports equipment alone in the UK in 1995 comprised

Table 8.2 Product sectors and sales in 1995 in sports equipment, sports clothing, and sports footwear

	1995 sales (£m)
Sports equipment: main product sectors	
Outdoor/waterproofs	65
Golf	180
Aerobics/indoor fitness	125
Football kit/boots/trainers	10
Swimwear	5
Racket sports	60
Snowsports	10
Snooker/billiards, darts	30
Sports clothing: main product sectors	
Outdoor/waterproofs	380
Tracksuits	250
Football kit	100
Swimwear	155
Aerobics/indoor fitness	80
Golf	95
Snowsports	50
Racket sports	50
Sports footwear: main product sectors	
General sports/leisure design	240
Running shoes	150
Outdoor boots	150
Football boots/black trainers	100
Aerobics/indoor fitness	100
Racket sports	65
Golf	30
Snowsports boots	5

Source: Department of Trade and Industry (1999).

imports of £390 million, exports of £201 million, giving a deficit of £189 million. Historically a big shift occurred in the balance of payments for sports equipment in the early 1980s: prior to this there was a large but decreasing surplus, but since 1981 there has been a steadily increasing deficit.

The DTI data also indicate just how international the sports equipment market has become. Imports represent 87 per cent of UK market sales, with domestic production accounting for just 13 per cent. Moreover, 78 per cent of UK manufacturers' production is exported. The UK is the seventh largest market world-wide for sports equipment, but the characteristics of the largest markets (typically advanced industrialised economies) are very different to the characteristics of the fastest growing markets (typically emerging economies such as India, China, Hungary, and the Philippines).

Table 8.2 gives the size of the various market segments in the sports equipment, sports clothing and sports footwear markets, the core sectors of the sports

Table 8.3 Leading suppliers of sports clothing and footwear

Company/brand	Type of Equipment/products	Sales (£m)	Year
Reebok UK	Athletics, aerobics, football, running, leisure	144.6	1996
Nike (UK)	Athletics, football, running, leisure	240	1996
Adidas (UK)	Athletics, football, tennis, rugby, gym, leisure	212.5	1996
Pentland Group: total		755.2	1997
Speedo	Swimwear	44.7	1997
Berghaus	Outdoor clothing, footwear and equipment	26.7	1997
Mitre Sports	Football and rugby boots, balls	16.1	1997
Ellesse Sports	Fashion clothing	86.1	1997
Umbro (UK)	Football, replica kits	123.4	1996
Pringle of Scotland	Golf brand owned by Dawson International	50.6	1996–7
Hi-Tec Sports	General trainers, racket sports, hiking, leisure	89.9	1997–8
Mizuno (UK)	Tennis, golf, football	23.2	1996
Fred Perry Sportswear	Tennis	20.1	1996–7
WL Gore Associates	Outdoor fabrics and garments	68.7	1996–7
Cainpari International	Outdoor, skiing	38.8	1995
J Barbour & Sons	Outdoor	43.8	1996–7
Fila (by Dashrace)	Tennis, women's fitness, fashion	40.5	1997

Source: Department of Trade and Industry (1999).

industry. Table 8.2 shows an interesting relationship with Table 5.3, which shows the levels of participation in various sport and recreation activities. Walking, by far the largest activity, is the activity generating the largest sector in the sports clothing market, but is a small part of the equipment market and joint second in the sports footwear market. The largest sector of the sports equipment market is golf, even though the 4-week participation rate in golf is only 5 per cent, about the same level as football. Golf equipment accounts for 18 times more expenditure than football. Similarly, skiing, with a participation rate of only 0.3%, appears prominently in equipment, clothing, and footwear markets because of the relatively high price of items related to skiing.

Table 8.3 lists the major companies supplying sports clothing and footwear. It is interesting to note that although the three global market leaders, Nike, Adidas, and Reebok, appear at the top of the table, another company, Pentland Group, has a higher turnover than all three together in the UK when we add the turnover of all its brands, although any one of its brands (such as Speedo or Mitre) has a relatively small turnover compared to Nike or Adidas.

Table 8.4 gives the leading suppliers of sports equipment to the British market. It is dominated by golf, racket sports, and fishing equipment suppliers, showing the relative importance of equipment costs in these three areas of sport compared with the low cost of equipment in the high-participation sports of walking and swimming.

Table 8.4 Leading suppliers of sports equipment

Company/brand	Type of equipment/products	Sales (£m)	Year
Dunlop Slazenger International Ltd	Golf, tennis, squash, badminton	108	1996
Wilson Sporting Goods Co. Ltd	Golf, rackets sports, basketball	42.8	1996
Accent Ltd	Golf	51.1	1997
Burghers Ltd	Camping and hiking (boots, fleeces)	26.7	1997
Grampian Holdings plc	Golf, clothing	244.3	1997–8
Mitre Sports International Ltd	Football and rugby balls and boots	18.9	1995
Daiwa Sports Ltd	Fishing tackle	10.1	1996–7
Spading Sports UK Ltd	Golf, tennis	15.6	1995–6
Christen (UK) Ltd	Golf (Ping brand)	15.1	1996
Leeda Ltd	Fishing tackle	14.8	1996–7
Lowe Alpine	Clothing, rucksacks	18.4	1996–7

Source: Department of Trade and Industry (1999).

Table 8.5 Sports goods market: channels of retail distribution, 1996

	Clothing		Footwear		Equipment		Total	
	£m	%	£m	%	£m	%	£m	%
All sports shops	678	57.8	461	52.6	230	35.4	1,369	50.7
Multiples	416	35.5	291	33.2	79	12.2	786	29.1
Independents	262	22.3	170	19.4	151	23.2	583	21.6
Home shopping	115	9.8	91	10.4	96	14.8	302	11.2
Clothing stores	182	15.5	14	1.6	–	–	196	7.2
Club shops	65	5.5	50	5.7	135	20.8	250	9.2
Department stores	76	6.5	59	6.7	34	5.2	169	6.3
Shoe stores	–	–	190	21.6	–	–	190	7.0
Mixed goods stores	53	4.5	7	0.8	120	18.4	180	6.7
Others	5	0.4	5	0.6	35	5.4	45	1.7
Total	1,174	1000.0	877	100.0	650	100.0	2,701	100.0

Source: Department of Trade and Industry (1999).

Table 8.5 gives the channels of retail distribution in 1996. It shows that only 50 per cent of retail sales goes through specialist sports retailers. This figure rises to 57 per cent for sports clothing but, perhaps surprisingly, drops to 35 per cent for sports equipment.

In the descriptive information above we have pointed out the lack of correspondence between sports participation statistics and major sectors of the equipment market in particular. There are specific economic reasons for this lack of correspondence, which we now investigate.

Sports goods and the accelerator effect

There is a potential source of instability and volatility in the sports goods market that is due to the fact that sports goods are durable consumption goods. The easiest way to illustrate this problem is by use of the economic theory of investment, which explains the quality of new capital goods a firm requires to produce its desired output. Just as a firm invests in capital equipment so as to yield a rate of return in the production process over time, households and individuals 'invest' in a range of sports equipment that can be used in the household 'production' of sporting activities. The investment model we use is the simple accelerator model.

The accelerator theory of investment, at its simplest level, is represented by

$$K = aO$$

where K is changes in capital stock (i.e. investment), O is the change in output (i.e. parent demand), and a is the accelerator coefficient (= capital/output ratio).

For our purposes, capital is sports equipment for an activity and output is the number of participants in an activity. a is the ratio of equipment to participants, i.e. the average value of equipment per participant. We can estimate such average prices by dividing the domestic market's equipment expenditure (i.e. domestic production minus exports plus imports) by the number of participants for any sport. A certain amount of investment in sports equipment is necessary to cover depreciation, so we have to make an assumption about the average length of life of sports equipment in any activity investigated.

To illustrate the accelerator effect, Table 8.6 and Figure 8.2 take three sports: squash, fishing and table tennis. We assume the following.

1   Squash and fishing have the same annual equipment costs to participants (£20), while table tennis costs only £5.
2   Fishing and table tennis equipment depreciates constantly over a 10-year period, after which it is replaced. Squash equipment depreciates faster and needs to be replaced after five years.
3   Each sport has four successive annual changes in participant numbers of 10%, 0%, 5%, 10%.

The accelerating effect of changes in participation on changes in equipment demand is clear to see. What appears to be the significant factor is not the price of equipment – Figure 8.2(b) and (c) have different prices – but the rate of depreciation of equipment. Where this depreciation differs, as in Figure 8.2(a) and (b), a different accelerator effect emerges. The longer the depreciation period (i.e. the slower the depreciation), the larger will be the accelerator effect.

So far we have talked in terms of depreciation as wear and tear of equipment. In sports equipment demand there will also be an element of 'relative depreciation' regardless of the physical state of the existing stock of equipment. This relative depreciation will be brought about by technological changes in equipment

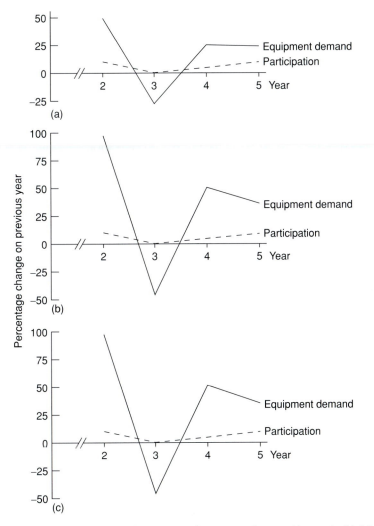

Figure 8.2 Illustration of the sports equipment accelerator: (a) squash; (b) fishing; (c) table
tennis.

construction, or by fashion changes in design which encourage sports participants to replace equipment before it is physically necessary to do so. It is in the
interests of sports equipment manufacturers to encourage such relative depreciation when their products have long depreciation periods. In fishing, for example,
fibreglass rods would often last a lifetime, but were superseded technically, first
by carbon fibre rods and then by boron rods, so that the fibreglass rods are
replaced sooner than is necessary. Similarly, ski equipment has undergone several important changes in design in recent years.

Table 8.6 The accelerator effect on sports equipment demand: an illustration

	Participants		Equipment stock (£m)	Desired equipment stock (£m)	Depreciation (£m)	Annual equipment demand* (£m)	% change
	Millions	% change					
Squash							
Year 1	1		20	20	4	4	
Year 2	1.1	10	20	22	4	6	50
Year 3	1.1	0	22	22	4.4	4.4	−27
Year 4	1.155	5	22	23.1	4.4	5.5	25
Year 5	1.2655	10	23.1	25.31	4.62	6.83	24
Fishing							
Year 1	1		20	20	2	2	
Year 2	1.1	10	20	22	2	4	100
Year 3	1.1	0	22	22	2.2	2.2	−45
Year 4	1.155	5	22	23.1	2.2	3.3	50
Year 5	1.2655	10	23.1	25.31	2.31	4.52	37
Table Tennis							
Year 1	1		5	5	0.5	0.5	
Year 2	1.1	10	5	5.5	0.5	1	100
Year 3	1.1	0	5.5	0.55	0.55	0.55	−45
Year 4	1.155	5	5.5	5.5	0.55	0.83	51
Year 5	1.2655	10	5.78	6.33	0.578	1.13	36

* Annual equipment demand = depreciation plus desired equipment stock minus equipment stock.

Thus we see that there are two ways for an equipment manufacturer to expand, and to reduce the volatility of its market: either by action to shorten the perceived length of life of sports equipment or by encouraging new participants. Although we have used the example of equipment here, in many ways the same applies to both sports clothing and footwear. In both cases, new materials create new products that make earlier versions obsolete even if not worn out. However, more important here is the role of fashion, where products become obsolete though being overtaken by new, more fashionable items. Such demand behaviour will reduce the 'depreciation' period and therefore reduce the volatility of demand changes in response to changes in the numbers participating. This means that replacement demand rises as a proportion of total demand; otherwise too much dependence on new participants' demand would increase the accelerator effect.

The major companies operating in these markets spend huge sums on marketing in order to promote their products globally. These companies have developed global brands partly as a way of expanding their customer base but also as a means to reduce the depreciation period on their products by constantly creating new ones that become more fashionable.

Global brands

One of the characteristics of the sports industry of recent years has been the development of the global sports business. There are two aspects to this globalisation of the sports industry: the setting up of global production and distribution networks, and the marketing of global brands through the association of the brand with major athletes and events. The company that has demonstrated this more than any other is Nike. In 1996 Nike became the 167th largest company in the world, moving up 175 places in the *Financial Times* league table of the Global 500 companies. We use Nike as a case-study of the archetypal global sports business corporation. We concentrate here on Nike's production and marketing strategies. Its sponsorship activities will be considered in more detail in the next chapter.

Nike: a case-study in the globalisation of the sports industry

Nike dominates the world sports shoe industry, an industry that has shown phenomenal growth over the past twenty years. Total sales of sports shoes worldwide were estimated at over $20 billion in 1997, and Nike accounts for 33 per cent of this.

Nike started out as a company called Blue Ribbon Sports, based in Oregon, USA, and distributing running shoes produced by a Japanese company, Onitsuka Sports. By the early 1970s the company had severed ties with Onitsuka and was designing, marketing, and distributing its own running shoes. In 1978 Blue Ribbon Sports changed its name to Nike. The company very quickly established itself in the lead in one of the fastest growing leisure markets in the world. Although Nike produces other sportswear, sports shoes are its main area of activity and two-thirds of the company's turnover comes from shoes.

There is some literature relating to the global production, distribution, and marketing approach of Nike (Clifford, 1992; Willigan, 1992). What is perhaps surprising is that Nike is not a manufacturing company at all. All manufacturing is done by contractors, 99 per cent of them in Asia. Clifford (1992) described how Nike keeps the cost of production down by constantly seeking out lowest cost producers:

> The company is forever on the lookout for cheap production sites. If costs in a particular country or factory move too far out of line, productivity will have to rise to compensate, or Nike will take its business elsewhere. The firm uses about 40 factories; 20 have closed in the past five years or so and another 35 have opened.

This tremendous dynamism and flexibility in the organisation of production is illustrated by Nike's response to soaring labour costs in South Korea in the late 1980s. In 1988, 68 per cent of Nike's shoes were produced in South Korea. By 1992, this percentage had fallen to 42 per cent (Clifford, 1992). Over this period

Nike switched an increasing proportion of production to contractors in the cheaper labour cost countries of China, Indonesia, and Thailand. In 1988, these countries accounted for less than 10 per cent of Nike's production. By 1992, this had increased to 44 per cent.

Not only is Nike able to move production rapidly in search of lower and lower costs, it is also able to alter its global distribution network in response to world events. Clifford (1992) reports that Nike was faced by a potentially dangerous commercial threat in September/October 1992. After Nike had moved much of the production of sports shoes to China, the US government became involved in a dispute with China over demands to open up the Chinese markets to American goods. The USA threatened to impose punitive tariffs on Chinese goods unless agreement was reached by 10 October. In response to this threat Nike planned to switch most of the output from Chinese factories to Europe. It also made an agreement with its Chinese suppliers that any loss resulting from any remaining shoes entering the US market would be split equally between Nike and the Chinese suppliers. In the end the dispute was resolved and no action was needed.

Willigan (1992) emphasised how Nike markets its products globally. One of Nike's major characteristics in marketing is the association of the product with the athlete: Michael Jordan with Air Jordan, the basketball shoe; John McEnroe, Andre Agassi, and Pete Sampras with tennis shoes and clothing. This association is an ideal way of marketing to a global market. The global media coverage of major sports events allows Nike to establish a global marketplace for its products as this quote from Ian Hamilton, Nike's tennis marketing director, illustrates:

> When I started at Nike tennis, John McEnroe was the most visible player in the world, and he was already part of the Nike Family. He epitomised the type of player Nike wanted in its shoes – talented, dedicated, and loud. He broke racquets, drew fines, and, most of all, won matches. His success and behaviour drew attention on and off the court and put a lot of people in Nikes.

A quote from Phil Knight stresses the importance of the association of the product with the athlete:

> The trick is to get athletes who not only can win but can stir up emotion. We want someone the public is going to love or hate, not just the leading scorer. . . . To create a lasting emotional tie with consumers, we use the athletes repeatedly throughout their careers and present them as whole people.

Thus as John McEnroe got older and Andre Agassi replaced him as the fiery newcomer, Agassi became the promoter of Challenge Court, the exciting and colourful tennis range, while John McEnroe launched a new, more subdued range, Supreme Court.

This policy of breaking down each individual sport into smaller and smaller sub-markets is another major characteristic of Nike's marketing approach. Twenty

Table 8.7 The cost structure of Nike's 'Air Pegasus' sport shoe, 1995

	$	%
Production costs	17.75	
Suppliers' profits	1.75	29
Shipping	0.50	
Cost to Nike	20.00	
Research and development	0.25	
Promotion, advertising	4.00	
Sales, distribution, administration	5.00	22
Nike profit	6.25	
Cost to retailer	35.50	
Retailers' costs	25.50	
Retailers' profits	9.00	49
Cost to consumer	70.00	

Source: *Washington Post* (1995).

years ago there was only one type of basketball shoe on the market and very few specialist running shoes. A trainer was an all-purpose sports shoe catering to a wide variety of sporting activities. Now there are different shoes and equipment for every sport. The Air Jordan basketball shoe was a concerted effort by Nike to create a completely new market for basketball shoes. It succeeded, and later Nike further segmented the market with two other basketball ranges, Flight and Force.

In the mid-1980s, Nike was losing out to Reebok, which was then the domin-ant force in the sport-shoe market. In 1987, Reebok had a 30 per cent market share of the US sports footwear market compared to Nike's 18 per cent. Nike's aggressive global marketing alongside its massive expenditure on athletes' endorse-ment contracts projected Nike way ahead of Reebok. By 1996, Nike had a 43 per cent share of the US footwear market while Reebok's share had dropped to 16 per cent. In the 1996–1997 financial year alone, Nike increased its global revenue by 42 per cent to $9.2 billion.

Nike spends around $1 billion annually on marketing and athlete endorse-ment contracts, compared with a spend of around $400 million by Reebok. In January 1998, Reebok announced that it would no longer attempt to compete head-on with Nike, largely because it could not match this massive investment in marketing its brand. Although Nike won the 'trainer wars' battle with Reebok, while it was going on, Adidas expanded in 1997 to become the second largest sports company in the world with global sales of over $5 billion spread across sports shoes, clothing, and equipment. Adidas has followed Nike in moving most of its manufacturing to Asia and aggressively marketing its brand with global advertising and athlete endorsement contracts.

Nike has demonstrated that, in a mature, post-industrial economy, design, marketing, and retailing can be more important for the sports economy than manufacturing. Table 8.7 demonstrates this for one of Nike's products.

Retailing constitutes 49 per cent of the total price of the shoe, while manufacturing is 29 per cent. Nike can look around globally for the cheapest manufacturing sites, and has shifted production three times, in Asia, in the past 20 years. However, retailing has to be conducted in the main markets, where costs are less negotiable, and margins are much higher.

This Nike case-study demonstrates not only the globalisation of the sports industry, but also the interrelationship between different elements of the commercial sector in sport. Nike is predominantly a sports design and marketing company. However, it has achieved its phenomenal success by using major sports events, and the global television audience for such events, as a major element in its marketing strategy. The company is also a major world-wide sponsor of professional team sports. The name of Nike will therefore also appear prominently in the four chapters of the next part, which deal with other commercial sports markets: sports sponsorship, major sports events, professional team sports, and sports broadcasting. However, before we move on to these markets, there is a need to consider the interrelationship between the three sectors on the supply side of the sports market.

The interrelationship between the government, voluntary and commercial sectors in sport

In this chapter and the previous two chapters, we have been examining the different roles that the commercial sector, government and the voluntary sector play on the supply side of the sports market. In this chapter we have defined the 'sports industry' as the commercial sector supplying sports goods and sports services. However, it is not always so easy in practice to put clear divisions between the commercial sector and the government and voluntary sectors. All three sectors are normally involved in the supply of sporting opportunities, and often we see direct competition between one sector and another. For instance, commercial health and fitness clubs may be in direct competition with similar facilities in a public sector leisure centre, or a voluntary sector sports club.

Gratton and Taylor (1991) showed that the commercial sector dominated expenditure on sporting excellence through expenditures on sports sponsorship and professional team sports (see Chapters 9 and 11). On the other hand, the market for mass participation sport gave a large role for the voluntary and government sectors. Since that study, we have seen more government resources devoted to excellence and more commercial market activity in the mass participation sector. Also, the voluntary sector has seen more of its economic activity taking place in the formal market economy, as paid labour time has replaced volunteer labour and as some voluntary sector clubs have become commercial operations (e.g. in rugby union).

In this section we investigate whether economics can help to explain why the supply of sports outputs is split between the different sectors in this way. Weisbrod (1978) provides a set of hypotheses that might be the first stage of an explanation. First of all he divides all outputs into three types: collective consumption goods, private good substitutes for collective goods, and pure private goods. Normally we expect to see government providing collective goods. However, Weisbrod argues that:

> the expectation is that supplementation of public sector provision (that is, financing) of any good, will either be overwhelmingly in the voluntary sector or overwhelmingly in the private, for-profit sector, depending on whether the publicly provided good is primarily a collective or an individual-type of good. In addition to the extent of 'collectiveness' of the govermentally financed good, the relative size of the voluntary and private sectors in an industry will depend on the state of technology – specifically on the degree of similarity between collective goods and their private-good substitutes, and on the relative production costs.

The first element in the argument, then, is that consumers first look to the public sector for the provision of collective goods. However, consumers are likely to be dissatisfied with the level of government provision for any particular collective good. As a result they look for additional output in the voluntary sector and the commercial sector. The quote above suggests that the more collective the good, the more likely it is to be provided in the voluntary sector. The more private the good, the more likely it is that the commercial sector will provide the additional output demanded. However, relative production costs in the two sectors are also an important influence.

The second stage in Weisbrod's argument relates to the nature of demand, in particular the heterogeneity of demand. The smaller the heterogeneity, the more likely it is that government will provide the major share of output. The greater the heterogeneity of demand, then the larger the share of total output provided by the voluntary and commercial sectors jointly. The reason for this is that government output is determined on the basis of a simple majority vote model. If consumers for a particular collective good are not big enough as a group to be an important influence on the voting process, they are unlikely to see government provision of the good.

The third element in Weisbrod's argument is what he calls his 'income hypothesis'. He argues that from the consumer's point of view there is likely to be an important disadvantage with the collective good compared with a private good substitute for it: the consumer will have a lower degree of individual control over its form, type of availability, and times of availability. He uses the example of a lighthouse, indicating that a particular lighthouse cannot be located differently for different users, nor turned on and off at different times to satisfy conflicting preferences. If we add to this a heterogeneity of demand for collective goods, then we are likely to see various aspects of demand undersatisfied. Private market substitutes will cater more to specific consumer demands. Since the degree of individual control desired by the consumer is likely to be positively related to income, the commercial supplier is likely to 'skim' the market and cater to the demands of the higher income consumer. The consumer who turns to the private-market option will expect to pay a higher charge, and in return will get a product closer to his or her individual demands. He or she is also likely to choose a form of the good that maximises his or her personal benefits, and probably minimises external benefits.

If we now turn to the sports market we can analyse to what extent Weisbrod's arguments are consistent with the evidence. In the market for participation, we have noted the dominance of provision by the public and voluntary sectors. And yet we have also noted that the nature of the product provided is more an individual-type good rather than a collective-type good. The benefits provided by public sector sports centres and swimming pools, and voluntary sector, participation sports clubs are neither non-rival nor non-excludable. The good provided is essentially a private good, although social benefits are provided through the generation of health benefits to participants and possibly in the reduction in crime and vandalism as discussed in Chapter 6. According to Weisbrod's first hypothesis, therefore, we would expect undersatisfied demand to be met by the commercial sector rather than the voluntary sector.

This is certainly the case for individual sports activities provided, for instance, by health and fitness clubs. The rapid rise in the commercial provision of such facilities in the 1990s has made this the single largest growth sector of commercial sport.

However, in team sports in particular, and in other competitive sports, the voluntary rather than the commercial sector is clearly the most important supplier. The reason for this lies in the 'relative production costs' of the two sectors. The voluntary sector, as indicated earlier, has the benefit of labour services provided at zero cost, and the commercial sector cannot compete with this. In fact, there is more to it than that. For many, volunteerism is part of the product. That is to say, many people who offer their services free within the voluntary sector actually receive utility from their contribution to voluntary sector output. If, for example, we take an amateur football club we can see that there will be many tasks to be done to organise a match on a Saturday afternoon. A group of people will pick the team, contact the players, organise the fixtures and the referees, make certain the kit is washed, provide refreshments after the game, etc. Some of this will be done by the players, but much will be done by non-players. Many of these non-players receive positive enjoyment from this voluntary activity. Their interest in the sport is fed through the positive involvement in its organisation. And so all these labour services are provided free of charge and are even regarded as a consumption rather than work by those providing them. Under such circumstances it is not surprising to see that the commercial sector cannot compete.

However, this picture of the voluntary sector may be a little old-fashioned. As we indicated in Chapter 7, time pressure has reduced the supply of sports volunteers and there is evidence to indicate that it is becoming more and more difficult to recruit younger volunteers. Many of the activities formerly provided by volunteer labour in sports clubs (running the bar, providing refreshments, cleaning, etc.) is increasingly being done by paid labour. The higher we move up the sports hierarchy, the greater is the level of market activity in the voluntary sector. Although the voluntary sector still possesses a relative production cost advantage over the commercial sector, this advantage is narrowing.

Weisbrod's second hypothesis indicates that the greater the heterogeneity of demand, the greater is the share of total output provided by the voluntary and commercial sectors. Chapter 5 clearly demonstrates that demand for sport is heterogeneous, with many sports involving only a small minority of the population.

It is not surprising that most of the demand for these minority sports is provided by the voluntary and commercial sectors. Sporting activities with a demand across a wider range of the population (e.g. indoor swimming), or at least certain age groups within the population (e.g. team sports for younger age groups), see more involvement by the government sector.

The third element of Weisbrod's hypothesis is that the commercial sector will 'skim' the market and provide more to the higher income consumer. If we look at the pattern of commercial provision for sport, this aspect can be identified. Golf is a sport that attracts high-income consumers, and we see commercial provision of golf courses and driving ranges. Similarly, the commercial sector provides exclusive health and fitness facilities with a greater range of customer services than would normally be seen in a voluntary or public sector club (and charges a much higher price as a result).

Thus we can see that all three elements of Weisbrod's argument can be identified in the market for sports participation services, and his analysis is useful in explaining the relative shares of each of the three sectors in the market. However, we have also seen that the situation is changing rapidly and the lines of demarcation between the three sectors are becoming blurred. We illustrate this by describing one specific problem that has arisen from this blurring in the United States.

Crompton (1998a) has suggested that in recent years it has become increasingly difficult to distinguish separate roles for the public sector and the commercial sector in the supply of sport and recreation opportunities. He identifies the reasons for the emergence of the problem:

> Three factors have contributed to blurring these sector boundaries. First, a host of new activities have emerged such as aerobics, mountain biking, power walking, in-line skating, skate-boarding, street hockey, jet skis, beach volleyball, cardiovascular machines and so on. These were not offered two decades ago by either sector. Since there was no established supplier tradition for these activities, response in some areas to the new demand came from the public sector while in others it was the private sector that supplied these services.
>
> A second factor is the reduced availability of public funds. . . . Agencies have responded by raising the prices of their existing services and by broadening their range of offerings by expanding into revenue-generating activities that were previously considered the exclusive preserve of private operators. The need to generate revenue was sufficiently central to the survival of some agencies, that it superseded any philosophical position they may have held with regard to avoiding competition with the private sector.

The third factor encouraging sector overlap is a corollary of the higher prices most agencies now charge for services. . . . When the prices of public recreation services were raised, the private sector was more able to offer a competitive programme because there was now a greater opportunity for generating a satisfactory return on the investment.

Crompton offers several different case studies where charges of unfair competition are made by the commercial sector provider against the government agency. These charges are based on the argument that competition is unfair because public sector agencies have lower cost, since they pay no property, sales or income taxes and they can invest in facilities without incurring commercial rates of borrowing for investment funds.

In Britain, the closest parallel we have to the situation described by Crompton is the competition between public sector leisure centres and commercial health and fitness clubs. As we saw in Chapter 5, the fastest rate of growth in participation over the past decade has been in fitness training and aerobics. Public sector facilities have responded to this change in demand by converting facilities with falling demand, such as squash courts, into fitness suites. The sports hall of a public sector facility is used more for aerobics classes than was the case ten years ago. Any new facilities constructed will closely resemble the facilities of commercial sector health clubs such as David Lloyd Centres or Esporta.

Crompton goes on to describe how the unfair competition charge has also been extended beyond the public sector against voluntary sector, or non-profit, organisations such as the YMCAs. Again, the problem has arisen as YMCAs have upgraded the quality of their facilities largely in response to the demands of members so that the sports facilities provided resemble those of a commercial health club. In Britain, many voluntary sector sports clubs are receiving substantial grants from the Sports Lottery Fund to do the same thing.

This problem of unfair competition raised in Crompton's article is largely caused by the failure of the publicly subsidised sector of sports provision to extend access to sport beyond the relatively affluent. It is still the case that sports subsidies predominantly benefit the better-off. As both the public and voluntary sectors have become more customer-oriented over the past decade, it is not surprising that the three sectors are producing facilities very similar to each other since all three sectors are competing for the same group of consumers: relatively affluent people in the rapidly expanding markets of health and fitness. It is these same consumers that have been generating profits for Nike, Adidas, and Reebok. There would be less of a problem if the government sector had been more successful in achieving its equity objective in sport, with more of the sports subsidies being received by the poorer sections of society.

Conclusions

Historically, sport was led by the voluntary sector. In the 1960s and 1970s, certainly in Western Europe, government took a much larger role, increasing public subsidies for sport and developing policy aimed at increasing participation and improving quality at the élite level. Since the beginning of the 1980s, however, the commercial sector of sport has shown the fastest rate of growth so that it is now the dominant economic sector in sport. In this chapter we have concentrated on the core element of the commercial sports business – the sports goods sector consisting of clothing, footwear, and equipment – and the delivery of sports services in commercial health and fitness clubs. However, in the 1990s, the most dynamic sectors of the commercial sector in sport were sports sponsorship, major sports events, professional team sports, and sports broadcasting, so much so that each warrants a chapter of its own in the next part.

Part IV

Contemporary issues in the economics of sport

9 Sports sponsorship

Introduction

Sports sponsorship hardly existed as an economic activity before 1970 in Britain, yet by 1999 it was estimated to be worth £350 million. Globally, sports sponsorship is a massive industry estimated to be worth around $20 billion in 1999, having grown in value by over 300 per cent in the 1990s alone. Sports sponsorship is the dominant form of sponsorship, accounting for over two-thirds of all sponsorship activity.

The economic viability of any major sports event is normally crucially dependent on the ability of the event organisers to raise substantial revenue through sponsorship. Every major professional sports team now raises a substantial share of its revenue from sponsorship. Sponsorship is pervasive throughout sport, not only at the narrow élite part of the sports hierarchy. Many amateur teams receive sponsorship. It is this pervasiveness that makes it difficult to measure accurately the true value of sponsorship. The problem is compounded by the unwillingness of many commercial companies to divulge the amount they spend on sports sponsorship.

Despite these problems, sport sponsorship has become important enough to attract the attention of both academics and business analysts, so that sufficient material is available in the public domain to illuminate the major issues in the economics of sports sponsorship.

What is sponsorship?

The Howell Report (CCPR, 1983) defined sports sponsorship as 'the support of a sport, sports event, sports organization or competition by an outside body or person for the mutual benefit of both parties'. The conclusion of the report was that 'the sponsorship of sport provides a service to the whole of sport and to the community which sport serves; in this respect therefore it also serves the public interest'.

Simkins (1980) picks out three characteristics of sponsorship:

- the sponsor makes a contribution, in cash or in kind, to the sport
- the sponsored activity is not part of the main commercial operations of the company

- the sponsor expects a return in terms of publicity which does not reflect adversely on the sponsor.

Kolah's (1999) definition of sponsorship is as follows.

> The term sponsorship describes an investment in cash or in kind activity, in return for access to the exploitable commercial potential associated with that activity.
>
> Sports sponsorship is generally of an event, a league, a governing body, a particular team or individual, or the broadcast of an event. Those capable of being sponsored are, in marketing terms, commonly referred to as 'properties'.

Sponsorship is a very varied activity. We tend to regard it as a relatively new phenomenon, yet there are examples in cricket going back over 120 years. The Howell Report catalogues the case of Spiers and Pond, an Australian catering firm, which sponsored the first England tour of Australia in 1861–1862 and made a profit of £11,000 from the deal.

However, there is no doubt that sports sponsorship has grown rapidly in the last decades of the twentieth century, both in absolute terms and in the breadth of activity that sponsorship encompasses.

The growth of sports sponsorship

The Central Council of Physical Recreation (CCPR) set up a Committee of Enquiry into Sports Sponsorship in 1981 with Dennis Howell, the former Minister of Sport, as Chairman. The reason for the setting-up of this committee was that:

> the CCPR decided that the issues were now so complicated and the reliance of sport upon sponsorship so complete that a major enquiry should be undertaken to analyse the situation and set a course for the future.
>
> (CCPR, 1983)

One of the first things this committee did was to make a concerted effort to establish accurate estimates of the level of sports sponsorship at that time and to chart its growth from the early 1970s. However, they encountered serious problems in this, mainly due to the fact that neither governing bodies of sport nor the sponsors themselves were willing to reveal the size of the financial commitment. The result of their efforts is reproduced in Figure 9.1, and Table 9.1 shows the sources of these estimates. Figure 9.1 shows a steady growth in money and real terms. However, such estimates are subject to a wide degree of error, as the alternative estimates for 1973 and 1981 indicate. Also, the 1981B, 1982 and 1983 figures include both 'visible' and 'invisible' expenditure, whereas the earlier estimates relate only to visible expenditure (although Head's 1981 adjustment (Head, 1982) for 'invisibles' is different from that of the Howell Enquiry).

£ million at current prices

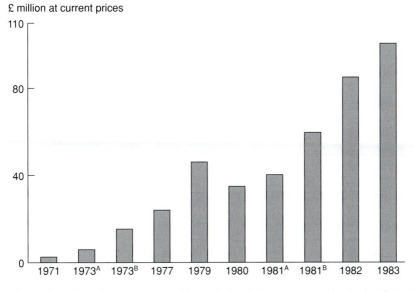

Figure 9.1 Estimated sports sponsorship 1971–1983 (alternative estimates are shown for 1973 and 1983).

Source: See Table 9.1

Table 9.1 Sources of sports sponsorship estimates in Figure 9.1

Year	Value of sports sponsorship (£ million, current prices)	Source of information
1971	2.5	Sports Council
1973[A]	6.0	System Communication
1973[B]	15.0	Economist Intelligence Unit
1977	24.0	Economist Intelligence Unit
1979	46.0	Economist Intelligence Unit
1980	35.0	Sports Council
1981[A]	40.0	Compton Report
1981[B]	60.0	Victor Head
1982	84.7	Howell Enquiry
1983	100.2	Howell Enquiry

Source: CCPR (1983).

'Visible' sponsorship is cash support openly revealed by the sponsors, but there are good reasons to expect this to be an understatement of the true amount of resources involved. Many sponsorship deals will never be revealed in statistics because they are at local or regional level and involve sponsorship arrangements between relatively small firms and small local sports organisations. The CCPR tried to find out through a questionnaire how important these local expenditures were, and estimated that they could account for up to 25–27 per cent of the national total. Thus, the values in Figure 9.1 and Table 9.1 would all be adjusted to this extent by the invisible aspect of sponsorship expenditure.

Probably the main reason why the 'visible' figure is such an underestimate, however, is that firms have to devote much more resources to the sport than is actually revealed in money expenditure figures. Often a large proportion of time and resources of the promotion and marketing departments of companies is taken up with sponsorship arrangements. Also, there are expenses associated with printing, publicity and entertainment in addition to the agreed sponsorship support.

In the period since the Howell Report, it has not become any easier to obtain accurate estimates of the total size and value of sports sponsorship in Britain. What is clear is that it has grown much faster than the economy as a whole between 1983 and 1999, fuelled by massive increases in the sponsorship of football following the turn around in the fortunes of professional football in Britain in the 1990s (see Chapter 11), and by large increases in the sponsorship of major sports events (see Chapter 10). Kolah (1999) indicates:

> Current estimates value sports sponsorship in Britain at £350 million in contract fees. The ISS (Institute of Sports Sponsorship) estimates that the overall worth of the market, including exploitation and other ancillary expenditure, is in the region of £1 billion.
>
> By 2002, sports sponsorship expenditure, valued by conventional rights fees is expected to be £500 million. Using the ISS calculation, this will give the market a total worth of £1.5 billion.

This quote suggests that the proportion of total sponsorship that is 'invisible' has increased tremendously since the early 1980s so that it is now double the 'visible' amount.

However, it is less relevant in the late 1990s to talk about sports sponsorship in any specific country. Increasingly it is appropriate to talk about the global market. A small but growing part of every country's sport market is international or global. Sporting competitions of truly global dimensions already exist: over two-thirds of the world's population (over 3.5 billion people) watched some part of the global television coverage of the 1996 Atlanta Olympic Games. The 1998 soccer World Cup in France attracted a cumulative global television audience of over 40 billion. Equally there are commercial companies that produce, distribute, and market their product on a global basis.

These sports mega events, the Olympics and the soccer World Cup, are ideal 'properties' for such companies to market their products to a global audience. The amounts global companies spend on their sponsorship of such events is huge. Euro 96 proved that the European Championship in soccer has joined the small number of global sports events. It is the second major international soccer tournament after the World Cup and attracts a world-wide television audience, with 445 million people watching the final of Euro 96 across 192 countries. Sponsorship Research International (SRI) estimated the cumulative television audience at 6.7 billion, with an average of 216 million for each of the 31 matches.

The Union of European Football Associations (UEFA), the governing body responsible for Euro 96, subcontracted the sponsorship contracting to ISL. There were eleven official sponsors (Carlsberg, Canon, Coca-Cola, Fuji, General Motors (Vauxhall), JVC, McDonald's, MasterCard, Philips, Snickers, and Umbro), which each paid £3.5 million. It is interesting to note that though this was a European Championship held in England, only one of these sponsors had its headquarters in England, with three in the rest of Europe, four in the USA, and three in Japan. Kolah (1999) describes the marketing programmes arranged around this sponsorship:

> The official sponsors all developed extensive marketing programs to support their individual Euro 96 sponsorships, with record levels of football-inspired promotional activity in showrooms, supermarkets, and stores in Europe. Promotional activities included above the line advertising, competitions offering the chance to win sponsors' products and match tickets, road shows and welcome centres at airports and railway stations in the eight host cities. As a result, sales increased, trade relationships were enhanced and new business contacts opened up.
>
> In addition, for the first time ever, a group of major international companies – the 11 Official Sponsors of Euro 96 – were featured together in the same TV commercial which appeared in British cinemas and on ITV and Eurosport. Entrenched brand strategies would normally make it impossible to create such an advertisement but these took a back seat for the sake of one common interest that brought the 11 together – namely football.

Research carried out by BMRB showed that Coca-Cola achieved the highest awareness score of any of the sponsors, followed by McDonald's. However, the same research showed that Nike came seventh in the awareness ratings, well ahead of many of the official sponsors, even though it did not sponsor any of the activities of Euro 96. It did, however, spend huge sums in television advertising and also embarked on a massive poster campaign.

A few weeks after Euro 96 ended, the Atlanta Olympics began. Sponsorship revenue has become the single most important source of revenue for the Olympics. There are three levels of sponsorship: the Olympic Programme (TOP), which is limited to a maximum of 12 sponsors that market their product on a global basis and is managed by the IOC; host country Organising Committee sponsors, to cover the costs of organising the Olympics; and individual country sponsors, managed by national Olympic associations to cover their national team costs. The TOP programme was implemented for the first time at the 1988 Calgary Winter Olympics. At Atlanta, there were ten global companies in the TOP programme, including Coca-Cola and McDonald's which also sponsored Euro 96. The total sponsorship revenue to the IOC from the TOP programme at Atlanta was $350 million. However, Kolah (1999) estimates that Coca-Cola alone spent $365 million on its sponsorship and promotion attached to the Atlanta Olympics in 1996, over ten times the amount it gave as direct revenue to the IOC as part of its sponsorship contract.

The different tiers of sponsorship developed by the IOC for the Olympic Games have been followed by other international governing bodies for the major global sports events. In the soccer World Cup in 1998 in France, ISL again handled the sponsorship arrangements. There were twelve major sponsors: Adidas, Canon, Coca-Cola, Gillette, Fuji, JVC, McDonald's, MasterCard, Opel, Philips, Snickers, and Budweiser. Each paid around £12.5 million for the global marketing rights. There were also other sponsors of France 98, the organising committee, and for individual national teams. England, for instance, had eight team sponsors paying £1 million each. Nike and Adidas are estimated to have spent $100 million each on the World Cup in 1998, although Adidas was an official sponsor of the event but Nike was not (Kolah, 1999).

It is the escalation in the sums committed by such companies that has driven the growth in size and value of sports sponsorship globally so that world-wide sports sponsorship was approaching $20 billion as we moved into the new millennium.

Ambush marketing

A new phenomenon of the 1990s was the increasing use by companies of ambush marketing. McAuley and Sutton (1999) argue that:

> New interdependence between corporate funding and sporting events bred a new kind of sponsorship landscape, out of which the concept of 'ambush marketing' was born. Tactics described as ambush marketing have altered the view of sponsorship both positively and negatively, and have forced the development of new marketing tools. Ambush marketing has changed the face of sport and sport sponsorship.

Kolah (1999) defines ambush marketing in the following way:

> Ambush marketing is a phrase that describes the actions of companies who seek to associate themselves with a sponsored event without paying the requisite fee. The ambush consists of giving the impression (sometimes false, sometimes not) to consumers that the ambush company or brand is actually a sponsor or is somehow affiliated with the event.

Bean's (1995) definition of ambush marketing, on the other hand, suggests that it is not so much the motive of the ambush marketer to associate the company with the event as to target a competitor that is an official sponsor of the event. He defines ambush marketing as the:

> direct efforts of one company to weaken or affect a competitor's official association with a sports organisation acquired through the payment of sponsorship fees. Through advertising and promotional campaigns, the ambushing company tries to confuse consumers and to misrepresent the official sponsorship of the event.

McAuley and Sutton (1999) agree that the increasing prevalence of ambush marketing has reduced the growth in the value of sponsorship in the late 1990s, as companies such as Coca-Cola and IBM have renegotiated or ended sponsorship contracts because ambush marketing has reduced the value of the sponsorship benefits to them. They see ambush marketing as a serious threat to the funding of sports organisations through sponsorship revenue.

They identify five major different types of ambush marketing.

1   Contests or sweepstakes: a company organises a contest around the outcome of a game, or has a competition where prizes are tickets to the game.
2   Broadcast sponsorship: a company sponsors a broadcast of an event or game, which will normally cost much less than sponsoring the event itself.
3   Television commercials: a company places commercials during breaks in the broadcast of an event which in terms of content can relate the company's name by implication to the event.
4   Sponsorship of a team or athlete: individual athletes or whole teams taking part in the event may be sponsored by a particular company although the company contributes nothing to the event organisers.
5   Promotional advertising/marketing collateral: this relates to flyers and giveaways distributed at the event, posters on billboards close to event venues, or specific marketing events staged in close proximity to the major sporting event.

Many companies use several of the above tactics at a specific event. At the 1998 World Cup, Nike was not an official sponsor but did have an endorsement contract with the favourites, Brazil. Nike brought advertising slots world-wide in the breaks in the games and featured the Brazilian team in the adverts. Nike also built a football village near Paris, and the Brazilian team was featured as a major attraction of the village. The campaign was backed by a major poster campaign. Nike achieved a slightly higher awareness rating for the World Cup than Adidas, its main rival and official sponsor of the event.

Ambush marketing fits in with Nike's image of an anti-establishment, innovative, aggressive company. Its adverts and endorsements have often concentrated on the non-conformist athlete, whether in behavioural terms, such as John McEnroe, or in dress/appearance, such as Andre Agassi. To be an official sponsor to some extent is in conflict with this image. Spending as much in ambush marketing as the official sponsors do in their sponsorship contract, and then achieving greater awareness, is consistent with Nike's image of winning by unconventional routes.

However, the growth of ambush marketing poses a clear danger to those involved in staging major sports events. Although the ambush marketers spend huge sums of money around the staging of the event, none of this money is revenue to the event organisers. Although broadcast sponsorship and athlete/team sponsorship do count as sports sponsorship, the other three types of ambush marketing would count as more generic advertising expenditure, and therefore the more companies that engage in these types of activities, the less will be the total value of sports sponsorship.

It is only recently that sports organisations have woken up to the threat of ambush marketing and started to combat the tactics of ambush marketers. There is little indication at the end of the twentieth century that they will be successful.

Ambush marketing creates a further uncertainty over any estimates of the value of sports sponsorship. Much ambush marketing activity, as indicated above, is not counted as sports sponsorship so that the higher the prevalence of ambush marketing in sport, the greater the underestimate of the true value of sports sponsorship will be the estimate that comes from contract fees.

The sponsorship decision of the firm

To understand why firms sponsor sport, one starting point is to look at the economics of advertising. The initial analysis of the advertising decision assumes the firm to have the overall objective of profit maximisation. Advertising aims to move the demand curve of the product to the right, although at the same time the costs of advertising will raise overall costs. Advertising increases profits as long as the increased sales revenue more than matches the increased cost. Koutsoyiannis (1982) indicates that such profit-maximising behaviour by a firm is not inconsistent with a simple rule of thumb that sets advertising expenditure as a constant proportion of revenue.

This rather simplistic view of advertising yields the direct conclusion that 'successful' advertising leads to increased sales. It is also relatively easy to test, since 'unsuccessful' firms will cease to advertise and hence we should find a strong positive relationship between advertising expenditure and the rate of growth of sales.

Many studies have attempted to estimate the effect of advertising on sales, but few have established any relationship at all. Koutsoyiannis (1982), reviewing all the empirical studies on the advertising–sales relationship, concludes that 'the effects of advertising on buyers have not been theoretically or empirically established in a satisfactory way'.

This economic research has indicated that one of the greatest problems with the advertising decision of the firm is the uncertainty associated with the return from this expenditure. This may explain why rules of thumb such as setting a constant advertising–sales ratio are the order of the day, with firms adjusting advertising expenditure to changes in revenue rather than revenue reacting to changes in advertising expenditure.

This risk or uncertainty associated with the advertising decision is compounded by the view of some economists that advertising should be treated as an investment, because it yields returns over a period of time. They argue that advertising is the main means by which a firm builds its name and goodwill over time. The longer the period of time over which the revenue stream is affected, the greater will be the risk and uncertainty associated with the advertising decision. Also this view indicates that the return to advertising involves immeasurable variables such as 'name and goodwill'.

Sponsorship can be viewed as part of the profit-maximising behaviour of a firm. In this context the primary motive is increased sales. The risk and uncertainty of revenue response to advertising expenditure would lead firms to diversify into alternative marketing strategies, of which sponsorship is one.

All the evidence on sports sponsorship by firms indicates that this type of marketing/advertising behaviour is highly risky in terms of expected returns. Because of the riskiness of this type of marketing strategy, we should expect some involvement (since returns could conceivably be large) but not too much. This is consistent with the observed behaviour of firms keeping sponsorship activity below 5 per cent of total marketing expenditure.

However, for some industries we could expect a much higher involvement in sponsorship. This may be because other forms of advertising strategies are prevented. In this case, in order to maintain a given advertising expenditure/revenue ratio, expenditure on sponsorship will have to increase. The tobacco industry has historically been the main sponsor of British sport. Moller (1983) indicated that by the early 1980s tobacco companies were increasingly attracted to sports sponsorship because it was the only way they could advertise cigarettes on television, since direct cigarette television advertising was banned. Moller illustrates how one particular sporting competition proved very effective for the sponsors:

> One of the greatest coups has been the annual Embassy World Professional Snooker Championship. During a 17-day period in April and May last year, no fewer than 81 hours' coverage was given on television to an audience of up to 10.8 million. For a sponsorship outlay of less than £200,000 Embassy gained a form of advertising that, at average television commercial rates, would have cost some £68 million.

Although tobacco companies still spend around £8 million a year on sports sponsorship, television coverage of tobacco-sponsored events such as the World Professional Snooker Championship became much more restricted in the late 1980s and 1990s. There is also a European Union directive imposing a ban on all tobacco advertising and sponsorship starting in 2001 and achieving full coverage by 2006.

The British government has pledged to ban tobacco sponsorship of sport earlier than that. Formula One motor racing has been exempted for the time being by the British government from this ban because of its strong dependence on tobacco sponsorship, and because of the impact such a ban would have on employment in Britain, where most of the jobs associated with Formula One are based.

The sports management and marketing literature has adopted a broader approach than the economic one to identifying benefits to the sponsoring firm. Crompton (1996) has indicated four motives of business for sponsoring sport: image enhancement, increase in awareness (of product or firm), hospitality opportunities, and product trial or sales opportunities.

Marketing expenditure aimed at building the corporate image is increasingly noticeable in Britain, and is closely associated with the investment motive for advertising. It is also often associated with some of the industries that are closely connected to sponsorship: banks, insurance companies, and oil companies. Since sport has a healthy image, the idea is to carry over the image to the company and its product. Strength, competitiveness, and the will to win are part of both sport and the competitive business environment. By associating élite performers with the product, the aim is to create an élite image for the company.

Another motive for sponsorship is to change the perceived image of a company to one more favourable to the company's products in a specific market. As an example of this, Crompton quotes Nunaghan's (1983) example of how Gillette lost its American image and gained ground against its British rival, Wilkinson, in the British market by its sponsorship of a traditional English sport, cricket.

Increase in awareness of both the company and the product is particularly important for those companies with a low level of awareness or for those who are introducing a new product and wish to raise awareness of it. Cornhill, with its sponsorship of Test cricket, showed how new sponsorship deals can have a dramatic effect on public awareness of the company's name, as this quote from the Howell Report indicates:

> When it began sponsorship of the Cornhill Test Series in 1977 the company rated twelfth among UK insurance companies and a survey showed that the public's 'spontaneous awareness' was 2 per cent. After five years of the sponsorships that awareness had increased to 17 per cent.
>
> Cornhill analysed the benefits from this sponsorship in 1981. During 140 hours of television coverage the company received 7,459 banner sitings on screen and 234 verbal mentions. In addition, there were 1,784 references on radio, 659 in the national press and 2,448 in the provincial press. There were also unexpected bonuses of publicity which included the 21 million telephone calls to British Telecom's cricket score service in 1980.
>
> The 250 tickets which Cornhill receives from each Test Match are also a valuable aid in customer contact. Cornhill's brokers tell them that policies are now much easier to sell as a result of the greater awareness of Cornhill's name and enhanced reputation and Cornhill itself estimates that an increased annual premium income of £10 million could be attributed to the sponsorship.

This quote also illustrates the hospitality opportunities offered by sports sponsorship. Many marketing managers regard entertainment and trade relations as the most important motive for sponsorship. Even here there appears to be a link with sales or profit maximisation, since the people the firm wishes to entertain are its customers. In certain cases the attraction of sport is the facility to entertain customers at national, prestigious, sporting occasions while at the same time having access to the best boxes, boardrooms, etc. due to the firm's sponsorship. This is particularly the case with big motor racing or horse racing occasions, but also applies to football matches, tennis tournaments, and cricket.

Perhaps the best example of product trial opportunities used by Crompton is the way computer companies demonstrate their products by offering in-kind assistance to sports events. When any time for an event or score appears on the television screen, the name of the company appears with it. Crompton uses the example of Olivetti quoted in Long (1993):

> Olivetti has been providing a timing service to Formula One motor racing for 13 years. Olivetti says it has processed 2 million race times, more than 500,000 laps, and calculated 700,000 top speeds. The computer team comprises 15 engineers, 10 km of cable and a dozen 386 PCs which make up the timing systems. The race and lap timer, based on a photocell at the finish line, feeds one set of PCs, while the telemetric system (whereby a small transmitter on the car sends the team confidential data on how it is running via antennae embedded in the track) supplies another. Two further systems stationed at other points on the circuit provide top speeds and intermediate times for all of the drivers. In 1992, at the Imola Grand Prix in Italy, it introduced a new system which takes timings from 15 points on the track, providing TV companies with even more statistics to push at the viewer. All of this represents a major investment, but the payoff is Olivetti's opportunity to demonstrate its technical excellence and have it recognized by the name on millions of TV screens around the world.

Slack and Bentz (1996) indicated a further motive for business to sponsor sport that is particularly relevant for small businesses: the enhancement of local community image.

Public relations and contact with the local community are the main objectives likely to be associated with small sponsorship deals at the local level rather than large, well-publicised deals. The rapid increase in marathon running in the early 1980s gave a big boost to this type of sponsorship, but local soccer teams and cricket teams now actively search for sponsors and many firms are willing to give small amounts to sporting teams in the local area. They can expect little advertising-type return from this, but such sponsorship could be useful politically if, for instance, the firm wishes to expand and needs, say, planning permission for a new development. Contributing to the community in terms of sports sponsorship could then be a useful asset at a public inquiry.

Because of the multiplicity of objectives associated with sponsorship it becomes difficult to monitor whether or not the sponsorship has been successful. If it were simply a matter of profit maximisation, or even sales maximisation, some testing would be possible. Even then, establishing any clear statistical links with this expenditure and sales is very difficult. Gillette relied on social survey methods and attempted to measure increasing awareness of the company's name through its sponsorship activity. Unfortunately, in the early 1980s, its research indicated that consumers were often more likely to associate Gillette with sport (particularly cricket) than with safety razors. The other problem Gillette found was that public consciousness of the company's sponsorship was not cumulative year after year. Repeated sponsorship of the same competition (for example, the Gillette Cup in cricket) seemed eventually to prove unproductive in reaching new consumers, as awareness levels reach a plateau and then stay there, or even fall away. The result of this evaluation was that Gillette withdrew from cricket sponsorship in 1981.

The quote from the Howell Report given earlier in this chapter regarding the Cornhill sponsorship of cricket indicated alternative methods of measuring the achievements of sponsorship expenditure, such as to monitor newspapers and television and count the number of column inches or television time that the company gets as a result of the sponsorship. This media coverage can then be costed at the price that similar space and air-time would have cost if purchased at market rates. We have already mentioned Moller's estimate of £68 million for the value of the media coverage achieved by Embassy in the 1982 World Professional Snooker Championship. The Howell Report details more closely where the media coverage came from.

(a)   Banners sited over the competitors' rest alcoves took up as much as one-eighth of the screen when the camera zoomed-in during actual play. During 17 days of competition there were more than 90 hours of scheduled viewing which grew to almost 100 hours when late-night programmes were allowed to over-run.

(b)   Verbal mentions were certainly more than two per programme during many longer transmissions, especially those covering six hours. There were 78 scheduled programmes with at least an entitlement of two mentions each for a minimum of 156 mentions.

(c)   *Radio Times* gave 28 mentions to Embassy in the published programme billings for the last 10 days, with as many as three on a single page.

(d)   Written captions of latest positions appeared regularly and Embassy was always in the heading.

These two examples, Cornhill and Embassy, indicate that benefits to the sponsoring firm can be substantial and that it is possible to put some monetary valuation on these benefits.

The benefits to the sponsored activity

The benefits to the sponsored activity seem fairly obvious. The sport receives payment from the sponsoring firm, which is an important source of income. A sport's governing body, or even an individual sports club, must raise its income from government subsidy, sponsorship, membership fees, or from selling its product (i.e. sales of admission tickets to sporting events). To some extent, one form of income is a substitute for another. If sponsorship income is increased then sport can become cheaper to the participant (lower membership fees) or the spectator (lower admission charges). In a way, then, sponsorship is a form of private market subsidy to sport.

Income, though, is not the only benefit to the sponsored sport: the sport is also receiving publicity. A sponsor will normally be willing to take steps to improve publicity for the sponsored event, and this automatically widens the market for the sport as well as for the product of the sponsoring company.

In the United Kingdom, the startling rise in the popularity of snooker indicated how this 'joint publicity' effect could create a virtuous circle of expanding demand for both product and sport. In the early 1970s, snooker was a low-interest sport with little media coverage. Sponsorship allowed the sport to move from smoky rooms to lavish surroundings for big competitions (most notably the Crucible Theatre, Sheffield). These surroundings attracted more media, in particular television coverage, which itself attracted more sponsors, giving higher prize money. The higher prize money and media coverage generated much wider interest which further encouraged the television companies and the sponsors, thus giving another boost to the upward spiral. Sponsorship, then, was a necessary condition for the promotion of the sport itself. By 1983, snooker was the fourth most televised sport in Britain, and had the second-highest participation rate for an indoor sport after darts.

Costs to the sponsored sport

Thus income, publicity and promotion for the sport are the main benefits to the sponsored sport. There may also be costs, though, to the sponsored sport. Sponsorship is essential to commercial activity and the sponsor expects a commercial rate of return on its investment. Because of this, sponsors may require some sort of control over the sponsored activity. Head (1982) comments:

> it is not difficult to predict that sponsors who feel they are getting a raw deal will either lose interest altogether or demand much greater control. By then we shall have moved into full scale promotion in which sport is run for the benefit of the promotion company and not primarily in the interests of sport itself.

This quote illustrates the underlying danger of the conflict in objectives between sponsor and sponsored. There is a worry over whether sponsorship somehow reduces the integrity of sport. Various questions are raised in this debate. Should the sport become more professional and commercial to satisfy the wishes of the sponsors? Should the rules of a sport be changed to make the game more interesting to television?

Some changes brought about by sponsorship are clearly beneficial and have attracted new audiences. The case of snooker is a good example. Others have been less welcome. Events created to provide sponsorship vehicles are not always in harmony with sporting programmes. Over-exposure on television can have damaging effects. All this can lead to the detriment of the long-term interests of sport. Serious reservations were expressed over the massive sponsorship of the Los Angeles Olympics. Some commentators referred to the 1984 Olympics as

'The $ Olympics' (*Observer*, 1984). The scale of the sponsorship involved is illustrated by this quote:

> US corporations are sinking $500 million into this summer's 23rd Olympic extravaganza in return for the right to use the games as a market-stall for their products. They mean to get their money's worth . . . This list runs through 30 major companies that have put down a minimum of $4 million apiece for 'exclusive rights' to use Olympian phrases and logos to market their wares. For most sponsoring firms, that $4 million is just a down payment. McDonald's, the Big Mac people, forked out a further $6 million to build Los Angeles a new swimming stadium. ABC-TV paid a staggering $225 million for TV rights.
>
> (Observer, 1984)

Although sponsorship on this scale meant that, for the first time for many years, the national and local government of the country staging the Olympics was not faced with a massive bill, many felt that the Olympic ideal had been lost in the race to attract sponsorship. The mayor of Olympia in Greece, home of the Olympic flame, felt so strongly that at one time he threatened to prevent the flame leaving Olympia since the Los Angeles Olympic Organizing Committee had sold off sections of its journey across the United States at $3,000 a kilometre.

Probably one of the most serious problems with sponsorship is that the sponsor, in order to gain maximum publicity, is normally interested only in the top, most prestigious, events and in the élite performers, the superstars. This creates several problems. First, a conflict has arisen in the past between the willingness of companies to sponsor élite sportsmen and the rules of sports federations on the amateur status of competitors. The current situation is less confused than in the 1980s, when some sports allowed sponsorship money to be used only for certain expenses and other sports allowed trust funds to be set up. Second, the top competitors are often subject to an excessively crowded schedule in order to satisfy the demands of the sponsors.

Third, conflicts arise between the governing body of a sport and the competitors because of sponsorship deals. Sponsorship of individual competitors often leads to a situation where the governing body receives no income from the sponsorship deal. The governing body has responsibility for the sport right down to grassroots level, and may feel that it has the right to a share in the sponsorship money received from the use of its competition. Such conflicts are often exacerbated by specialist agencies that arrange sponsorship deals between competitors and companies. These agencies sometimes cut across the responsibilities of the governing bodies by staging their own events, but essentially by putting themselves between the sport and the individual competitor, they create a possible area of conflict.

Another problem for the sport is the lack of continuity that characterises much sponsorship activity. Sponsors often withdraw from a sport with little notice.

This volatility in income can cause serious problems for a governing body of sport. As indicated earlier, Gillette withdrew from the Gillette Cup after nearly 20 years in 1981. As the Howell Report comments:

> There is an important lesson here for sport, companies have to take hard commercial decisions about their investments. Gillette fully appreciated that the very success of the competition which it had initiated meant that its value to sport was now probably more than its own sponsorship would sustain.

This raises another important point. In order to achieve the sponsor's commercial objectives it may be necessary to change events continually. In this case Gillette switched its sponsorship to the London Marathon, which it then dropped after two years.

This volatility in sponsorship incomes means that sports have to be wary of dependence on sponsorship as a whole, and on one sponsor in particular. The Howell Report suggested that 'governing bodies should guard against an over-reliance upon sponsorship income and should maintain as wide a portfolio of sponsorship as is practical in order to minimise the dangers when sponsors end their involvement'.

A final problem with sponsorship is the association of sport with tobacco, gambling and alcohol, three industries that provide the bulk of sponsorship money. Our model of the sponsorship decision by the firm indicates that it is the banning of other forms of advertising for tobacco products that directly leads to more sponsorship money being available from this industry. Here we have a serious conflict: an activity, sport, that is actively encouraged because of the positive externalities generated by participation, becomes linked with other activities – smoking, drinking and gambling – that are known to have negative externalities associated with their consumption. We indicated above that the end of tobacco sponsorship of sport has already been announced. For the moment, the same fate is not intended for alcohol and gambling sponsorship.

Conclusions

Sports sponsorship is a $20 billion global industry dominated by the USA, which accounts for about a quarter of the total. It is estimated to be growing at an annual rate of 10 per cent, fuelled by escalation in the sponsorship fees for major sports events and professional team sports. However, whatever figures are quoted are likely to underestimate the true value of sports sponsorship due to the difficulty of identifying the true level of resources involved in any sponsorship deal and the problems caused by ambush marketing, which disguises sponsorship expenditure under the generic advertising and marketing budget.

In this chapter we have attempted to analyse the market for sports sponsorship. We have shown that the market is rather fragmented and patchy. There is a small number of élite events, teams, and athletes for which there is an excess supply of sponsors, resulting in the bidding-up of sponsorship fees. There are a much larger number of events, teams and athletes in a situation of excess demand for sponsorship funds.

Another major feature of the sponsorship market is its volatility. Thirty years ago the market did not exist outside the USA. Today, major sponsors, such as IBM in the Olympics, can suddenly decide to end their sponsorship of the event. Any sport may find that a major source of revenue disappears overnight for reasons that do not always have anything to do with the behaviour of the sport. It is potentially the most volatile form of revenue support for sport. Although we have tried to identify the reasons why firms sponsor sport and the benefits they seek, many firms cannot prove that these benefits have been achieved, and if changes in the firm's core business pose threats to the economic viability of the firm, sponsorship expenditure is often the first to be cut.

Despite these problems, the sheer size of sponsorship revenue support for sport means that sport can no longer live without it. At the present time, many sports in Europe are fighting to replace tobacco sponsorship revenue faced with a European Union ban from 2001 onwards. It is not proving an easy task.

One relationship that is crucial to sponsorship has pervaded the discussion in this chapter: the dependence of sponsorship on television broadcasting of the event, team, or athlete. All the major sponsorship contracts are dependent on television exposure. We will return to this issue in detail in Chapter 12.

10 Major sports events

Introduction

Until the 1980s, hosting major sporting events such as the Olympics was thought of as a financial and administrative burden to the organising city and country. This view was confirmed by Montreal's loss of £692 million in the staging of the 1976 summer Olympics. The previous summer Olympics in Munich in 1972 made a loss of £178 million.

Following these escalating losses, it seemed as if any host city would have to accept such a financial burden if it were to stage the Olympic Games or any other major sports event. However, the 1984 Los Angeles Olympics made a surplus of £215 million. This financial success changed the way cities and governments regarded the hosting of major sports events. Partly as a result of this, but also because there developed a greater understanding of the broader economic benefits to a city and country that could result from the staging of a major sports event, cities started to compete fiercely to host major World and European championships across a wide range of sports, and other special sports events such as Grand Prix athletics.

The economic importance of major events

The study of hallmark events or mega-events also became an important area of the tourism and leisure literature in the 1980s. The economic benefits of these events have been the main focus of such literature, although broader-based multidisciplinary approaches have been suggested (Hall, 1992; Getz, 1991). Within the area of mega-events, sports events have attracted a significant amount of attention.

One of the first major studies in this area was on the impact of the 1985 Adelaide Grand Prix (Burns *et al.*, 1986). This was followed by an in-depth study of the 1988 Calgary Winter Olympics (Ritchie, 1984; Ritchie and Aitken, 1984, 1985; Ritchie and Lyons, 1987, 1990; Ritchie and Smith, 1991).

Mules and Faulkner (1996) point out that even such mega-events as Grand Prix races and the Olympics are not always an unequivocal economic benefit to the cities that host them. They emphasise that, in general, staging major sports

Table 10.1 Financial costs and economic impact of various events

Event	Financial loss (A$ million)	Impact on GSP (A$ million)
1985 Adelaide Grand Prix	2.6	23.6
1992 Adelaide Grand Prix	4.0	37.4
1991 Eastern Creek Motor Cycle Grand Prix	4.8	13.6
1994 Brisbane World Masters Games	2.8	50.6

Source: Mules and Faulkner (1996).

events often results in the city authorities losing money even though the city itself benefits greatly in terms of additional spending in it. Table 10.1 gives the losses made by Australian cities hosting major sporting events, and indicates the increase in Gross State Product (GSP) as a direct result of the event. Thus the 1994 Brisbane World Masters Games cost A$2.8 million to put on but generated a massive A$50.6 million of additional economic activity in the State economy. Mules and Faulkner's basic point is that the public sector is normally required to be in the role of staging the event and incurring these losses in order to generate the benefits to the local economy:

> This financial structure is common to many special events, and results in the losses alluded to above. It seems unlikely that private operators would be willing to take on the running of such events because of their low chance of breaking even let alone turning a profit. The reason why governments host such events and lose taxpayers' money in the process lies in spillover effects or externalities.

It is not a straightforward job, however, to establish a profit and loss account for a specific event. Major sports events require investment in new sports facilities, and often this is paid for in part by central government or even international sports bodies. Thus some of this investment expenditure represents a net addition to the local economy, since the money comes in from outside. Also, such facilities remain after the event has finished, acting as a platform for future activities that can generate additional tourist expenditure (Mules and Faulkner, 1996). Sports events are part of a broader strategy aimed at raising the profile of a city, and therefore success cannot be judged simply on profit and loss basics.

Often the attraction of events is linked to a re-imaging process, and in the case of many UK cities it is invariably linked to strategies of urban regeneration and tourism development (Bianchini, 1991; Bramwell, 1995; Loftman and Spirou, 1996; Roche, 1994). Major events, if successful, can project a new image and identity for a city. The hosting of major sports events is often justified by the host city in terms of long-term economic and social consequences directly or indirectly resulting from the staging of the event (Mules and Faulkner, 1996). These effects are primarily justified in economic terms, by estimating the additional expenditure generated in the local economy as the result of the event, in terms of the benefits injected from tourism-related activity and the subsequent re-imaging of the city following the success of the event (Roche, 1992).

Cities staging major sports events have a unique opportunity to market themselves to the world. As we will see in Chapter 12, increasing competition between broadcasters to secure broadcasting rights to major sports events has led to a massive escalation in fees for such rights, which in turn means that broadcasters give blanket coverage at peak times for such events, enhancing the marketing benefits to the cities that stage them.

Measuring the economic impact of major sports events

The economic impact of major sports events is normally assessed using multiplier analysis. Multiplier analysis converts the total amount of additional expenditure in the host city to a net amount of income retained within the city after allowing for 'leakages' from the local economy. For example, the total amount of money spent in a hotel will not necessarily all be recirculated within a given city. Some of the money will be spent on wages, food suppliers, beverage suppliers, etc., the recipients of which may well be outside the city. Thus the multiplier is a device that converts total additional expenditure into the amount of local income retained within the local economy.

The ultimate purpose of multiplier calculations is that they can be used as the basis for further economic analysis such as making estimates of job creation attributable to a given inflow of income into a local economy. Sustained additional income into a local economy will lead to the creation of additional jobs within that economy.

There are many different multipliers, but the one used most commonly for studies of events is called the proportional multiplier. The proportional income multiplier is expressed as:

$$\frac{\text{direct} + \text{indirect} + \text{induced income}}{\text{initial visitor expenditure}}$$

Once the initial visitor expenditure has been measured, economic impact in terms of additional local income can be estimated by multiplying this initial expenditure by the local multiplier.

Direct income is the first round effect of outside visitor spending. It represents additional wages, salaries, and profits to local residents working in businesses that were the direct recipients of the additional visitor expenditures. Indirect income is the income to other businesses and individuals within the local economy as a result of the additional expenditures of the visitors but which were not the direct recipients of this visitor expenditure (e.g. local suppliers to the shops, restaurants, hotels, etc., that were the recipients of visitor expenditures). Induced income is the income resulting from the respending of additional income earned directly or indirectly on locally produced goods and services.

In practice, the value of the local multiplier is 'borrowed' from other studies in related cities since it is both complicated and costly to estimate the value directly. In Sheffield, for instance, which is our case-study city later in the chapter, a local proportional multiplier of 0.2 (meaning that only 20 per cent of the additional visitor expenditure is retained in the city as additional local income) has been used for several previous economic impact studies. The larger the city, the less the leakages, and, in general, the higher the value of the multiplier. A multiplier value of 0.2 was used for the events held in Sheffield, Glasgow, and Birmingham reported later in the chapter, and 0.1 for the golf championships in Sunningdale, as the leakages from the local economy in this case of a rural economy would be substantial.

By dividing additional local income by an average annual full-time wage for the sector where the income is received (e.g. hotel and catering), the number of additional jobs created can be obtained, and this is expressed in full-time equivalent job years. One full-time equivalent job year is the employment equivalent of one full-time job for one year. In reality, few, if any, full-time jobs lasting as long as one year are generated by any single, one-off, sports event. Most of the employment effect is normally seen in short-term and part-time employment. The average annual income figure that is used in such calculations, therefore, is normally lower than the national average wage to reflect this employment structure. In the UK studies referred to below, a figure of £12,500 was used.

Sports events in the UK

In the UK there has been a recent acknowledgement of the economic and social benefits that major events can have upon the host city, region, or country. The setting-up of the Major Events Support Group, now the Major Events Steering Group (MESG), in 1994 by the Sports Council was an attempt to assist governing bodies and local authorities in bidding for, and staging, major sports events. A report by the former National Heritage Committee (1995) provided a framework for a co-ordinated approach to attracting events. The report indicated that the UK had started to fall behind other countries in its approach to attracting major sports events, and that the UK had lacked a consistent approach for bidding for events. One of the principal objectives in setting up the UK Sports Council was to rationalise the system. The UK Sports Council has since adopted a Policy and Strategy for Major Events, and funding is now available from the National Lottery to support major sports events.

The National Heritage Committee (1995) report stated:

> It is clear that bids to stage major sporting events ... can operate as a catalyst to stimulate economic regeneration even if they do not ultimately prove successful.

The report used the case of Sheffield and Manchester to highlight the regenerative impact of sports events in the UK:

... once the initial redevelopment has taken place, the existence of high quality facilities means that the cities concerned are able to attract other sports events. The impact however does not stop there. Many of the facilities are suitable for other uses such as conferences and concerts. In addition the favourable publicity which can follow from a successful event may increase the attractiveness of a city, raise its profile overseas, and enable it to attract an increasing number of tourists.

Euro 96

The economic importance of major sports events became an increasingly important issue following the economic success of the Euro 96 football championship, which attracted 280,000 overseas visiting supporters, spending around £120 million in the eight host cities and surrounding regions (Dobson *et al.* 1997). If we include the impact of spending by domestic visitors not resident in the host cities, the total economic impact generated in the host cities by all spectators and media/officials to Euro 96 was £195 million.

Euro 96 was estimated to have increased Britain's net earnings from travel and tourism in the second quarter of 1996 by 3 per cent and generated an extra 0.25 per cent of UK exports of goods and services. The impact on the whole economy was estimated at an added 0.1 per cent on British Gross Domestic Product (GDP) in the period from April to June, a quarter of the total growth of 0.4 per cent. The tourist boom during the championship helped push Britain's trade balance into its first surplus since the beginning of 1995.

According to estimates from Deloitte & Touche, the government also experienced £64 million gains as a result of England hosting the tournament: £40m from the tournament through VAT on ticket sales, merchandising, corporate hospitality and other Euro 96 spending; £5 million from betting tax from the £80 million wagers on Euro 96 matches; £3 million from taxation on the incomes of competition organisers; and £16 million from companies paying corporation tax on commercial profit. The government received this revenue boost while contributing only relatively small amounts through National Heritage Department grants. The costs of organising, promoting, and policing the tournament and associated cultural events were borne by local authorities, private companies, and the Football Association.

The tournament itself made a record profit of £69 million for UEFA (Europe's governing body of football), £49 million of which was given as prize money to the competing countries. Although the FA made an operating loss of £1.7 million on the tournament, a £2.5 million overall surplus was made after taking account of England's prize money as a result of reaching the semi-finals.

Euro 96 had a significant impact on the UK hotel industry. Outside London average room occupancies and average room rates were up by 14 and 22 per cent respectively in June 1996 over their level in June 1995. In Manchester, there was a 57 per cent increase in room yield and room occupancy directly attributable to Euro 96. However, the displacement of business and conference trade dampened the impact in some areas of the country.

Euro 96 was the largest sports event to be held in Britain since the 1966 World Cup. The evidence discussed above shows that it was an economic success story for the host cities and the British tourism industry. It has also led to an increased demand for more major sports events to be staged in Britain in the future, most notably the bids to stage the 2006 soccer World Cup and the 2012 Olympic Games. The UK also hosted the 1999 Rugby Union and Cricket World Cups, and will host the 2002 Commonwealth Games.

Also, every year in the UK there is a rolling programme of major sports events, some of which are of global significance. The Sports Council's Calendar of Major Sporting Events lists 291 major sports events that took place in Great Britain in 1997. Forty-six of the events would attract major television coverage outside as well as inside Britain. These would include the Six Nations Rugby Tournament, Wimbledon, the Open Golf Championship, the FA Cup Final, the Boat Race, and the Grand National. Britain probably has the broadest portfolio of annual major sports events in relation to its population size of any country in the world. This gives an expertise and experience that represents a competitive advantage in this rapidly growing global market. It also signals a need to understand more fully how sport events can generate benefits to the cities that host them.

In the UK, three cities – Sheffield, Glasgow, and Birmingham – have adopted an economic strategy based on attracting major sports events to their area as a catalyst to stimulate economic regeneration. These three cities have been designated 'National Cities of Sport' and two of these, Sheffield and Birmingham, were also host cities in Euro 96. A look at developments in one of these cities, Sheffield, allows us to assess the extent to which sports events can contribute to economic regeneration.

Sports events and economic regeneration: a case-study of Sheffield

Between 1978 and 1988 Sheffield suffered a severe local economic recession as its coal, steel and engineering industries declined with the loss of over 60,000 jobs, leaving unemployment in some areas of the city as high as 20 per cent. Faced with few realistic alternatives and with little hope of any help from central government, Sheffield embarked on an adventurous event-led tourism strategy to attempt to replace lost employment by expansion in the sport, leisure, and tourism industries. The 1991 World Student Games (WSG) were attracted to Sheffield, involving £150 million of new investment in sports facilities including an athletics stadium, an indoor arena, and an international competition swimming pool.

Sheffield became then an economic experiment to test the hypothesis discussed above that hosting sports events could make a significant contribution to the local economy, as well as changing the historical image of the city as a dirty industrial city. Given Sheffield's industrial heritage in the steel industry, it was a massive reorientation of policy to aim to attract visitors to the city to watch or take part in sports events.

The strategic policies set out in the 1980s for regeneration were quick to evolve, and as Roche (1992) comments:

> One feature of such strategies has often been at first sight the rather implausible looking project of creating out of unpromising material a new urban tourism industry.

The World Student Games made an operating loss of £10 million, but no economic impact study was carried out so there were no estimates of the economic activity generated by visitors to Sheffield as a direct result of the staging of the event. Thus, only one side of the economic equation outlined in Table 10.1 was measured, and this proved a political burden in the early years of the strategy. However, the investment in the new sports facilities for the WSG provided the platform for a continuous programme of events held in Sheffield since 1991. Since 1991, over 300 sports events have been staged in Sheffield and the additional expenditure in the local economy that visitors to Sheffield have generated as a direct result of these events is estimated at over £30 million.

Over £9 million of this total was generated in a 24-day period (15 event days) in June and July in 1996 by two events: the three first-round games of Group D in Euro 96 and the World Masters Swimming Championships that followed immediately afterwards. Both of these events were the subject of economic impact studies carried out by the Leisure Industries Research Centre. These two events are particularly interesting because one is a major spectator attraction also attracting major media attention (Euro 96) while the other attracts few spectators but a large number of competitors (World Masters Swimming Championships).

The three Euro 96 matches attracted a total attendance of nearly 69,000, of which just over 61,000 were visitors to Sheffield. Only 24 per cent of these, however, spent at least one night in Sheffield. Although Euro 96 attracted a large number of spectators from other countries, a surprisingly high percentage of these were day-visitors and returned home, by boat or plane, after each match. These day visitors, however, on average spent more than £50 per day, much higher than would be expected for other day-visitor tourist attractions, with the result that the overall additional spend in Sheffield by visitors as a result of these three games was £5.8 million.

Whereas the Euro 96 games attracted a large number of mainly overseas visitors to Sheffield to spectate at a major sports event and had global media coverage, the World Masters Swimming Championships, which began three days after the last Group D match of Euro 96, attracted few spectators and little media attention. The Championships began on 22 June 1996 and finished on 3 July. There were 6,500 competitors and officials, plus a few spectators who were normally friends or family of the competitors. However, over 80 per cent of these visitors stayed at least one night in Sheffield, with the average length of stay being 5.4 nights. The average daily expenditure of those staying overnight was over £80, resulting in a total additional spend by visitors to Sheffield as a result of the event of £3.6 million.

Thus the World Masters Swimming Championships attracted around 10 per cent of the number of visitors brought to Sheffield by the Euro 96 games but generated over 60 per cent of the additional expenditure of visitors to these games. This is because the visitors attracted to the event, who were mostly the competitors themselves, stayed longer in Sheffield and spent more money. Masters events are now recognised as particularly beneficial to the host city in the generation of significant economic impact since they attract older, more affluent competitors who stay in the host city for a significant period of time. As Table 10.1 indicates, the 1994 World Masters Games in Brisbane generated over A\$50 million of economic activity in the host city. The 25,000 competitors that took part made it the world's largest multi-sport participation event.

The economic importance of major sports events: a study of six events

This section reports the results of a study of six major sports events held in the United Kingdom between May and August 1997. The research was carried out on behalf of the UK, English and Scottish Sports Councils by the Leisure Industries Research Centre. The study aimed to evaluate the economic impact of these events on the local economies of host cities and towns as well as to investigate the complicated economics of staging major sports events.

In total, 4,306 questionnaires were completed by visitors to the six events. In addition to the social survey information, additional information was collected from local authorities in the host cities, governing bodies involved in staging the event, and hotels in the host cities. The sample survey information, together with ticket sales data, was used to provide estimates of additional expenditure by visitors from outside the local economy. Estimates of additional local income generated and additional jobs created were provided using a proportional income multiplier approach. A summary of results, on an event-by-event basis, is provided below.

The six events studied were:

1	19 May–1 June	World Badminton Championships and Sudirman Cup, Glasgow
2	31 May–8 June	European Junior Boxing Championships, Birmingham
3	5–9 June	1st Cornhill Test Match, England/Australia, Edgbaston
4	29 June	International Amateur Athletics Federation Grand Prix, Sheffield
5	31 July–3 August	European Junior Swimming Championships, Glasgow
6	14–17 August	Weetabix Women's British Open Golf Championship, Sunningdale

This study showed the wide variety in the economic impact generated by the six events. The two junior events (boxing and swimming) generated a relatively small economic impact on the host city given that one (boxing) lasted 9 days and

Table 10.2 Source of additional visitor spending in host city

	Badminton	Boxing	Cricket	Athletics	Swimming	Golf
Visiting spectators	31%	65%	91%	75%	8%	90%
Officials, competitors, and media	69%	35%	9%	25%	92%	10%
Total additional spend	£1,926,692	£244,374	£4,571,225	£150,936	£257,802	£1,645,244

the other (swimming) 4 days. Athletics also generated a small impact, but this event lasted less than 5 hours. Cricket generated by far the highest level (£5.1 million) of additional expenditure in the host city, and also attracted the highest number of spectators. Badminton and golf generated a similar level of additional expenditure, but badminton lasted for 14 days and golf for 4 days.

Table 10.2 compares the overall additional visitor spending generated by each of the six events, and breaks down the total additional expenditure in the host city by the source of this spending. The table shows that the events differ in the relative share of total additional spending generated by visiting spectators on the one hand, and competitors, officials, and media representatives on the other. The cricket and golf stand out as spectator-driven in the economic impact with 91 and 90 per cent respectively of the additional expenditure generated by visiting spectators. Athletics is also spectator-driven, with 75 per cent of total additional expenditure generated by visiting spectators. In the case of athletics, most of the spectators were day visitors, whereas the much smaller number of competitors and officials had a higher proportion of them staying overnight, and spending considerably more in the host city. Consequently, the percentage contributed by spectators is less than in the cricket and golf events.

At the other extreme, at the swimming in Glasgow, 92 per cent of the additional expenditure generated resulted from the spending of competitors, officials, and media representatives. For badminton around one-third of the additional spending was due to spectators, with most of the other two-thirds being due to competitors, officials, and media representatives. For boxing, the proportions were reversed, with around two-thirds of the additional spend being due to visiting spectators.

Overall, then, if we consider a spectrum from spectator-driven to competitor-driven, cricket and golf are at the spectator-driven end and swimming is at the competitor-driven end. The other three events lie in between, with athletics and boxing on the spectator-driven side and badminton on the competitor-driven side (as in Figure 10.1).

The level of additional expenditure generated by competitors, officials, and media should be relatively easy to forecast in advance, since it depends on the numbers of competitors and officials visiting and the number of event days. Hence, forecasting the economic impact of competitor-driven events is not a major problem. In Glasgow, it was possible to build up a profile of expenditure on the main items of accommodation and food by investigating the terms offered

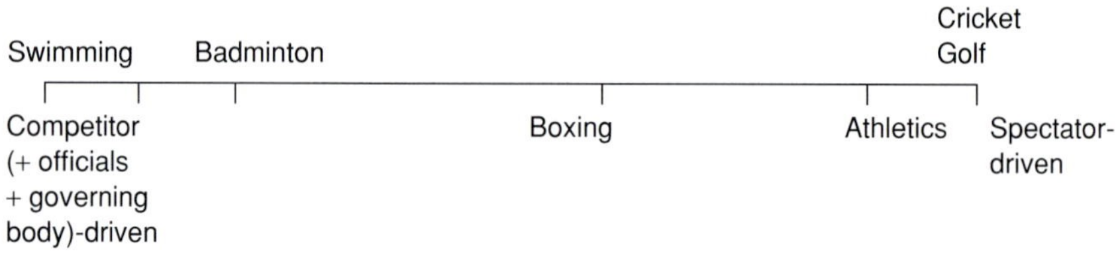

Figure 10.1 The spectrum from competitor-driven to spectator-driven.

Table 10.3 Predicted and actual spectator attendance

	Predicted total attendance	*Actual total attendance*
Badminton	35,000–40,000	21,642
Boxing	35,000–40,000	1,690
Cricket	63,000–70,000	72,693
Athletics	25,000	16,025
Swimming	1,500– 2,000	990
Golf	40,000	50,000

by the hotels to the visiting teams and officials. Since this was a junior event, there was little expenditure in addition to that on accommodation and food. In such circumstances it is possible before the event to build up a very accurate forecast of its economic impact, by investigating the number of competitors, officials, and media present at previous stagings of the same championship and the number of days for which the championship ran.

Predicting the impact of spectators is much more difficult. Table 10.3 shows the projected attendance at each of the events as given to us by the English Sports Council at the beginning of the study and prior to the events, and the actual total spectator attendance at the events.

The boxing and badminton estimates of the likely attendances were considerable overestimates. The athletics event in Sheffield also attracted many fewer than expected, even after tickets were distributed to Sheffield residents and schools at a heavily discounted price. Only in the case of the two main spectator events, cricket and golf, were the forecasts of attendances relatively close to the actuals. Both these events are annual events, and therefore relatively easy to predict. However, both are susceptible to the weather, and cricket is susceptible to the way the match develops. Test matches sometimes finish in three days, considerably reducing the economic impact. In the case of the golf championships, very good weather in August gave rise to attendances above expectations.

This illustrates the danger of staging special 'one-off' events. Projected attendances have a high error margin and mistakes can have a dramatic effect on the final budget out-turn as well as on the economic impact of the event in the local economy.

Table 10.4 Average additional visitor expenditure per event day

Badminton	£137,621
Boxing	£27,153
Cricket	£1,142,806
Athletics	£176,937
Swimming	£64,451
Golf	£411,311

Table 10.5 Percentage expenditure on various items

	Badminton	*Boxing*	*Cricket*	*Athletics*	*Swimming*	*Golf*
Accommodation	52	31	25	21	82	55
Food and drink	21	26	35	24	7	23
Entertainment	5	7	15	5	2	2
Programmes and merchandise	1	3	7	12	1	6
Shopping and souvenirs	11	19	5	18	6	7
Travel	6	8	8	14	1	4
Other	3	6	4	7	1	2

Table 10.2 shows that, overall, the cricket generated the highest level of economic impact, followed by badminton and golf. However, the impact of the badminton was to a large extent due to the fact it was by far the longest event, with 14 event days. Table 10.4 gives average additional spend per day. Cricket has by far the highest visitor expenditure per day, over twice the level of the next highest spend, golf, and 42 times the spend per day of the lowest, boxing. Badminton slips to fourth out of the six on this measure, behind cricket, golf, and athletics. The table shows more clearly the distinction between those events that generate significant economic impacts and those that generate little.

Table 10.5 gives the distribution of additional expenditure due to the event over the different items of expenditure. It is interesting that swimming has by far the highest proportionate expenditure on accommodation. This is not surprising, since additional expenditure due to this event is almost totally generated by competitors and officials staying in full-board accommodation for the duration of the competition. In general, the more competitor-driven the event is, the higher the proportion of expenditure that will go on accommodation. Thus, we see that badminton also has a high proportion of total expenditure on accommodation. The exception is golf, which is a spectator-driven event but has a high proportion of expenditure on accommodation. This is because a higher proportion of spectators stayed overnight than in the other spectator-driven events, there was a large absolute number of competitors, officials, and media representatives staying for long periods (even though this number was small in relation to the total number of spectators), and the cost of the accommodation was relatively high.

Athletics showed the smallest percentage expenditure on accommodation due to the high proportion of day-visit spectators. Cricket showed by far the highest percentage spend on food and drink, again not surprising given the nature of the event. Overall, Table 10.5 shows a large degree of variability in the percentage breakdown of expenditure, but is broadly consistent in that most events have more than 60 per cent of total expenditure on accommodation and food and drink, the main exception being athletics where programmes, shopping and travel took up a higher than normal proportion of total spend.

Implications for the economic importance of sports events in the UK

Of the six events studied in this project, two were part of the normal annual cycle of sports events in Great Britain, three were special 'one-off' or irregular events that would not normally take place in Britain, and one (the athletics Grand Prix) normally takes place in Britain, but not in Sheffield. If we add to this typology the extent to which the event is capable of generating significant economic impact (either on a per day basis or overall), then it is possible to consider the following typology for major sports events.

A   Irregular, one-off, major international spectator events generating significant economic activity and media interest (e.g. Olympics, World Cup, European Football Championship).

B   Major spectator events generating significant economic activity, media interest and part of an annual cycle of sports events (e.g. FA Cup final, Six Nations Rugby Union Internationals, Test Match Cricket, Open Golf, Wimbledon).

C   Irregular, one-off, major international spectator/competitor events generating limited economic activity (e.g. European Junior Boxing Championships, European Junior Swimming Championships, World Badminton Championships, IAAF Grand Prix).

D   Major competitor events generating limited economic activity and part of an annual cycle of sports events (e.g. national championships in most sports).

Use of the word 'major' in each of these categories is to signify the importance of sporting outcomes of such events (e.g. national, European, or World Championships) rather than the economic importance. The typology serves to indicate that not all events that are 'major' in sporting terms are important in economic terms.

The majority of sports events in any one year are of types C and D, and this balance is reflected in the six case-studies of this project. However, it is the type A and B events that will dominate the contribution to economic impact in any one year.

Type D events, though of limited economic significance, also have limited additional costs of staging, since they are annual events and the governing bodies have long-term experience in terms of putting on such events.

Type C are special events that take place on a one-off or irregular basis. Even if they take place regularly, from any one country's point of view they will be irregular since they move from country to country. Such events have to be planned and managed from scratch, and potentially pose a major organisational problem for the governing bodies and the cities in which they take place, since they will not have had experience in hosting that particular event. Mega-events such as the Olympics and the World Cup, which pose a similar problem, have proved that the costs of staging such events are easily matched by the economic benefits generated. However, for smaller events such as the World Badminton Championships the true costs of the organisation and staging of the event are probably greater than or equivalent to the economic benefits. In addition, it is very difficult to predict the level of spectator interest in such an event. Whereas the World Badminton Championships attracts huge interest in Asia, it would have been difficult to forecast the level of spectator demand in Glasgow. The more competitor-driven the event, the easier it is to forecast the economic impact, but the less the impact is likely to be.

For type D events, the benefits do not cover the costs in economic terms and the rationale for bidding for such events must lie outside the purely economic domain.

Type A and B events will generate the largest economic benefits to the cities that host them. This is already well known for type A events, hence the fierce competition between cities to host them. The majority of type B events either do not move venues for year to year (e.g. Wimbledon) or, if they do, cities cannot bid to host them. What is not generally realised, however, is that Britain is unusual in having a very high number of such events. This means that the sports event business is a significant industry in Britain and we have a competitive advantage over most other nations in having considerable expertise and experience in staging major sports events.

Type B events are a low-risk investment for any hosting city, since spectator demand is relatively easy to predict. However, for cities trying to follow an event-led tourism strategy, such events are not normally 'on the market'. The result is that cities compete to stage type C events, which is the most uncertain category in terms of economic impact. The results of this study, together with previous event impact studies, allow us to make certain generalisations about Type C events:

1   the economic impact of competitor-driven events is relatively easy to forecast in advance;
2   in general, junior competitor-driven events generate small impacts;
3   the more senior the event and the longer the event, then the larger the economic impact, with World Masters events, in particular, generating significant impacts as large numbers of relatively affluent competitors stay in the host city for several weeks;
4   spectator forecasts are subject to large error margins and the tendency is to make highly optimistic forecasts that rarely materialise, with the result that higher than expected losses are made on the event.

As more and more economic impact studies of sports events are carried out it will be possible to identify with more certainty the parameters of events that categorise their economic significance. Twenty years ago little was known about the economic significance of type A and B events. The challenge for the next ten years is to find out more about the economics of type C events.

Conclusions

Major sports events are now a significant part of Britain's tourism industry. Britain has, partly by historical accident rather than by design, become the global market leader in the staging of major sports events because many of our annual domestic sporting competitions such as the FA Cup Final and Wimbledon attract a large number of overseas visitors and a global television audience. Major sports events held in Britain are a crucial ingredient in the creation of the tourist image of Britain. The evidence presented above indicates that the major sports events also have the potential to generate significant economic impact. This is most recognised in the USA and Australia, and less so in Britain. The Australian Tourist Commission estimates that major events contribute 5 per cent of Australia's total tourism income each year. Although Britain has a headstart in the global competition to stage major sports events, the competition is now fierce and UK Sport has recently launched its Major Events Strategy to ensure that the United Kingdom stays in contention.

11 Professional team sports

Introduction

The literature on the economics of professional team sports has grown rapidly since articles first started to appear in the 1950s. Most of the literature has been generated in North America and deals mainly with issues of restriction of competition in the product and labour markets that characterise major American professional team sports, American football, baseball, ice-hockey and basketball. Much of the analysis developed in North America has also been applied to UK professional team sports, in particular to football and cricket.

The economics of professional team sports has become particularly relevant over the past decade because of the changes that have taken place in both UK and European professional team sports: the setting up of the Premier League in English professional football in 1992; the move to Super League in rugby league in 1996; the professionalisation of rugby union in 1996; and the restructuring of the European Cup in football in 1999. This chapter will focus particularly on English professional football, but first we will discuss the major ingredients of the 'peculiar' economics of professional team sports (Neale, 1964) as developed in North America.

Uncertainty of outcome

One of the key features that makes the economics of professional team sports 'peculiar' is that demand for the product (i.e. the game) is positively related to the uncertainty of outcome, as El-Hodiri and Quirk (1971) state:

> the essential economic fact concerning professional team sports is that gate receipts depend crucially on the uncertainty of the outcome of the games played within the league. As the probability of either team winning approaches one, gate receipts fall substantially, consequently, every team has an economic motive for not becoming too superior in playing talent compared to other teams in the league.

Economists have highlighted this as the crucial feature of the professional team sport industry that distinguishes it from all other industries. The conventional textbook firm in economic theory has an interest in increasing its market power and ultimately it maximises its own interest (and profit) when it achieves maximum market power as a monopolist. In professional team sport once a team became a monopolist, revenue would disappear altogether; output would be zero since it would be impossible to stage a match.

One major function of the league is to ensure that no team achieves too much market power, or excessive dominance. The league therefore aims to restrict competition. This explains why price competition between clubs is effectively prevented. Other non-competitive characteristics of professional team sports' leagues include labour market restrictions giving clubs property rights in players and the pooling of revenues so that poorer clubs are cross-subsidised by the richer ones. As Noll (1974) points out:

> Nearly every phase of a team or league is influenced by practices and rules that limit economic competition within the industry. In most cases government has either sanctioned or failed to attack effectively these anti-competitive practices. Consequently professional team sports provide economists with a unique opportunity to study the operation and performance of an effective and well-organised control.

Despite almost universal acceptance by economists writing in this area that uncertainty of outcome is the key to demand analysis in professional team sports, Cairns *et al.* (1986) point out the lack of conclusive empirical evidence in support of this contention:

> Given the importance of uncertainty of outcome to professional team sports research, it is unfortunate that not only has empirical testing of the key relationship between demand and uncertainty of outcome been limited, but also that the discussion of this central concept has been unmethodical, if not confused. Inadequate attention has been paid to determining the appropriate empirical specifications of the underlying theoretical notions.

They go on to point out that at least three distinct versions of the uncertainty of outcome hypothesis have appeared in the literature: uncertainty of match outcome, uncertainty of seasonal outcome, and uncertainty of outcome in the sense of the absence of long-run domination by one club.

Quirk and Fort (1992) incorporate all three aspects of the uncertainty of outcome hypothesis in their measure of competitive balance in American professional sports leagues:

> Our primary emphasis, however, is in the dispersion ('spread') of W/L [win/lose] percentages in a league and the concentration of championships and high W/L percentages among league teams. A league in which team W/L percentages are bunched together around .500 displays more competitive balance than does a league in which team W/L percentages are

widely dispersed; and the more concentrated is the winning of champion-ships and high W/L percentage among a few teams, the less competitive balance there is in a league.

The approach Quirk and Fort (1992) take is based on the work of Noll (1988). This approach is effectively comparing the actual performance of a league to the performance that would have occurred if the league had the maximum degree of competitive balance in the sense that all teams had equal playing strengths. The degree of competitive balance is greater the smaller the deviation of actual league performance from that of the ideal league where all teams have equal playing strengths. They carried out this analysis for all the five major American professional team sports leagues (National Football League (NFL), National Bas-ketball Association (NBA), National Hockey League (NHL), and the two baseball leagues, the American League (AL) and the National League (NL)) for each decade from 1901 to 1990.

Quirk and Fort (1992) found that all five leagues operated with a significant degree of competitive imbalance. The NFL had the most competitive balance, and the NBA the least, but even the NFL fell a long way short of the ideal league. They concluded:

> One obvious conclusion from our extended look at historical data on com-petitive balance in the five major team sports leagues is that none of the leagues comes close to achieving the ideal of equal playing strengths. There is ample evidence of long-term competitive imbalance in each league, despite the league rules that are supposedly designed to equalise team strengths. On the other hand, with all their flaws, the leagues have not only survived but have flourished, with growth in numbers of teams, in geographic coverage, in attendance and public interest, and in profitability.

One interpretation of their conclusion would be that uncertainty of outcome and maintenance of competitive balance are not as important to the success of pro-fessional team sports leagues as the previous economic literature has suggested. Another interpretation would be that the various restrictions on competition im-posed by American sports leagues have achieved sufficient competitive balance to make the leagues successful. It is to this restriction that we now turn.

Restriction of competition in professional team sports

Although uncertainty of outcome may be a major determinant of attendances at a whole league over a season, each individual club is mainly concerned about its own home gates. One major determinant of this is the size of the local market, in terms of population. Also, the number of clubs competing in the local catchment area will influence the size of each club's attendances.

A major determinant, however, of any one club's demand will be playing success. In general, other things being equal, the more successful the club, the higher the attendance will be. This is an obvious conflict with the uncertainty of outcome hypothesis discussed above. Whereas each club can maximise its attendances by maximising the number of wins, the league as a whole may suffer by a reduced uncertainty of outcome. This conflict is a major feature of the supply side of professional team sports.

Sloane (1980) stresses the need for the league to operate strong anti-competitive controls so that the league is not dominated by one or a few teams:

> The more the uncertainty of the results of the games, the higher the public demand for the sport. The more equal the quality of competing teams, the more the uncertainty of the result. Uncertainty of result is threatened by the tendency of wealthy clubs to enjoy a virtuous circle of playing success and rising revenue, and others to be caught in a vicious circle of relative poverty and playing failure. To diminish this possibility sports league organisations claim justification for operating as cartels, redistributing revenue among member clubs, restricting price competition between them, and limiting their property rights in players. With the recent weakening of labour market controls in professional team sports, revenue sharing may have become even more necessary to promote equality of performance among clubs.

There are several such restrictions in force in American professional team sports. Leagues operate revenue-sharing arrangements where television and some sponsorship revenues are negotiated centrally by the league and revenues shared equally between clubs. The draft system operates so that the weakest teams from the previous season get first choice of the college players coming through to the professional league for the new season. Salary caps prevent the richest and most successful clubs from bidding up players' wages to attract them.

One of the most controversial restrictions is the reserve clause that restricts players' bargaining rights in the labour market by keeping the player tied to the club that holds his registration. In Britain, an equivalent scheme, the retain and transfer scheme, operated in British professional football until 1978. Owners of clubs in North America have consistently argued that the reserve clause was essential for maintaining competitive balance. However, it has increasingly caused disputes between clubs and players and was abolished in 1976 in baseball and basketball. In their historical analysis Quirk and Fort (1992) analysed the level of competitive balance in both these sports pre-1976 and post-1976. They concluded:

> The argument of owners that the reserve-option clause is needed for competitive balance is offered no support at all by microeconomic theory. Instead, that theory asserts that there will be the same degree of competitive balance in a league with a reserve-option clause and unrestricted sale of players as there would be in a league with a free competitive labour market. The evidence from free agency in baseball and basketball is consistent with microeconomic theory and not with the claims of owners – there are no indications that

introducing competitive labour markets into baseball and basketball has had any measurable impact on competitive balance in those leagues.

Despite this conclusion, it is generally accepted that the role of the league is to operate as a cartel to restrict open competition between clubs in both the product and labour markets so that no one club becomes too dominant (Cairns *et al.*, 1986). The cartel model as a representation of the sports league is based on the assumption of profit maximisation of both the club and the league. In order for the league to secure profit maximisation for the group of clubs that make up the league, it is necessary for the league to impose restrictions on the profit maximisation of individual clubs.

The role of the league in managing the collective interests of all clubs is in direct conflict with the individual profit maximisation interests of the most successful clubs, which would be more profitable without the restrictions imposed by the league. The league has the objective of ensuring uncertainty of outcome and competitive balance. Each individual club has the objective of maximising sporting success and the consequent economic benefits of television, sponsorship, and gate money revenue. This conflict of interest between the objectives of the cartel and those of its individual members is the classic scenario of the economics of cartels. Normally, the cartel's role is not only to impose product and labour market restrictions on members, but also to restrict output in order to keep the price high. In American team sports, in the NFL for instance, this restriction of output is exhibited by no team playing more than one game a week, and the length of the season is restricted to one-third of the year. The number of teams is also strictly controlled, with only 30 teams in the NFL.

Broadcasting demand

Traditionally clubs in professional team sports have earned income primarily from sales of tickets to games. Hence the theory, put forward in earlier sections of this chapter, that, to maximise profits and revenue, the league must maintain uncertainty of outcome and competitive balance in order to maximise attendances. However, in recent years other sources of revenue and profit have become much more important, although revenue from sales of tickets to games still remains the single most important element of total revenue. Chapter 9 examined the increasing importance of sponsorship income in professional team sports. The most important factor in recent years, however, has been the sharp rise in the economic value of broadcasting rights to professional team sports.

In early 1998, American broadcasters agreed to pay $18 billion for the rights to the National Football League for 8 years. The previous deal, for 1995–1998, was for $1.58 billion and was with Rupert Murdoch's News Corporation, also owners of BSkyB, and this deal projected Fox to be one of the big four broadcasters in the United States together with NBC, CBC and ABC.

The top eight television programmes in the United States are sports events. Around 130 million watch the Super Bowl on television. The result is that advertising rates are at a premium during the televising of such events. Thirty seconds of advertising during the Super Bowl costs over $1 million, and it is the large sports companies such as Nike, Adidas and Reebok that will want to attach their advertising slots to this and other major televised sports competitions.

The reason for this in America is that these games are broadcast on free-to-air channels and attract massive audiences – half the American population in the case of the Super Bowl. The motive of the television companies in bidding for them is the ability to sell advertising slots at hugely inflated prices during such games, which last two or three times longer than the equivalent in Europe, and are broken more frequently by advertising slots than is the case in Europe.

The importance of American football to the television companies is illustrated by a *Financial Times* article (17 January 1998) discussing the latest $18 billion deal for the right to the NFL. The article indicated how no major network TV station could afford to be without football:

> CBS learnt that lesson in 1993 when it allowed Fox, which is owned by Rupert Murdoch's News Corp, to outbid it in the previous auction of broadcast rights for football. With the loss of the sport, the network plunged from first to third in the rankings, where it languishes. The fledgling Fox was promoted overnight, and the Big Three which had hitherto dominated viewing become the Big Four.
>
> CBS this week attempted to restore its fortunes by paying $4 billion (twice the old price) to show some American football games. Fox stumped up $4.4 billion for another package of games, and Walt Disney, which owns ABC and the ESPN cable sports channel, followed with a $9.2 billion deal, a grand total of almost $18 billion. That left NBC, the top-rated network, with no football on its schedule for the first time in decades. Time Warner's TNT, the most popular cable channel in the US was also pushed out of the game.
>
> The NFL, which started the decade earning $500 million a year from TV rights and last year collected just over $1 billion, will enter the next century with annual small-screen revenues of $2.2 billion.

This escalation in the sale of broadcasting rights to the games of major professional team sports is a phenomenon that started in the United States but, as we will see later in this chapter and in the next, was quickly imported into Britain.

The American professional team sports model

We can identify, therefore, certain clear characteristics of the American professional team sports model.

- Both clubs and leagues clearly have profit maximisation as the priority.
- The conflict between the behaviour required to ensure profit-maximising behaviour by the league as a whole and maximisation of profits for the most successful clubs in the league requires that the league act as a cartel to

impose restrictions on output (the number of clubs, number of games, price competition, salaries paid to players, and the operations of the labour market). In addition, the leagues have traditionally employed revenue-sharing arrangements so that the economic gap between the richest and the poorest clubs is narrowed.

- These restrictions on competition in both the product and labour markets is accepted by the competition (anti-trust) regulators in the USA as necessary to maintain the competitive balance (or uncertainty of outcome) that is a necessary condition for the successful operation of professional team sports leagues.

- The sale of broadcasting rights has become an increasingly important source of revenue to professional team sports leagues and clubs.

These are the critical aspects of the economics of professional team sports in the USA that we need to bear in mind when we analyse the situation in both Britain and the rest of Europe.

Before we leave the North American scene, however, one other issue needs to be noted. It is the issue raised by Crompton (1998c):

> Cities do not use public money to build skyscrapers and then hand them over gratis to IBM or Telecom, even though such businesses are likely to have positive economic impact on a community. However, in the US they do use public money to build stadia for professional football and baseball teams, and arenas for professional hockey and basketball teams, and then give them to the millionaire owners of those teams. This largesse is particularly remarkable given the conditions of financial crises and infrastructure deterioration that prevail in major cities. . . .
>
> In 1997 there were 113 major league professional franchises in the four sports listed above. Between 1989 and 1997, 31 of them had a new stadium or arena built; and in 1997, an additional 39 teams were actively seeking new facilities, finalising a deal to build one, or waiting to move into one (Noll and Zimbalist, 1997). All of these were built with public money or leased to the owners for either no rental fee or nominal sums which do not approach the amount needed to cover the debt charges involved. These facilities are not cheap. The typical arena cost for hockey and basketball is around $150 million while for football and baseball stadia the typical cost increases to approximately $250 million.

The rationale for local governments providing these massive subsidies to profit-maximising sports businesses is that local businesses will benefit from the spending of spectators attracted to the games that take place in these stadia and arenas.

This argument has been critically evaluated in Chapter 10. For the moment, we simply note that it is a rather unusual situation for a profit-maximising business to receive such a huge subsidy from local government. Another significant effect of this phenomenon of cities willing to build new stadia and arenas for

American professional sports teams is that these teams move around from city to city, dependent on which city gives them the best offer in terms of facilities. As we shall see, this is a major difference from the European situation.

The economics of English professional football

Until the late 1980s there seemed little relationship between the American professional team sports model described in the previous sections and the way the major professional team sport in England, football, operated. Many of the major differences between Britain and North America in relation to professional team sports were noted in the literature.

One major area of difference was in the objectives of clubs. In North America, profit maximisation is the clearly established objective. Noll (1974) concluded that 'there is no evidence that the prime motivation of the vast majority of the owners is any consideration other than profits'.

A similar statement would not be true for British football, or other British professional team sports, prior to the 1990s. The PEP Report on professional football (1966) stated that the objective of the professional football club is: 'to provide entertainment in the form of a football match. The objective is not to maximise profit but to achieve playing success while remaining solvent'.

Many league clubs operated at a loss and only stayed in existence through directors' donations, supporters club activities, transfer fee revenues and the use of lotteries.

Sloane (1971) regarded utility maximisation as the objective of most clubs. He suggested that supporters and directors were willing to outlay money without regard to pecuniary rewards, playing success being the ultimate objective of the clubs. His theory was that clubs strove to maximise utility subject to financial viability, or a maximum security constraint.

Wiseman (1977) indicated that the motives of directors may not be too dissimilar to those we identified for sponsorship in Chapter 9:

> Club directors are often fanatical supporters and find their involvement a rewarding hobby in itself. But of course philanthropy is not all. Directors are given the best seats, free boardroom hospitality and the chance to mix with men in similar positions as themselves. In addition to these social and business contacts, a directorship (and especially a chairmanship) of a league club is excellent for a man's prestige, local standing and business.

Wiseman goes on to suggest that, whereas profits are not the objective, the pursuit of playing success can lead to larger attendances, and hence greater revenue. This might indicate that utility maximisation and profit maximisation objectives may yield the same predictions. However, Sloane argues that the utility maximisation objective will give quite different predictions to that of profit maximisation. He quotes Rottenberg (1956), who suggests that a profit-maximising club may not want to maximise playing success:

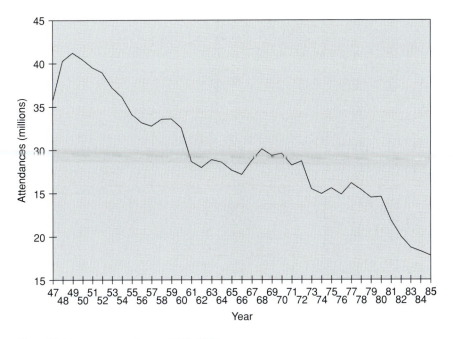

Figure 11.1 League attendances 1947–1985.
Source: *Rothmans Football Yearbook*

It should not be thought that wealthy teams will invariably want to assemble winning combinations of players. . . . A team will seek to maximise the difference between its revenues and its costs. If this quantity is maximised, for any given club, by assembling a team of players who are of lower quality than those of another club in its league, it will pay the former to run behind.

Such 'running behind' would not occur under utility maximisation. However, it is difficult to envisage how a club could maximise profits in the Premier League by this type of behaviour. There are many examples of clubs that have assembled 'a team of players . . . of lower quality', often by deliberately selling star players in order to raise revenue. The end result has tended to be relegation to a lower division, reduced attendances and lower profits (or more likely, bigger losses). Cairns (1983) concludes that: 'it is not clear that we are capable in principle of empirically distinguishing utility and profit maximising behaviour'.

Whatever the objective of the clubs, the reality was that neither the profit-maximising nor the utility-maximising objective was achieved by the majority of clubs prior to the 1990s. Figure 11.1 shows the long decline in attendances from the peak of 41.3 million in the 1948–49 season. Except for a brief revival following England's World Cup success in 1966, attendances fell steadily from then until reaching their lowest point at just over 16 million in the 1985–86 season. May 1985 proved to be a particularly low point for English professional football.

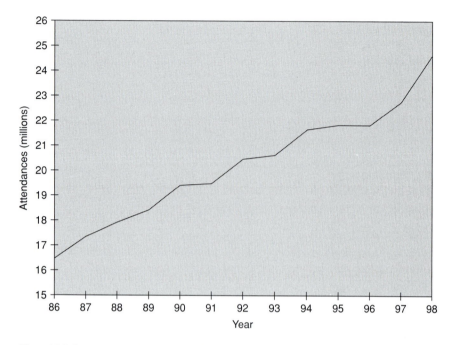

Figure 11.2 League attendances 1986–1996.
Source: *Rothmans Football Yearbook*

In that month, fifty-five people were killed and over 200 were injured when there was a fire in the old wooden stand at Bradford City Football Club. A few weeks later a 15-year-old boy died during rioting by supporters of Leeds United and Birmingham City. On 30 May 1985, thirty-eight Juventus supporters died at the European Cup Final in the Heysel stadium in Brussels when Liverpool supporters chased them into a wall that collapsed and caused people to be crushed. The result was the banning of all English clubs from European competitions.

Critcher (1985) questioned whether English football would survive.

> Football will no doubt survive in British culture in one form or another. It will remain a strength in regions where traditional male working-class culture persists. . . . Perhaps football belonged to an earlier phase of industrialisation and has only a tenuous place in post-industrial society.

However, 1985 proved to be the end of English football's long decline. Since then attendances have risen consistently (Figure 11.2), as have revenues to the major clubs. It is not easy to explain why the long decline changed around in this way in the mid-1980s, particularly since before the 1980s had finished, the Hillsborough disaster at the FA Cup semi-final in 1989 that led to ninety-six dying seemed to sink another nail in the coffin of English professional football.

However, it is easier to explain why the economics of English professional football became much healthier in the 1990s.

Several factors contributed to this. First, as a direct result of the Hillsborough disaster, the Taylor Report (1990) recommended that all the football grounds in the top league become all-seater stadia by the start of the 1994–95 season. This resulted in the highest level of new investment in British football grounds in the twentieth century taking place in the first four years of the 1990s. Second, the top twenty-two clubs in the country broke away from the Football League and formed the FA Carling Premier League, which began life on 15 August 1992. Third, a few clubs floated on the Stock Market and became publicly quoted companies with a clear responsibility to shareholders to operate on sensible commercial grounds (i.e. profit maximisation). Prior to 1995 only four clubs – Millwall, Preston, Tottenham Hotspur, and Manchester United – had taken this route, and only Manchester United could claim it had been successful. In 1995 and 1996 many more clubs followed, and certainly in 1996 football club shares were City favourites.

However, the single largest change to English professional football was the increasing importance of revenue from broadcasting rights.

The escalating revenue from the sale of broadcasting rights for football

Table 11.1 gives the history of the contracts for televised football from 1983, when the first televised live Football League matches were shown, until 1997, when BSkyB signed a 4-year deal for £670 million for the broadcasting of

Table 11.1 The cost of the rights to live league matches from the top division in England, 1983 to 1997

| | *Start year of the contract* | | | | | |
	1983	*1985*	*1986*	*1988*	*1992*	*1997*
Length of contract (years)	2	0.5	2	4	5	4
Broadcaster	BBC/ITV	BBC	BBC/ITV	ITV	BSkyB	BSkyB
Rights fee (£m)	5.2	1.3	6.2	44	191.5	670
Annual rights fee (£m)*	2.6	2.6	3.1	11	38.3	167.5
Number of live matches per season	10	6	14	18	60	60
Fees per live match (£m)	0.26	0.43	0.22	0.61	0.64	2.79

Source: MMC (1999).

* Based on the rights fee divided by the number of years in the contract. There have been variations in annual rights fees. For example, the annual rights fees for the 1992 Premier League contract were £35.5 million in 1992–93, £37.5 million in 1993–94 and £39.5 million in each of the last three years of the contract. The payments in the current 4-year contract for rights to the Premier League are £50 million paid when the offer was accepted, £135 million in 1997–98, £145 million in 1998–99, £160 million in 1999–2000 and £180 million in 2000–01.

Premier League matches. Deals for 1983–85 and 1986–88 were joint deals with the BBC and ITV, with the annual rights fee rising slightly from £2.6 million in the 1983–85 period to 3.1 million in the 1986–88 period.

The major escalation came when ITV pushed up the annual fee to £11 million in 1988–92 for its exclusive coverage, with a large increase in the number of live televised matches to 18 per year. This 250 per cent increase over the previous level of fees for televised football was matched in 1992, when BSkyB won the rights for 60 live matches at a cost of £38 million per year. When the deal was negotiated in 1997 there was a further 337 per cent rise in the annual rights (Monopolies and Mergers Commission, 1999).

Table 11.2 gives the distribution of television revenues over the Premier League clubs from 1992 to 1998. It shows how the leading five clubs – Manchester United, Arsenal, Liverpool, Chelsea, and Leeds – accounted on average for over 30 per cent of total TV payments over this period, in contrast to the revenue-sharing arrangements that are seen in American team sports.

It is also notable that most of the revenue from the sale of broadcasting rights is distributed back to the Premier League clubs. In 1998–99, less than 14 per cent of this television revenue went to other football-related bodies, mainly the Football League, the Professional Footballers' Association and the Football Trust. In 1998–99, various youth development schemes together received a total of £200,000 and the English Schools FA £25,000 out of total television revenue to the Premier League of £168 million (Monopolies and Mergers Commission, 1999).

The importance of television revenues to Premier League clubs can be seen from Table 11.3, which shows that although Manchester United received the second largest television payment (after Arsenal) in 1996–97, this accounted for a smaller percentage of the overall turnover of Manchester United than for any other Premier League club. The reason for this is given in Table 11.4, which shows the tremendous variation in the level of turnover between Premier League clubs. Manchester United had the highest turnover in 1996–97 at £88 million: over twice that of the next club, Newcastle United, at £41 million.

The lowest turnover for 1996–97 was Southampton at £9.2 million, with Wimbledon the second lowest. However, Wimbledon tops Table 11.3 with 42 per cent of its turnover coming from television revenues, and Southampton is second at 35 per cent. Manchester United, on the other hand, is bottom of Table 11.3 with only 7 per cent of its total turnover coming from television revenue, because it had the highest gate receipt revenue (£30 million) of any club (although this accounted for only 34 per cent of total revenue in 1996–97). Sponsorship and advertising accounted for a further 13 per cent, conferences and catering 6 per cent, and 'merchandising and other' a massive 33 per cent, almost equal to gate receipts.

This massive increase in revenue from the sale of broadcasting rights to the Premiership has been the single largest factor affecting the economic fortunes of Premiership clubs. However, little of this money trickles down to clubs in the Football League, many of which had not seen a change in economic fortunes

Table 11.2 Total TV payments to Premier League clubs, 1992–93 to 1997–98

Club	1992–93	1993–94	1994–95	1995–96	1996–97	1997–98	Average for 1992–93 to 1997–98
Arsenal	4.83	5.30	4.19	5.54	6.85	7.52	6.31
Manchester United	6.85	7.24	7.42	7.81	7.58	7.38	7.41
Liverpool	5.66	5.30	5.71	6.49	6.95	6.79	6.42
Chelsea	4.68	3.75	4.31	4.53	5.59	6.45	5.37
Leeds United	4.17	5.83	5.08	4.47	4.71	5.82	5.18
Blackburn Rovers	5.78	6.82	6.86	5.25	4.44	5.61	5.58
Aston Villa	6.44	4.81	3.78	5.81	5.49	5.20	5.26
West Ham United	–	4.06	4.39	5.18	4.52	5.01	4.26
Derby County	–	–	–	–	4.38	4.95	2.78
Newcastle United	–	5.82	5.29	8.11	6.76	4.73	5.26
Coventry City	3.84	4.42	4.11	3.87	3.71	4.66	4.19
Leicester City	–	–	3.24	–	4.73	4.61	3.09
Tottenham Hotspur	4.84	4.56	4.95	5.68	5.24	4.52	4.89
Southampton	3.55	3.34	4.35	3.74	3.85	4.38	4.00
Everton	4.08	3.63	3.87	5.54	4.21	4.25	4.25
Wimbledon	3.96	4.82	4.24	3.84	5.31	4.00	4.39
Bolton Wanderers	–	–	–	3.09	–	3.82	1.69
Sheffield Wednesday	4.53	4.89	4.43	3.94	4.99	3.61	4.27
Crystal Palace	3.32	–	3.34	–	–	3.37	1.89
Barnsley	–	–	–	–	–	3.30	1.18
Other	33.48	25.40	20.42	17.11	10.70	0.00	12.31
Total TV payments(£m)	35.25	36.05	39.59	38.27	83.04	129.11	361.32

Source: MMC (1999).

Table 11.3 The proportion of revenue accounted for by BSkyB's coverage of the Premier League, 1996–97 (%)

Wimbledon	42.3
Southampton	34.6
Derby County	34.0
Sheffield Wednesday	28.9
Blackburn Rovers	25.8
Coventry City	25.1
West Ham United	24.6
Leicester City	22.7
Sunderland	22.3
Arsenal	20.9
Aston Villa	20.6
Chelsea	19.6
Nottingham Forest	19.3
Everton	18.5
Leeds United	17.9
Tottenham Hotspur	15.6
Liverpool	14.7
Middlesborough	13.8
Newcastle United	13.6
Manchester United	7.2
Total (£m)	83.0

Source: MMC calculations based on data in Deloitte & Touche (1998).

Table 11.4 Revenue excluding transfer fees in 1996–97 and 1992–93

	1992–93 revenue (£m)	1992–93 (%)	1996–97 revenue (£m)	1996–97 (%)	Growth in revenue (%)
Manchester United	25,177	13.6	87,939	19.0	249.3
Newcastle United	8,743	4.7	41,134	8.9	370.5
Liverpool	17,496	9.4	39,153	8.4	123.8
Tottenham Hotspur	16,594	9.0	27,874	6.0	68.0
Arsenal	15,342	8.3	27,158	5.9	77.0
Chelsea	7,891	4.3	23,729	5.1	200.1
Middlesborough	3,968	2.1	22,502	4.9	467.1
Aston Villa	10,175	5.5	22,079	4.8	117.0
Leeds United	13,324	7.2	21,785	4.7	63.5
Everton	7,994	4.3	18,882	4.1	136.2
Leicester City	4,775	2.6	17,320	3.7	262.7
West Ham United	6,571	3.5	15,256	3.3	132.2
Notts Forest	7,651	4.1	14,435	3.1	88.7
Sheffield Wednesday	12,806	6.9	14,335	3.1	11.9
Blackburn Rovers	6,305	3.4	14,302	3.1	126.8
Sunderland	3,806	2.1	13,415	2.9	252.5
Coventry City	4,592	2.5	12,265	2.6	167.1
Derby County	4,183	2.3	10,738	2.3	156.7
Wimbledon	3,556	1.9	10,410	2.2	192.7
Southampton	4,307	2.3	9,238	2.0	114.5
Total	185,256	100.00	463,949	100.00	150.4

Source: MMC calculations based on data in Deloitte & Touche (1998).

from the 1980s, even though BSkyB currently has a 5-year contract to show Football League games for a total fee of £125 million. The escalation in the fees for broadcasting rights for Premiership football has only served to widen the gap between the richest and poorest clubs. Whereas each Premier League club receives around £8 million a season from television revenue, each First Division club receives around £0.5 million.

The American model and British professional team sports

The development of the Premier League in British football in the 1990s, to-gether with the flotation of clubs on the Stock Market and massively increased revenues from sports sponsorship, merchandising and the scale of broadcasting rights, has led some commentators to argue that this increasing commercialisa-tion of British football, and other British professional team sports, is an indica-tion that the American model has been adopted in British professional team sports.

There are certainly greater similarities with the American model than was the case in the 1980s. As we have already pointed out, one of the major topics of discussion in the literature in the 1970s and 1980s was the differences in the objectives of clubs between American and British professional team sports. Whereas profit maximisation was the norm in America, maximising playing success or 'utility maximisation' was the role in Britain, and the rest of Europe.

This has effectively changed for many Premier League and some Football League and Scottish clubs by the flotation of the clubs on either the London Stock Exchange or the Alternative Investment Market. In the 1998–99 season seven Premier League clubs (Aston Villa, Leeds Sporting (Leeds United), Lei-cester City, Manchester United, Newcastle United, Southampton Leisure, and Tottenham Hotspur) were quoted on the London Stock Exchange and a further three (Charlton Athletic, Chelsea Village, and Nottingham Forest) were quoted on AIM. A further five clubs from other divisions (Burnden Leisure (Bolton), Heart of Midlothian, Millwall, Sheffield United, and Sunderland) were quoted on the London Stock Exchange and five more (Birmingham City, Celtic, Loftus Road (QPR/Wasps), Preston North End, West Bromwich Albion) were quoted on AIM. Of these 20 quoted clubs, only Manchester United (1991), Millwall (1989), and Tottenham Hotspur (1983) were quoted prior to 1995 (Deloitte & Touche, 1998). Thus, this is a new development in the financing of British (in particular, Premier League) clubs that puts increasing emphasis on stronger commercial management of the clubs. Flotation automatically involves greater emphasis on profits in the objectives of clubs, and results show that profits of some clubs have improved tremendously in the 1990s.

A quote from the Deloitte & Touche (1998) analysis of financial results for 1996–97 indicates the increased profitability of (mainly) Premier League clubs but also the growing gap between the Premier League and the Football League:

Turnover grew significantly for the Premier League (34%), Division One (26%) and Division Two (32%), although turnover fell 1% in Division Three. The Premier league now accounts for 68.7% of football revenues. . . . The top five finishers in the Premier League (Manchester United, Newcastle United, Arsenal, Liverpool, and Aston Villa) had a combined turnover greater than that of all the 72 Football League clubs. . . .

The Deloitte and Touche report goes on to indicate that the aggregate profits of all clubs in the Premier League in 1996–97 increased to £86 million from £52 million in 1995–96. On the other hand, aggregating profit and loss for all clubs in each of the Football League divisions yields a net loss for each division.

This evidence suggests that the Premier League has, at least in some ways, started to exhibit the characteristics of the American professional team sports leagues with increasing revenues from sponsorship, merchandising, and sale of broadcasting rights leading to higher profits. However, one crucial difference between the American model and British professional football is the lack of restriction of output in terms of the number of clubs and number of games. The NFL in the USA has 30 clubs for a population of 260 million. England and Wales have 92 Premier and Football League clubs with a further 40 clubs in Scotland for a total population of 56 million.

Whereas clubs in American professional sports leagues play once a week for three months of the year, clubs in British football begin in August and finish in May. Also, international competition, at either club or country level, for most of America's professional team sports is not an important factor. The World and European Championships in football mean that every two years international football goes on into July and, in the intervening years, qualifiers for these tournaments are played in June. Within these long seasons, clubs will often play twice a week. The reorganisation of the European Champions' League in 1999 substantially increased the number of games for Europe's major clubs.

Another characteristic not evident in British football has been the movement of franchises from one city to another, often on the basis of incentives such as a new stadium provided out of taxpayers' money, that has been so common in North America. There is a stronger history of community attachment to clubs in Britain that makes it much more difficult for clubs to move cities.

There are two other major differences between what has happened in British football and the American professional team sports model. First, neither the Premier League nor the Football League has imposed the restrictions on competition, revenue-sharing and salary caps regarded as essential in the American model to generate uncertainty of outcome. In the NFL, 90 per cent of revenues are shared and gate receipts are split 60:40 in favour of the home team. In the Premier League and the Football League, the home team takes all the gate receipts. This favours the bigger clubs with larger capacity grounds and good support. Even in the Premier League, commentators have suggested two or three different leagues are operating since only a small number of richer clubs stand any realistic chance of winning the Championship or the major cup competitions, another group battles for mid-table positions, and a third group struggles to stay in the Premier League, with a sub-group of them yo-yoing up and down between the First Division and the Premier League (Deloitte & Touche, 1998).

This lack of attention by the league to its role in maintaining competitive balance is a major difference between Britain and America. The success of the Green Bay Packers, a small city team, in recent years is evidence that measures to ensure competitive balance do allow smaller clubs to achieve success. Green Bay's success would be the equivalent in Britain to Port Vale winning the Premier League title or the FA Cup: hardly imaginable in the current economic climate of British professional football.

The second major difference between Britain and America in the economics of professional team sports, however, has not been well recognised and is a greater potential long-term threat to the economic health of British professional team sports than any of the factors mentioned above.

Britain has followed America in the escalation of fees for broadcasting rights for the major professional team sports. There is a clear difference, however, between the motives of the American broadcasters competing for the rights to the NFL and the motives of BSkyB, 40 per cent owned by Rupert Murdoch's News Corporation, for acquiring the rights to Premiership football. American broadcasters bid up the rights to the NFL because of its importance in winning them market share, and also because of the ability to increase advertising revenues for advertisements during football games. BSkyB bids for Premiership rights to increase revenue from subscriptions to its pay-per-view channels.

While in the American scenario there is correspondence of the objectives of clubs, broadcasters, the league, advertisers and major sponsors, since they all get maximum exposure to the country's largest television audiences, in the British case there is conflict between the objectives of the broadcaster (maximum subscriptions) and those of the league, clubs, advertisers, and major sponsors (maximum exposure). To some extent, this conflict is reduced in British football by the fact that there is major football coverage on the BBC with the *Match of the Day* highlights programmes and on ITV with the European Champions' League coverage, matches which achieved the highest television audiences of any sports programmes in the 1998–99 season. Whereas audiences for BSkyB's live Premiership matches vary between 1 million and 2 million, with the odd key match getting slightly more than 2 million, *Match of the Day* viewing figures often exceed 10 million although average viewing figures are around 6 million. ITV's live coverage of Manchester United versus Bayern Munich in May 1999 attracted an audience of 15.6 million in Britain (with a peak of 18.8 million).

Although football has managed to avoid the negative effects of reduced exposure on BSkyB, other professional team sports in Britain, in particular rugby league and rugby union, have not fared as well. Both these sports, encouraged by the success of the Premier League, signed exclusive contracts with BSkyB in 1996. Rugby league made the biggest change to its structure with the formation of Super League, playing in summer rather than winter, to fit in with Rupert Murdoch's Super League World Club Challenge involving Australian and New

Zealand teams. However, in the case of rugby league, the normal television audience of 2.5–3.5 million that they achieved on BBC's *Grandstand* dropped to 100,000–200,000 on BSkyB. This represents a serious reduction in exposure and marketing of the sport.

Similarly, rugby union internationals involving England used to attract 4 million on the BBC, but have dropped to below 500,000 on BSkyB. England is the least watched of all the Six Nations teams despite a highlights programme on ITV following the live coverage on BSkyB. This is particularly a problem for the impact these sports will have through their exposure to younger generations, with potentially serious implications for the future economic health of these sports.

Conclusions

The economics of professional team sports developed as a recognised area of applied economics well before other areas of the economics of sport were recognised. This longer pedigree stems from the 'peculiar' nature of the economics of team sports and the need for leagues to control competition in order to maintain competitive balance or uncertainty of outcome.

The British literature developed later than its North American counterpart, and mainly concentrated on how British professional team sports were different to North American equivalents, in particular in the objectives of owners.

This difference is not so easy to establish in the late 1990s for the top level of British team sports, in particular the Premier League. However, this convergence of objectives between major Premier League clubs and NFL clubs in the United States has not led to convergence in other areas of the American model of professional team sports. The largest differences relate to the lack of revenue-sharing mechanisms in British professional team sports and the restrictions in overall exposure that the British broadcasting deals have led to. The end result is that rather than the Premier League achieving maximum profits, it is a small group of clubs in that league that achieve most benefits. Since this pattern is reflected in other European countries, the closest we might see to an American model of professional team sports is the new European Champions' League, with a large number of more equal clubs, more revenue-sharing, and greater exposure through free-to-air channels.

12 Sport and broadcasting

Introduction

The last three chapters have emphasised the importance of broadcasting to sport sponsorship, major sports events, and professional team sports. All major sponsorship deals, for events or for teams, will depend on the guarantee of widespread television coverage of the event or the team. The teams and events with the largest television audiences will attract the most sponsors at the highest prices. We have already given the examples of the Olympics, the soccer World Cup, and the Super Bowl in the United States. The analysis in the last three chapters has looked at the sales of broadcasting rights as an increasingly important part of the economics of sport sponsorship, major sports events, and professional team sports.

However, these chapters looked at broadcasting through its effects on each of these sectors of the sport market. In this chapter we look at the effect of sport on the broadcasting market. We attempt to define the broadcasting market and then look at the role of sport in it. We then go on to analyse the nature of the interaction between the sports market as a whole and the broadcasting market. This task is made easier by the publication in 1999 of the Monopolies and Mergers Commission (MMC) report on the proposed merger between British Sky Broadcasting Group plc and Manchester United plc (Monopolies and Mergers Commission, 1999). This report is, to date, the most comprehensive analysis of the economic relationship between the sports and broadcasting markets in Britain, and provides the basis of much of this chapter. Consequently, the case-study of BSkyB and Manchester United also features prominently. However, we begin by looking briefly at the history of the relationship between sport and television.

The history of sport and broadcasting

The last three chapters have emphasised that the effect of television on sport has grown enormously over the recent past, most particularly in the money coming into sport from the sale of broadcasting rights. However, Holt (1989) indicates that there has always been a strong relationship between sport and broadcasting:

In fact, broadcasting first through radio and then even more dramatically on television, has been the single most important influence on the development of sport in this century. The number of radio licences rose from two to eight million between 1926 and 1939 with 71 per cent of all households having a wireless by the Second World War. The first sports broadcast, ironically at the suggestion of the *Daily Mail*, was a fight between Kid Lewis and Georges Carpentier in 1922. Sport came to have an important place in the BBC canon of 'good' entertainment, though boxing did not meet with full official approval. The aim of the new Director-General was to promote sport as well as Christianity. Reith was the true successor of the Victorian headmaster, rapidly establishing a range of sporting events which the BBC in its capacity as the sole arbiter of airways deemed to be of *national* significance. A few big events joined the list of approved patriotic 'moments' like Remembrance Day – the Wembley crowd even sang 'Abide With Me' – and in Reith's words permitted the British people to be 'present equally at functions and ceremonials upon which national sentiment is consecrated'. Test cricket, rugby internationals, the Derby, and the Cup Final were established favourites. The annual rowing contest between the two ancient universities was a great London event with many ordinary families taking sides and wearing favours but it was hardly a matter of 'national' concern until the BBC included the Boat Race in the select band of truly British events. 'Look how that's come to the fore,' remarked a Bristol listener, 'we never used to know anything about it and now there's many wouldn't miss it'. Seventy per cent of the audience panel of a BBC survey in 1939 listened to the Boat Race followed by 51 per cent for boxing, 50 per cent for soccer, and 50 per cent for cricket; soccer and boxing were predictably the favourites of the working-class respondents but the 34 per cent overall interest in Wimbledon was a clear indication that hitherto bourgeois sports were broadening their appeal.

The first sports television broadcast in Britain was in June 1937, when 25 minutes of a men's single match from Wimbledon was televised. The BBC televised the international match between England and Scotland on 9 April 1938, the world's first live television pictures of a soccer match. A few weeks later the BBC gave the first television broadcast of the FA Cup Final on 30 April between Huddersfield Town and Preston North End (Barnett, 1990).

However, although these events were pioneering in broadcast terms, so few people had a television that they made little impact on the country as a whole. As Holt (1989) comments: 'In the early 1950s no more than 10 per cent of households had a television. By the late 1960s only 10 per cent did not.'

During this period, the BBC used sport (and football in particular) to encourage '. . . working people to buy or hire televisions in the 1950s with the slogan "When they are talking about the big match on TV will you have to remain silent?"' (Holt, 1989).

BSkyB, then, was not the first broadcaster in Britain to sell subscriptions (or licences in the case of the BBC) by the offer of exclusive coverage of football or other sports.

Over this period the BBC dominated sports coverage in Britain, televising all the major national sporting spectacles, and establishing the annual cycle of major sports events beginning in January with the Five Nations rugby union tournament, then the Boat Race, the Grand National, rugby league Challenge Cup final, FA Cup Final, the Derby, Cricket Test matches, Wimbledon, and the Open golf championship.

Whannel (1992) suggests that there were good economic reasons for the BBC to put so much emphasis on sport. Whannel indicates the inequality of market power between the buyers and sellers of broadcasting rights for sports events in the early part of the post-war period:

> The dominance of the BBC in the field of broadcasting was matched by its dominance over the organisations of sport. Until the arrival of ITV in 1955, the BBC was the only purchaser of a commodity, sporting competitions, for which there were many suppliers. These suppliers, the sporting organisations, were rarely able to band together out of mutual interest. Television sport in the United Kingdom has generally been a buyer's market. . . .
>
> In its negotiations with outside bodies the BBC claimed that its right to cover events was analogous to that of the press. Consequently fees were regarded as 'facility fees' – payment offered by way of compensation for inconvenience – and did not constitute a payment for broadcast rights. . . .
>
> During the immediate post-war period, the BBC attempted to settle on a fee of 25 guineas as standard. It was to become a point of contention with the athletics authorities that, as a facilities fee, the BBC held that this payment included an allowance for lost seats at camera positions, and consequently no extra compensation was paid.

However, as the 1950s progressed it became increasingly evident that such a policy could not be sustained. The arrival of ITV in 1955 destroyed the BBC's monopoly on the buying side of the market and increased the level of fees. However, the BBC continued to dominate the broadcasting of sport.

Holt (1989) provides a possible explanation for this BBC dominance:

> In Britain the pattern of televised sport has in many respects followed the natural preferences of the 'amateur' establishment. With the exception of the Cup Final, the independent channels have concentrated on racing and on wrestling for Saturday afternoon entertainment and do not show golf or cricket. Currently the ITV sports budget is around £14 million. 'In newspaper terms, the BBC is much more *Telegraph* and we are the *Mirror* or even the *Sun*', remarked ITV's head of sport recently. As an established 'national' institution the BBC head of sport claims 'we don't approach life from a purely business point of view'. Historically the BBC has been in a privileged position to negotiate coverage with the 'gentlemen amateurs' of the MCC, the Committee of the All-England Club, and the four rugby unions. 'I have never attempted to conceal my belief that "Wimbledon" treated us generously', wrote the Head of Outside Broadcasts in 1952. 'I assumed it was the

deliberate policy of an amateur sport towards a "public service".' From early on the government underpinned this advantage by laying down that certain 'national' events could not be contractually monopolised by either side. This had the effect of giving the BBC an effective monopoly as advertising revenue could best be maximised by providing an alternative to sport on independent television.

Whannel (1992) gives three reasons why ITV did not in the 1950s and 1960s provide stronger competition with the BBC. First, the BBC had a headstart. It had developed a substantial competitive advantage with its outside broadcasting expertise. It had also tied up many sports on long-term exclusive contracts.

Second, the regional structure of ITV meant that no single company had a big enough audience to justify substantial investment in outside broadcasting facilities or to make large enough bids for exclusive contracts:

> Competition with the BBC required co-operation between the companies, which was hard to establish, with the network system itself only gradually taking shape in an *ad hoc* manner . . . had the companies opted to establish along with Independent Television News (ITN), a nationally based, jointly owned sport company, ITV sport would have been in a stronger position.
>
> (Whannel, 1992)

Third, in the 1950s it was not clearly established that sport was an obvious audience winner.

Holt (1989) points out that the BBC's historical lead over ITV also provided a subtle barrier to entry from competition. The BBC's commentators in the various sports – Harry Carpenter in boxing; Eddie Waring in rugby league; David Coleman in soccer and athletics; John Arlott and Brian Johnston in cricket – were themselves household names and their voices were part of the broadcast event, making it more difficult for ITV to compete.

With these advantages the BBC was also enjoying an economic advantage in that sports broadcasting was still relatively cheap despite a rise in fees for broadcasting rights as a result of competition with ITV. Whannel (1992) states that in the early 1960s, *Grandstand* cost approximately £2,000 per hour, compared to an average of £3,000 per hour for a studio programme:

> Major rugby matches cost £2,500, cricket Test matches £1,600 per day, top show jumping events £1,200 per day, and athletics £2,000 or less, while Wimbledon was a bargain at less than £600 per day.

The coverage of televised sports broadened considerably in the 1960s, beginning with the international coverage of the Rome Olympics in 1960. The power of sport in television was demonstrated in 1966 when the World Cup Final between England and West Germany gathered the whole nation around television screens. The pictures from this final still appear regularly in Britain, most notably in the introduction to the comedy sports quiz *They Think It's All Over*, these words being those of the BBC's TV commentator, Kenneth Wolstenholme, seconds before Geoff Hurst scored the fourth goal that sealed England's victory.

This particular game is also picked out by Cashmore (1996) to indicate how the television coverage was used to contribute to the post-match discussion, again lasting years rather than weeks, on whether England's third goal actually crossed the line:

> It was at this event that the advantage of the camera over the naked eye was fully appreciated. In the championship game, the English team's third goal arrived gift-wrapped for television. The ball thundered against the under-side of the West German team's crossbar, appearing momentarily to bounce over the goal line before rebounding into the field of play. If the *whole* ball had crossed (not just broken as in American football) the plane of the goal line, then it was a goal. The referee said 'yes', the Germans said 'no'. The cameras slowed down the action, freeze-framed it, reversed the angle; and it could still not prove conclusively whether or not the ball had crossed the line. The arguments raged and the footage rolled and rolled.

ITV was dealt a further competitive blow by the introduction of BBC2 in 1964. This gave the BBC a tremendous advantage for those events that took place over a long period of time: cricket Test matches, Wimbledon, major snooker champion-ships. Barnett (1990) indicates how the introduction of BBC2 enhanced the BBC's competitive advantage:

> By switching coverage from BBC1 to BBC2 during the course of a day, thereby allowing one channel to maintain its regular programmes, the BBC has avoided alienating those with no appetite for the particular televised event, while simultaneously satisfying its responsibilities to the followers of sport. Six hours of cricket, golf, tennis, or snooker coverage would be unsustainable for a single-channel public broadcaster and unprofitable for a single commercial channel. Blessed with the flexibility of two-channel cover-age, the BBC has been able to satisfy most of its sports fans, its other licence payers, and – just as importantly – a commitment to major sporting bodies to provide full uninterrupted coverage of their sport.

During the 1960s and 1970s, ITV did attempt to match the BBC in one sport – football. In 1964, 'the BBC initiated what was to become the hallmark of British football coverage and the centrepiece of Saturday night programming – recorded highlights on *Match of the Day*' (Barnett, 1990). *The Big Match* on Sunday afternoons was ITV's answer to *Match of the Day* and was introduced in the 1968–69 season. It proved popular, but as Barnett (1990) pointed out, ITV's regional structure held back its audience since it was never shown in the Granada, Yorkshire, or Central television areas. The FA Cup Final was shown by both the BBC and ITV over this period, but the audience for the BBC coverage was twice that of ITV.

Throughout the 1970s football coverage was handled by negotiation between the BBC and ITV, and the Football League and the Football Association in what Whannel (1992) describes as 'the old cosy BBC/ITV sharing of football'. ITV made an attempt to break free of the dominance of the BBC in sports broadcasting in 1979, as Barnett (1990) describes:

> In 1979, the peace was shattered. In their determination to overcome a long-standing and irritating subservience to the BBC's soccer coverage, under Michael Grade's stewardship as Director of Programmes at LWT, ITV decided to break ranks with the BBC and secure exclusive rights to League football coverage. If the BBC could not be beaten within the ruling spirit of co-operation, the spirit would simply have to be sacrificed. Behind closed doors, and unknown to the BBC, the deal was signed and announced to an unsuspecting public. Uproar ensued. While the contract was perfectly legal, and entitled ITV alone to coverage of English League soccer matches, it was somehow not fair play to exclude the country's national broadcaster from showing the country's national sport. Representations were made, strings were pulled, even the Office of Fair Trading was asked to intervene. What in America had become a customary feature of the television sporting land-scape created in Britain a furious backlash which ITV was unable to withstand. 'In the end', says Bromley [Head of ITV Sport], 'we had to concede it – we couldn't sustain the deal.'

Following the failure of this attempt, it was not until the late 1980s that ITV became a serious threat to the BBC in football coverage when it pushed up the price of broadcasting rights for the 1988–1992 period by 250 per cent and outbid the BBC to obtain exclusive rights.

Before this, however, another major change in the relationship between sport and broadcasting occurred when Channel 4 began transmitting in 1982. Channel 4 did not have the resources to compete with the BBC and ITV for the major British sports events. Instead it chose to have foreign sports such as American football, basketball, and sumo. As Whannel (1996) points out, Channel 4 for the first time set out to educate the audience in how to understand and appreciate these sports, whereas formerly British television had treated them as exotic nov-elties. In the early years of Channel 4, American football and sumo were particu-larly successful in attracting a new audience. Channel 4 also successfully introduced day-by-day coverage of the Tour de France cycle race, again spending the time to explain to the audience the critical stages of the race. In the 1990s, its live coverage of Italian football on Sunday afternoons attracted audiences of between 2 and 3 million (Whannel, 1996).

Barnett (1990) showed how the approach taken by Channel 4 had also resulted in relatively cheap programmes. Channel 4 produced a breakdown of programme costs for 1986–1987, which showed that sport was cheaper per hour than all other programme costs other than films and cartoons. Although Barnett criticises the concept of an average cost per hour for sports programmes, because this disguises tremendous variability, he illustrates the cost per hour to Channel 4 of American football which at the time was one of the prime elements of the sports coverage of Channel 4:

> Although a great deal of editing, packaging, interviews and previews are incorporated, the core of these programmes is the pictures and commentaries produced by the American networks. The bulk of the cost, therefore – about two-thirds – is devoted to editing in both the US and the UK. The weekly cost for two 75-minute programmes is £30,000, representing a notional hourly budget of £12,000.

This compares with £42,600 per hour for drama, £37,200 for news, and £33,700 for current affairs. Channel 4 had entered the sports broadcasting market and introduced a novel menu of new sports, but at the same time cleverly used the peculiar economics of sports broadcasting, in particular the relative cheapness of replicating the sports output of foreign television stations, to its own economic advantage.

It was not, however, until BSkyB entered the scene, most notably with its bid for football's Premiership matches for the 1992–1997 period, that the landscape of sports broadcasting in Britain changed dramatically. BSkyB, with owners used to the much stronger competition for broadcasting rights in the United States, simply raised the price for the rights from its artificially depressed level.

For BSkyB, however, sport became much more important economically than it ever was for the BBC. The BBC received its revenue from the licence fee and had a responsibility to provide a breadth of programmes to satisfy 'the national interest'. This included prominence for sport because of the historically important role of sport in British culture. However, the BBC could never dedicate the share of its income (over 30 per cent) that BSkyB dedicates to sport, as this would be regarded as unbalanced for a public service provider.

BSkyB is not bound by such considerations. Sport has proved the difference between high levels of profit and bankruptcy for BSkyB. Most financial analysts see BSkyB's share value as crucially dependent on its ownership of broadcasting rights in sport. It is this dependency that led BSkyB to offer £625 million for the ownership of the most commercially successful football club in the world, Manchester United, in 1999. Before we consider this bid in more detail, we need to define the broadcasting markets in which BSkyB operates.

The broadcasting market

The Monopolies and Mergers Commission (1999) report split the TV broadcasting market into a vertical chain consisting of four main markets:

(a)   the supply of rights for TV broadcasting purposes, for example for sports events or musical performances; the owners of rights do not usually participate in other levels of the industry;

(b) the supply of programmes; the makers of programmes may need to buy rights to produce certain types of programmes, in particular films and sport; suppliers of programmes may or may not participate at other levels;

(c) the supply of channels at the wholesale level; channel providers package programmes into channels; they may distribute and retail their own channels or supply them wholesale to other pay TV retailers or both; and

(d) the distribution and retailing of channels to subscribers; following the introduction of digital TV, there are currently five separated distribution platforms: analogue terrestrial, digital terrestrial (DTT), analogue satellite, digital satellite and analogue cable; digital cable services are expected shortly.

In Britain, TV channels are provided either free-to-air (by the BBC or the ITV Network Limited Companies) or by payment of a subscription to a cable or satellite operator. BBC, ITV, Channel 4 and Channel 5 are available to all subscribers who pay the television licence fee, which provides the main source of revenue to the BBC. ITV, Channel 4 and Channel 5 receive their revenue from the sale of advertising and other commercial activities. Cable, satellite and digital terrestrial (mainly ONdigital) operators receive revenue by selling subscriptions and advertising. Some channels may be provided free as bonus channels when other premium channels (in particular, sport or movie channels) are subscribed to.

  In order to understand how the four main markets referred to above operate, it is useful to look at the main pay TV operator, BSkyB. Figure 12.1 shows the different levels in the supply chain and the role of BSkyB in it. The MMC (1999) report describes the chain:

> The chain begins with the rights' suppliers that sell the rights to their contents to programme makers, the second level in the chain. Programmes are made into channels by channel providers. For example, the Premier League has sold the rights to live coverage of the Premier League to BSkyB which features these contents on its Sky Sports 1 channel. Channel providers wholesale channels to retailers who sell the channels to viewers via particular platforms. For example, Sky Sports 1 is provided to viewers via the cable platform by the retailer NTL and by other cable companies, via the satellite platform by the retailer BSkyB and via the digital terrestrial platform by the retailer ONdigital.

By September 1998 there were 3.3 million subscribers to satellite television and 2.9 million subscribers to cable TV, compared with 23 million households that have television and receive analogue terrestrial channels. BSkyB's influence is not limited, however, to its 3.3 million subscribers, as Figure 12.1 indicates. Both cable and Digital Terrestrial Television (DTT) take channels from BSkyB and provide additional subscriptions through these platforms:

> BSkyB's total subscriber numbers in the UK and the Republic of Ireland (including cable and DTT) increased from 3.9 million in 1994 to 6.9 million

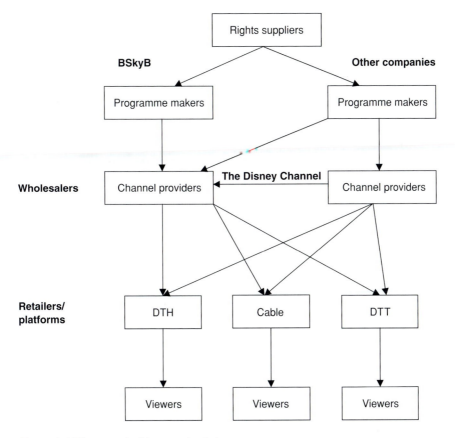

Figure 12.1 The pay television supply chain.
Source: Monopolies and Mergers Commission (1999)

in 1998. The greatest growth has been in cable subscribers such that this category now makes up approximately 49 per cent of total subscribers for one or more channels broadcast by BSkyB in 1998 against 35 per cent in 1994.

(MMC, 1999)

More importantly, BSkyB provides (as a wholesaler) all the main premium sports channels on pay TV (with the exception of MUTV and The Racing Channel). MUTV (Manchester United TV) is jointly owned by BSkyB, Granada Television, and Manchester United, each with a third share. As the MMC (1999) report comments: 'BSkyB's premium sports channels account for virtually all of the viewing figures of all premium sports channels at the wholesale level'.

There were 2.7 million subscribers to one or more Sky Sports channels in 1998. Of all those that have Sky Sports, 82 per cent regularly watched football and 47 per cent regarded football as the single favourite sport on Sky Sports.

The most watched sport after football was cricket, which 38 per cent of Sky Sport subscribers watched regularly, but only 7 per cent regarded cricket as the single most favourite sport on Sky Sports channels. These results came from a NOP Media survey of satellite and cable households in 1996. The same survey asked respondents for their main reason for subscribing to satellite or cable. Forty-nine per cent said their main reason was more choice of programmes/ channels. However, 40 per cent of respondents mentioned sport as the main reason, and football was mentioned by many more respondents than any other sport, as the MMC (1999) report indicates:

> 10 per cent of respondents gave football as their main reason and 5 per cent gave live Premier League football. No other particular sport was mentioned by more than 1 per cent of respondents.

These results indicate that sport, and football in particular, has a crucial role in the sale of subscriptions to pay television.

BSkyB and Manchester United

As Chapter 11 indicated, Manchester United has been by far the most successful club economically since the Premier League began. In addition to having double the turnover of any other Premier League club, MMC (1999) points out that Manchester United was of particular importance to BSkyB:

> In each of the last five full seasons, the match with the highest viewing figures for live Premier League football on BSkyB featured Manchester United. In 1993/94 Manchester United played in all of the top four matches in terms of BSkyB's live Premier League football audiences. In 1994/95 Manchester United matches had the largest two audiences. In 1995/96 and 1996/97 matches involving Manchester United had two of the three largest audiences and in 1997/98 they had the three largest audiences.

Since the Premiership began in the 1992–93 season, Manchester United has clearly been the most successful club in football as well as in economic terms, winning the Premiership five times and coming second on the two other occasions. In this period, it won the double of Premier League Championship and FA Cup on three occasions. In 1999, it added the European Champions' Cup to the FA Cup and Premier League titles to become the first English club to win this treble.

Deloitte & Touche (1999) established that Manchester United was the most commercially successful soccer club in the world. It is not surprising, therefore, that the most successful and profitable sports broadcaster in Europe should want to take it over. The question is, why should the government prevent such a take-over?

The MMC (1999) identified two public interest issues raised by the proposed merger between BSkyB and Manchester United: the effects of the merger on the competition for TV rights and the effects of the merger on football.

Effects of the merger on the competition for TV rights

The Monopolies and Mergers Commission crucially concluded that it was appropriate to treat pay TV as a separate market from free-to-air TV, and that within the pay TV market there were distinct separable markets for sports and movie channels.

The reasoning for this was based on the arguments put forward by the Office of Fair Trading (1996) and the European Commission (1998). The latter argued that in terms of the application of European competition law to the broadcasting of sports events, the relevant market was probably as narrow as football broadcasting. The Office of Fair Trading (1996) concluded that free-to-air TV was unlikely to provide sustained and effective competition to pay TV in sports programming because:

(a) free-to-air TV was capacity constrained and could only make limited time available for sports programmes whereas dedicated sports channels offered subscribers the option to watch sport at any time; and
(b) the ability to levy subscription charges made many sports events potentially far more valuable to a pay TV broadcaster than to a free-to-air broadcaster, giving the former the ability to pay more for broadcasting rights.

We have seen earlier in this chapter how the economics of sports broadcasting meant that even to free-to-air broadcasters, hour-by-hour, or viewer-by-viewer, it has been relatively cheap television for most of the history of sports broadcasting. The limits that the free-to-air broadcaster must put on sports broadcasting in terms of hours of programming limits its ability to benefit from this. Premium sports channels have unlimited sports programming and also charge extra for it. It is these economic facts that set premium sports channels apart as a separate market.

Within the premium sports channel market in Britain, BSkyB is already effectively a monopolist. Despite its profitability in the mid-to late-1990s, no new entrants have entered the market, suggesting that BSkyB's control of the broadcasting rights for football, rugby and other major sports events was acting as a barrier to entry of potential competitors. The MMC (1999) concluded that a merger with Manchester United would 'gain influence over and information about the Premier League's selling of rights that would not be available to its competitors. It would also benefit from its ownership stake in Premier League rights, providing a further advantage in the bidding process.'

The conclusion then was that the merger would increase the market power of BSkyB from its already powerful position in the sports premium channel market and reduce competition for Premier League broadcasting rights. The MMC also stated that it was this consideration that led it to conclude that the merger would operate against the public interest. However, there were also public interest issues from the effects of the merger on football.

Effects of the merger on football

The main public interest issue of the effect of the merger on football related to the argument that the merger would widen the economic gap between Manchester United and other Premier League clubs, making Manchester United too strong and reducing uncertainty of outcome for the Premier League as a whole.

For Manchester United, European competition would be stronger than the Premier League and the end result would be the devaluation of the Premier League as a championship. This argument is clearly based on the economics of professional team sports discussed in the last chapter. The MMC concluded:

> In our view the increase in the inequality of wealth between clubs, arising from the merger, would be likely to have the consequences put to us, namely it would put at risk the ability of many clubs to compete and ultimately could hasten the demise of some smaller clubs. This may be expected to have the adverse effect of damaging the quality of British football.

The use of the word 'hasten' in the penultimate sentence of this quote suggests that the current levels of inequality in British football are already so high that the merger would be just one more nail in the coffin for the poorer clubs. This may be why the emphasis of the MMC ruling against the merger was on the basis of its adverse effects on the broadcasting market.

Conclusion

In this chapter we have tried to bring together the importance of broadcasting to sport that has run through the other three chapters in this part of the book, and more importantly, to emphasise the importance of sport to broadcasting. Over the post-war period as a whole, the BBC has clearly emphasised how important sport is in its programming, initially because of its belief in the importance of sport in British culture. The BBC's rather peculiar choice of major sports events, including the Boat Race, itself defined the major sporting events calendar in Britain. ITV entered the market in 1955 but it was not until the 1980s that it seriously challenged BBC's premier place in sports broadcasting. Soon after, BSkyB effectively changed the nature of competition for broadcasting rights in British television and became one of the most profitable broadcasters in Europe as a result.

However, in 1999 there is more sport on free-to-air television in Britain than at any other time in history. The largest television audiences for *Match of the Day* are more than five times the best achieved for live football on BSkyB. In 1998, the single largest sports broadcast was England against Argentina in the World Cup. In 1999, it was ITV's live coverage of the European Cup Final between Manchester United and Bayern Munich. In some ways, BSkyB's competition for broadcasting rights has led to a higher quality of sports broadcasts across the free-to-air channels.

Bibliography

Allied Dunbar National Fitness Survey (1992) Sports Council and Health Education Authority, London.

Andreff, W. (1994) *The Economic Importance of Sport in Europe: Financing and Economic Impact*, Committee for the Development of Sport, Council of Europe, Strasbourg.

Audit Commission (1989) *Sport for Whom? Clarifying the Local Authority Role in Sport and Recreation*, HMSO, London.

Baade, R. and Dye, R. (1988) 'Sports stadiums and area development: a critical review', *Economic Development Quarterly*, **2**, No. 3, 265–275.

Barclay, Sir P. (1995) *Joseph Rowntree Foundation Inquiry into the Distribution of Income and Wealth in the UK*, Joseph Rowntree Foundation, York.

Barnett, S. (1990) *Games and Sets: The Changing Face of Sport on Television*, British Film Institute, London.

Barrett, J. and Greenaway, R. (1995) *Why Adventure?* Foundation for Outdoor Adventure, Coventry.

BBC (1965) *The People's Activities*, BBC, London.

BBC (1978) *The People's Activities and Use of Time*, BBC, London.

Bean, L. (1995) Ambush marketing: sports sponsorship confusion and the Lanhan Act, *Boston University Law Review*, **75**, 1099.

Becker, G.S. (1964) *Human Capital*, Columbia University Press, New York.

Becker, G.S. (1965) 'A theory of the allocation of time', *Economic Journal*, **75**, 3.

Becker, J.W. (1991) *The End of The Work Society*, Social and Cultural Planning Office, Pijswijk, The Netherlands.

Bianchini, F. (1991) 'Re-imagining the city', *Enterprise and Heritage*, 214–234.

Bramwell, B. (1991) 'Sheffield: tourism planning in an industrial city', *Insights*, March, 23–28.

Bramwell, B. (1995) Event Tourism in Sheffield: A Sustainable Approach to Urban Development? Unpublished paper, Centre for Tourism, Sheffield Hallam University.

British Travel Association/University of Keele (1967) *The Pilot National Recreation Survey*, London and Keele.

Buchanan, J.M. (1965) 'An economic theory of clubs', *Economica*, **32**, 1–14.

Burns, J.P.A., Hatch, J.H. and Mules, F.J. (eds) (1986) *The Adelaide Grand Prix: The Impact of a Special Event*, The Centre for South Australian Economic Studies, Adelaide.

Cairns, J. (1983) *Economic Analysis of League Sports – A Critical Review of the Literature*, University of Aberdeen, Department of Political Economy Discussion Paper No. 83-01, Aberdeen.

Cairns, J., Jennett, N. and Sloane, P.J. (1986) 'The economics of professional team sports: a survey of theory and evidence', *Journal of Economic Studies*, **13**, 1–80.

Cashmore, E. (1996) *Making Sense of Sports*, Routledge, London.

CCPR (1983) *Committee of Enquiry into Sports Sponsorship: 'The Howell Report'*, Central Council for Physical Recreation, London.

Centre for Advanced Studies in the Social Sciences (1995) *The Economic Impact of Sport in Wales*, Sports Council for Wales, Cardiff.

Centre for Leisure Research (1993) The impact of variations in changes on usage levels at local authority sports facilities: economic analysis, *Scottish Sports Council Research Digest*, No. 34, Edinburgh.

Charlesworth, K. (1996) *Are Managers under Stress? A Survey of Management Morale*, Institute of Management Research Report, Sept.

Cicchetti, C.J. (1973) *Forecasting Recreation in the US*, Lexington Books, Lexington, MA.

Cicchetti, C.J., Seneca, J.J. and Davidson, P. (1969) *The Demand and Supply of Outdoor Recreation: An Econometric Analysis*, Bureau of Outdoor Recreation, Washington, DC.

Clifford, M. (1992) Nike Roars, *Far Eastern Economic Review*, Nov.

Coalter, F. (1990) 'Sport and anti-social behaviour', in Long, J. (ed.) *Leisure, Health and Well Being*, Leisure Studies Association, Eastbourne.

Coalter, F. (1993) Sports participation: price or priorities? Leisure Studies, **12**, 171–182.

Coalter, F. (1996) *Sport and Anti-social Behaviour: a Policy-related Review* (SSC research digest no. 41), Scottish Sports Council, Edinburgh.

Coe, S. (1985) *Olympic Review: Preparing for '88*, Sports Council, London.

Commission for Social Justice (1994) *Social Justice: Strategies for National Renewal*, Vintage, London.

Compass (1999) *Sports Participation in Europe*, UK Sport, London.

Coopers and Lybrand (1994) *Preventative Strategy for Young People in Trouble*, Prince's Trust, London.

Council of Europe (1980) *European Sport for All Charter*, Strasbourg.

Council of Europe (1992) *European Sports Charter*, Strasbourg.

Cox, B.D., Blaxter, M., Buckle, A., Fenner, N., Golding, J., Gore, M., Roth, M., Stark, J., Wadsworth, M. and Whitelow, M. (1987) *The Health and Lifestyle Survey*, Health Promotion Research Trust, Cambridge.

Critcher, C. (1985) Professional football in Britain: Reading the signs, in Meijer, E. (ed.), *Everyday Life, Leisure and Culture*, Tilburg University Press, Tilburg, The Netherlands, 141–147.

Critcher, C. (1991) 'Sporting civic pride: Sheffield and the World Student Games of 1991', in *Leisure in the 1990's: Rolling Back the Welfare State*, LSA Conference 1991, LSA Publication No. 46, 193–204, Brighton.

Crompton, J.L. (1996) 'The potential contributions of sports sponsorship in impacting the product adoption process', *Managing Leisure*, **1**, No. 4, 199–212.

Crompton, J.L. (1998a) 'Emergence of the unfair competition issue in United States recreation', *Managing Leisure*, **3**, No. 2, 57–70.

Crompton J.L. (1998b) 'Ethical challenges and misapplications of economic impact studies undertaken by and for professional sport franchises in the USA', paper given to *Sport in the City*, Sheffield Hallam University, 2–4 July.

Crompton, J.L. (1998c) Analysis of sources of momentum that underlie the investment of local public funds on major sporting facilities and events, paper given to *Sport in the City*, Sheffield Hallam University, 2–4 July.

Csikszentmihalyi, M. (1975) *Beyond Boredom and Anxiety*, Jossey Bass, San Francisco, CA.

Cullis, J.G. and West, P.A. (1979) *The Economics of Health: An Introduction*, Martin Robertson, London.

Culyer, A.J. (1980) *The Political Economy of Social Policy*, Martin Robertson, London.

Daily Telegraph (1996a) Euro 96 nets UK trade surplus, 25 September.

Daily Telegraph (1996b) FA hope UEFA can ease Euro loss, 12 October.

Davis Smith, J. (1998) *The 1997 National Survey of Volunteering*, National Centre for Volunteering, London.

Deloitte & Touche (1998) *Deloitte & Touche Annual Review of Football Finance*, Manchester.

Deloitte & Touche (1999) *20 Richest Clubs in the World*, Manchester.

Department of the Environment (1977) *Policy for Inner Cities*, Cmnd 6845, HMSO, London.

Department of Trade and Industry (1999) Competitiveness Analysis of the UK Sporting Goods Industry, London.

Dobson, N., Holliday, S. and Gratton, C. (1997) *Football Came Home: The Economic Impact of Euro 96*, Leisure Industries Research Centre, Sheffield.

Dower, M., Rapoport, R., Strelitz, Z. and Kew, S. (1981) *Leisure Provision and People's Needs*, HMSO, London.

Durnin, J.V.A. and Pasmore, R. (1967) *Energy, Work and Leisure*, Heinemann, London.

El-Hodiri, M. and Quirk, J. (1971) An economic model of a professional sports league, *Journal of Political Economy*, **79**, 1302–1319.

European Commission (1998) Broadcasting of sports events and competition law, *Competition Policy Newsletter*, 2 June.

Ewart, A. (1983) *Outdoor Adventures and Self-Concept: A Research Analysis*, Centre for Leisure Studies, University of Oregon, Portland, Oregon.

Fentem, P.H. and Bassey, E.J. (1978) *The Case for Exercise*, Sports Council, London.

Fentem, P.H. and Bassey, E.J. (1981) *Exercise: The Facts*, Oxford University Press, London.

Financial Times (1979) A Swag of Sponsors, October.

Fine, B. (1990) *Consumer Behaviour and the Social Sciences: A Critical Review*, Queen Mary College, London.

Fletcher, J.E. (1989) Input–output analysis and tourism impact studies, *Annals of Tourism Research*, **16**, 514–529.

Foley, P. (1991) 'The impact of the World Student Games on Sheffield', *Environment and Planning C: Government and Policy*, **9**, 65–78.

Gershuny, J. (1996) *High Income People Want Less Work*, ESRC Research Centre on Micro-Social Change Working Paper, University of Esset.

Gershuny, J. (1997) Time for the family, *Prospect*, Jan., 56–57.

Gershuny, J.I. (1979) The informal economy: its role in post-industrial society, *Futures*, **12**, No. 1, 3–15.

Gershuny, J.I. and Thomas, G.S. (1980) *Changing Patterns of Time Use*, University of Sussex, Science Policy Research Unit, Brighton.

Getz, D. (1991) *Festivals, Special Events, and Tourism*, Van Nostrand Reinhold, New York.

Gibson, P. (1979) 'Therapeutic aspects of wilderness programmes: a comprehensive literature review', *Therapeutic Recreation Journal*, No. 2.

Glyptis, S. and Jackson, G. (1993) 'Sport and tourism: mutual benefits and future prospects', paper presented at the international Leisure Studies Association conference, *Leisure in Different Worlds*, Loughborough, July.

Gratton, C. (1984) Efficiency and equity aspects of public subsidies to sport and recreation, *Local Government Studies*, **10**, 53–74.

Gratton, C. and Taylor, P.D. (1985) *Sport and Recreation: an Economic Analysis*, E & FN Spon, London.

Gratton, C. and Taylor, P.D. (1991) *Government and the Economics of Sport*, Longman, Harlow.

Gratton, C. and Taylor, P.D. (1994) The impact of variations in charges on usage levels at local authority sports facilities: economic analysis, *Scottish Sports Council Research Digest*, **34**, Edinburgh.

Gratton, C. and Taylor, P. (1995) 'From economic theory to leisure practice via empirics: the case of demand and price', *Leisure Studies*, **14**, 245–261.

Gratton, C. and Taylor, P. (1996) *Economic Benefits of Sport*, SSC research digest no. 44, Scottish Sports Council, Edinburgh.

Gratton, C. and Taylor, P.D. (1997) *Leisure in Britain*, Leisure Publications (Letchworth).

Gratton, C. and Tice, A. (1987) 'Leisure participation, lifestyle and health', paper delivered to the *International Conference on the Future of Adult Life*, Leeuwenhorst Conference Centre, Holland, April.

Gratton, C. and Tice, A. (1989) 'Sports participation and health', *Leisure Studies*, **8**, No. 1, 77–92.

Gratton, C. and Tice, A. (1994) Trends in sports participation in Britain: 1977–1986, *Leisure Studies*, **13**, No. 1, 49–66.

Greene, Belfield-Smith (1996) *The Impact of Euro '96 on Hotels: A Summary of Results*, Deloitte & Touche Consulting Group.

Greenley, D.A., Walsh, R.G. and Young, R.A. (1981) Option value: empirical evidence from a case study of recreation and water quality, *Quarterly Journal of Economics*, **XCVI**, No. 4, 657–673.

Grossman, M. (1972) On the concept of health capital and the demand for health, *Journal of Political Economy*, **80**, No. 2, 223–255.

Hall, C.M. (1992) *Hallmark Tourist Events: Impacts, Management and Planning*, Belhaven Press, London.

Harada, H. (1996) 'Work and leisure in Japan', in Gratton, C. (ed.) *Work, Leisure, and the Quality of Life: A Global Perspective*, Leisure Industries Research Centre, Sheffield.

Head, V. (1982) *Sponsorship: The Newest Marketing Skill*, Woodhead-Faulkner, Cambridge.

Heflebower, R. (1967) 'The theory and effects of non-price competition', in Kuenne, R.E. (ed.) *Monopolistic Competition Studies in Impact*, Wiley, London.

Hendry, L.B., Shucksmith, J., Love, J.G. and Glendinning, A. (1993) *Young People's Leisure and Lifestyles*, Routledge, London.

Henley Centre for Forecasting (1986) *The Economic Impact and Importance of Sport in the UK*, SC study 30, Sports Council, London.

Henley Centre for Forecasting (1989) *The Economic Impact and Importance of Sport in Two Local Areas: Bracknell and the Wirral*, SC study 33, Sports Council, London.

Henley Centre for Forecasting (1990) *The Economic Impact and Importance of Sport in the Welsh Economy*, Sports Council for Wales, Cardiff.

Henley Centre for Forecasting (1992a) *The Economic Impact and Importance of Sport in the UK Economy in 1990*, Sports Council, London.

Henley Centre for Forecasting (1992b) *The Economic Impact and Importance of Sport in the Northern Ireland Economy*, Sports Council for Northern Ireland, Belfast.

Henzler, H. (1992) The new era of Eurocapitalism, *Harvard Business Review*, Jul.–Aug., 57–68.

Holliday, S. (1996) 'Trends in British work and leisure', in Gratton, C. (ed.) *Work, Leisure, and the Quality of Life: A Global Perspective*, Leisure Industries Research Centre, Sheffield.

Holt, R. (1989) *Sport and the British: A Modern History*, Clarendon Press, Oxford.

Hopkins, D. and Putnam, R. (1993) *Personal Growth through Adventure*, David Fulton, London.

Hosseini, H. (1990) The archaic, the obsolete and the mythical in neoclassical economics, *American Journal of Economics and Sociology*, **49**, No. 1, 81–92.

Hughes, H. (1993) 'The role of hallmark event tourism in urban regeneration', paper to the *First International Conference on Investment and Financing in the Tourism Industry*, Jerusalem, May 1993.

Institute of Leisure and Amenity Management (1994) *Purposeful Leisure as an Alternative to Crime and Punishment*, Policy position statement 4, ILAM, Reading.

Investors Chronicle (1996) Euro '96. Shooting for Net Profits, June.

Jones, H. (1989) *The Economic Impact and Importance of Sport: A European Study*, Council of Europe, Strasbourg.

Kalter, R.J. and Gosse, L. (1970) Recreation demand functions and the identification problem, *Journal of Leisure Research*, **12**, 43–53.

Kolah, A. (1999) *Maximising the Value of Sports Sponsorship*, Financial Times Media, London.

Koutsoyiannis, A. (1982) *Non-Price Decisions*, Macmillan, London.

Lancaster, K. (1966) 'A new approach to consumer theory', *Journal of Political Economy*, **74**,132–157.

Law, C.M. (1994) *Urban Tourism: Attracting Visitors to Large Cities*, Mansell, London.

Le Grand, J. (1982) *The Strategy of Equality: Redistribution and the Social Services*, George Allen and Unwin, London.

Leisure Consultants (1992) *Activity Holidays: The Growth Market in Tourism*, Leisure Consultants, London.

Linder, S. (1970) *The Harried Leisure Class*, Columbia University Press, New York.

Long, C. (1993) Sporting link wins marketing results, *The Sunday Times*, 19 Sept.

LIRC (1996) *Valuing Volunteers in UK Sport*, Sports Council, London.

LIRC (1997a) *A Review of the Economic Impact of Sport*, report for the Sports Council, London.

LIRC (1997b) *Economic Impact of Sport in Wales, 1995*, report for the Sports Council, London.

LIRC (1997c) *Economic Impact of Sport in Scotland, 1995*, report for the Sports Council, London.

LIRC (1997d) *Economic Impact of Sport in Northern Ireland, 1995*, report for the Sports Council, London.

Loftman, P. and Spirou, C.S. (1996) 'Sports, stadiums and urban regeneration: the British and United States experience', paper to the conference *Tourism and Culture: Towards the 21st Century*, Durham, September 1996.

Loomis, J.B. and Walsh, R.G. (1997) *Recreation Economic Decisions: Comparing Benefits and Costs*, Venture, Pennsylvania.

Lynn, P. and Davis-Smith, J. (1991) *The 1991 National Survey of Voluntary Activity in the UK*, Volunteer Centre UK, London.

McAuley, A. and Sutton, W.A. (1999) 'In search of a new defender: the threat of ambush marketing in the global sport arena', *Sports Marketing & Sponsorship*, **1**, No. 1, 64–86.

McCarville, R.E. and Crompton, J.L. (1987) An empirical investigation of the influence of information on reference prices for public swimming pools, *Journal of Leisure Research*, **19**, 223–235.

McCarville, R.E., Crompton, J.L. and Sell, J.A. (1993) The influence of outcome messages on reference prices, Leisure Sciences, **15**, 115–130.

Mitchell, R.C. and Carson, R.T. (1989) *Using Surveys to Value Public Goods: The Contingent Valuation Method*, Resources for the Future, Washington, DC.

Moller, D. (1983) 'Sponsorship: Tobacco's Deadly New Ingredient', *Readers' Digest*, 121.

Monopolies and Mergers Commission (1999*) British Sky Broadcasting plc and Manchester United PLC: A Report on the Proposed Merger*, The Stationery Office, London.

Morris, J.N., Chave, S.P., Adam, C. *et al.* (1973) 'Vigorous exercise in leisure time and the incidence of coronary heart disease', *Lancet*, 1, 333–339.

Morris, J.N., Everitt, M.G., Pollard., R., Chave, S.P. and Semmence, A.M. (1980) 'Vigorous exercise in leisure time: protection against coronary heart disease', *Lancet*, 2, 1207–1210.

Morris, J.N., Heady, J.A., Roberts, C.G. and Parks, J.W. (1953) 'Coronary heart disease and physical activity of work', *Lancet* 2, 1111–1120.

Mules, T. and Faulkner, B. (1996) An economic perspective on special events, *Tourism Economics*, **12**, No. 2, 107–117.

Myerscough, J. (1988) *The Economic Importance of the Arts in Britain*, Policy Studies Institute, London.

National Heritage Committee (1995) *Bids to Stage International Sporting Events*, House of Commons, London, HMSO.

Neale, W.C. (1964) The peculiar economics of professional sports, *Quarterly Journal of Economics*, **78**, No. 1, 1–14.

Nicholl, J.P., Coleman, P. and Brazier, J.E. (1994) 'Health and healthcare costs and benefits of exercise', *PharmacoEconomics*, **5**, No. 2, 109–122.

Nicholl, J.P., Coleman, P. and Williams, B.T. (1991) *Injuries in Sport*, Sports Council, London.

Nichols, G. (1994) 'Major issues in evaluation of the impact of outdoor-based experiences, *Journal of Adventure Education and Outdoor Leadership*, **11**, No. 1, 11–14.

Nichols, G.S. and Booth, P. (1999) *Programmes to Reduce Crime and Which are Supported by Local Authority Leisure Departments*, Institute of Sport and Recreation Management, Melton Mowbray.

Nichols, G.S. and Taylor, P.D. (1995) 'A justification of public subsidy of the British Sports Council's National Mountain Centre using a contingent valuation approach', *Journal of Applied Recreation Research*, **20**, No. 4, 235–247.

Nichols, G.S. and Taylor, P.D. (1996) *West Yorkshire Sports Counselling Final Evaluation Report*, West Yorkshire Sports Counselling Association, Wakefield.

Nichols, G.S. and Taylor, P.D. (1998) 'Volunteers: the Sports Council strikes back', *Recreation*, December.

Nishi, M. (1993) Emerging work and leisure time patterns in Japan, in Brent Ritchie, J.R. and Howkins, D.E. (eds), *World Travel and Tourism Review: Indicators, Trends and Issues*, Vol. 3, CAB International, Oxford.

Noll, R.G. (ed.) (1974) *Government and the Sports Business*, Brookings Institution, Washington, DC.

Noll, R. (1988) Professional Basketball, Stanford University Studies in Industrial Economics, Paper no. 144.

Noll, G. and Zimbalist, A. (1997) Build the stadium – create the jobs, in Noll, G. and Zimbalist, A. (eds), *Sports, Jobs and Taxes*, Brookings Institution, Washington, DC, pp. 1–54.

Observer (1984) 'The $ Olympics', 5 February.

Office of Fair Trading (1996) *The Director General's Review of BSkyB's Position in the Wholesale Pay TV Market*, London, December.

Office for National Statistics (1998) *Living in Britain: Results from the 1996 General Household Survey*, The Stationery Office, London.

Office of Population Censuses and Surveys (1976) *The General Household Survey, 1973*, HMSO, London.

Office of Population Censuses and Surveys (1979) *The General Household Survey, 1977*, HMSO, London.

Office of Population Censuses and Surveys (1985) *The General Household Survey, 1983*, HMSO, London.

Office of Population Censuses and Surveys (1989) *The General Household Survey, 1986*, HMSO, London.

Oldenbroom, E.R., Hopstaken, P. and van der Meer, F. (1996) *De nationale bestedingen aan sport*, Stichting voor Economisch Onderzoek der Universiteint Van Amsterdam, Amsterdam.

Olson, M. (1965) *The Logic of Collective Action: Public Goods and the Theory of Groups*, Harvard University Press, Cambridge, MA.

Ono, A. (1991) Working time in Japan: 200 hours longer than in statistics, *Economist*, **B12**, 74–77 (in Japanese).

Owen, J.D. (1979) *Working Hours: An Economic Analysis*, Lexington Books, Lexington, MA.

Paulhus, D. (1983) Sphere-specific measures of perceived control, *Journal of Personality and Social Psychology*, **44**, No. 6, 1253–1265.

PEP (Political and Economic Planning) (1966) 'English professional football', *Planning*, **32**, No. 496.

Pieda (1991) *Sport and the Economy of Scotland*, SSC research report no. 18, Scottish Sports Council, Edinburgh.

Pieda (1994) *Sport and the Northern Regional Economy*, Sports Council Northern Region, Manchester.

Purdy, D.A. and Richard, S.F. (1983) 'Sport and juvenile delinquency: an examination and assessment of four major theories', *Journal of Sport Behaviour*, **6**, No. 4, 179–183.

Quirk, J. and Fort, R.D. (1992) *Pay Dirt: The Business of Professional Team Sports*, Princeton University Press, Princeton, NJ.

Rawls, J. (1971) *A Theory of Justice*, Clarendon Press, Oxford.

Reeves, M. and Jackson, G. (1996) 'Evidencing the sports–tourism interrelationship: a case-study of élite British athletes', paper delivered to the 4th International WLRA Conference, *Free Time and Quality of Life for the 21st Century*, Cardiff, July.

Riiskjaer, S. (1990) 'Economic behaviour and cultural perspectives in voluntary sport', *Sport Science Review*, 13, Jan., 44–51.

Ritchie, J.R.B. and Aitken, C.E. (1984) Assessing the impacts of the 1988 Olympic Winter Games: the research program and initial results, *Journal of Travel Research*, **22**, No. 3, 17–25.

Ritchie, J.R.B. and Aitken, C.E. (1985) 'OLYMPULSE II – evolving resident attitudes towards the 1988 Olympics', *Journal of Travel Research*, **23**, Winter, 28–33.

Ritchie, J.R.B. (1984) 'Assessing the impact of hallmark event: conceptual and research issues', *Journal of Travel Research*, **23**, No. 1, 2–11.

Ritchie, J.R.B. and Lyons, M.M. (1987) 'OLYMPULSE III/IV: a mid term report on resident attitudes concerning the 1988 Olympic Winter Games', *Journal of Travel Research*, **26**, Summer, 18–26.

Ritchie, J.R.B. and Lyons, M.M. (1990) 'OLYMPULSE VI: a post-event assessment of resident reaction to the XV Olympic Winter Games, *Journal of Travel Research*, **28**, No. 3, 14–23.

Ritchie, J.R.B. and Smith, B.H. (1991) The impact of a mega event on host region awareness: a longitudinal study, *Journal of Travel Research*, **30**, No. 1, 3–10.

Roberts, K. and Brodie, D.A. (1992) *Inner-city Sport: Who Plays and What Are the Benefits?* Giordano Bruno, Culemborg, The Netherlands.

Robins, D. (1990) *Sport as Prevention: The Role of Sport in Crime Prevention Programmes Aimed at Young People*, occasional paper 12, Centre for Criminological Research, University of Oxford.

Roche, M. (1992) 'Mega-event planning and citizenship: problems of rationality and democracy in Sheffield's Universiade 1991, *Vrijetijd en Samenleving*, **10**, No. 4, 47–67.

Roche, M. (1994) 'Mega-events and urban policy', *Annals of Tourism Research*, **21**, No. 1.

Rodgers, B. (1977) *Rationalizing Sports Policies; Sport in its Social Context: International Comparisons*, Council of Europe, Strasbourg.

Rodgers, B. (1978) *Rationalizing Sports Policies; Sport in its Social Context: Technical Supplement*, Council of Europe, Strasbourg.

Ross, R. and Fabiano, E. (1985) *Time to Think: A Cognitive Model of Delinquency Prevention and Offender Rehabilitation*, T3 Associates, Ottawa.

Rottenberg, S. (1956) 'The baseball players labour market', *Journal of Political Economy*, **64**, 243–258.

Sandler, T. and Tschirhart, J.T. (1980) 'The economic theory of clubs: an evaluative survey', *Journal of Economic Literature*, **XVIII**, 1481–1521.

Schor, J.B. (1991) *The Overworked American: The Unexpected Decline of Leisure*, Basic Books.

Schor, J.B. (1996) 'Work, time and leisure in the USA', in Gratton, C. (ed.) *Work, Leisure, and the Quality of Life: A Global Perspective*, Leisure Industries Research Centre, Sheffield.

Scitovsky, T. (1976) *The Joyless Economy*, Oxford University Press, New York.

Scitovsky, T. (1981) 'The desire for excitement in modern society', *Kylos*, **34**, 3–13.

Shepherd, R.J. (1990) Sport, physical fitness and the costs of sport, *Science Review*, 13.

Sillitoe, K.K. (1969) *Planning for Leisure*, Government Social Survey, HMSO, London.

Simkins, J. (1980) *Sponsorship 1980/81*, special report no. 86, Economist Intelligence Unit, London.

Skjei, S.S. (1977) Identification in the estimation of recreation demand curves from cross-section data: how important is it?, *Journal of Leisure Research*, **9**, No. 4, 301–309.

Slack, T. and Bentz, L. (1996) 'The involvement of small business in sport sponsorship', *Managing Leisure*, **1**, No. 3, 175–184.

Sloane, P.J. (1971) 'The economics of professional football: the football club as a utility maximiser', *Scottish Journal of Political Economy*, **18**, 121–146.

Sloane, P.J. (1980) *Sport in the Market*, Institute of Economic Affairs, London.

Smith, Y. (1991) 'The World Student Games, Sheffield 1991: an initial appraisal', *Regional Review*, No. 5, 8–10.

Sport England (1999) *Best Value through Sport: A Survey of Sports Halls and Swimming Pools in England*, Sport England, London.

Sports Council Reseach Unit, North West (1990) *Solent Sports Counselling Project: Final Evaluation Report*, Sports Council, London.

Szalai, A. (1972) *The Use of Time*, Mouton, The Hague.

Taylor, P.D. and Foote, C. (1996) *Passport to Leisure Schemes*, Institute of Sport and Recreation Management, Melton Mowbray.

Taylor, P.D. (1993) *The Financing of Excellence in Sport*, Sports Council, London.

Taylor, P.D., Crow, I., Irvine, D. and Nichols, G. (1999) *Demanding Physical Programmes for Young Offenders under Probation Supervision*, Home Office, London.

Taylor, P.D. and Page, K. (1994) *The Financing of Local Authority Sport and Recreation: A Service under Threat?* Institute of Sport and Recreation Management, Melton Mowbray.

Thomas, G.S., Lee, P.R., Franks, S.P. and Paffenbarger, R.S. (1981) *Exercise and Health: The Evidence and the Implications*, Gunn and Hain, Oelgeschlager.

Trujillo, C.M. (1983) 'The effect of weight training and running exercise intervention programmes on the self-esteem of college women', *International Journal of Sports Psychology*, **14**, 162–173.

Turco, D. and Kelsey, C. (1992) *Measuring the Economic Impact of Special Events*, NRPA, Alexandria, VA.

UKTS (1998) *The UK Tourist: Statistics 1997*, English, Scottish, Wales and Northern Ireland Tourist Boards.

Utting, D. (1996) *Reducing Criminality among Young People: A Sample of Relevant Programmes in the United Kingdom*, Home Office Research Study 161, Research and Statistics Directorate, Home Office, London.

Van Puffelen, F., Reijnen, J. and Velthuijsen, J.W. (1988) *De Macro Economische Betekenis Van Sport*, Stichting voor Economisch Onderzoek der Universiteint Van Amsterdam, Amsterdam.

Vaughan, D.R. (1986) *Estimating the Level of Tourism-Related Employment: An Assessment of Two Non-survey Techniques*, BTA/ETB, London.

Veal, A.J. (1976) *Leisure and Recreation in England and Wales: 1973*, Countryside Commission, Cheltenham.

Veal, A.J. (1981) Using Sports Centres, unpublished report to the Sports Council, London.

Veal, A.J. (1982) 'Planning for leisure: alternative approaches', papers in *Leisure Studies*, No. 5, Polytechnic of North London.

Vickerman, R.W. (1975a) 'Demand and derived demand for recreation', *Hull University Economics Research Papers*, No. 5, Hull.

Vickerman, R.W. (1975b) *The Economics of Leisure and Recreation*, Macmillan, London.

Vickerman, R.W. (1980) 'The new leisure Society: an economic analysis', *Futures*, **12**, 191–199.

The Volunteer Centre UK (1995) *The Economic Value of Volunteering*, research bulletin 1, The Volunteer Centre UK, London.

Vuori, I. and Fentem, P. (1995) *Health: Position Paper*, Council of Europe, Strasbourg.

Weisbrod, B.A. (1968) 'Income redistribution effects and benefit–cost analysis', in Chase, S.B. Jr (ed.) *Problems in Public Expenditure Analysis*, Brookings Institution, Washington, DC.

Weisbrod, B.A. (1978) *The Voluntary Non-Profit Sector*, Lexington Books, Lexington, MA.

Weisbrod, B.A. (1988) *The Non-Profit Economy*, Harvard University Press, Cambridge, MA.

Whannel, G. (1992) *Fields in Vision: Television Sport and Cultural Transformation*, Routledge, London.

Whannel, G. (1996) 'Imported sport on British television: a feast of sport', in Collins, M. (ed.) *Leisure in Industrial and Post-industrial Societies*, Leisure Studies Association, Brighton.

Wilkinson, J. (1994) Using a reconviction predictor to make sense of reconviction rates in the probation service, *British Journal of Social Work*, **24**, No. 4, 461–475.

Willigan, G. (1992) High performance marketing: Nike, *Harvard Business Review*, July/Aug., **70**, No. 4, 90–101.

Wiseman, N.C. (1977) 'The economics of football', *Lloyds Bank Review*, Jan., 29–43.

Young, M. and Willmott, M. (1973) *The Symmetrical Family*, Routledge, London.

Index